Re

CW00391945

An unlikely ride from club cyclist to World Champion via liver transplantation

Richard Smith

Acknowledgments

When you have been through the experience I have you pretty much have to thank or apologise to everybody. That's not possible here so, first and foremost, I would like to thank my donor and his family, my Dad and all those involved in the pointy end of saving my life back in February 1993, including the friends who gathered around me at that time, the team at the Queen Elizabeth hospital and Dr Dave Mutimer in particular.

I have taken inspiration from those I have been fortunate to compete with over the years in transplant and non – transplant related sport and would personally like to thank those who have taken the time and trouble to give me a kicking on the bike. No really, thanks a lot.

For putting up with me whilst writing this and for other reasons too numerous to mention I would like to thank my partner Helen, my children Charlie and Grace for continued inspiration, my brother Ian and Anne, my step-mum, who helped nurse me back to health.

I would like to thank the members of Wrekinsport Cycling Club, the Birmingham Transplant Games Team and the Great Britain Transplant Games Team for never letting me take myself too seriously, for keeping me sane and for providing me with so much material for this book.

More latterly, I would like to thank Andy Britton and John Ireson my co-directors at Mamil Cycling Ltd and those cyclists, particularly the youth and junior riders, who give me such hope for the future.

From a practical perspective, I'd like to thank Liz Foster who tirelessly proof read ReCycled and offered invaluable advice on how to make it readable. She has a lot to answer for.

4

Contents

Introduction

I inhabit two worlds of cycling. In one, I am a British, European and World Champion and the fastest cyclist in the world: I get the occasional request for an autograph and people ask to have their photograph taken with me. In the other, the one more closely associated with reality, I'm a 3rd Category road racer and the 17th fastest 25-mile time trialist in Shropshire: I get changed in lay-bys in the back of a car like everybody else.

This being the case, I feel it only right and proper to point out that my seemingly preposterous claim to be a cycling champion and my eligibility to represent Great Britain, comes not from prodigious cycling talent alone. Or at all. Ask anybody who has ridden with me and they'll happily tell you. It comes by virtue of me having had a liver transplant at the ripe old age of 26.

It's all marvellously sudden, dramatic and exciting, as you will discover if you choose to read on. I feel compelled to mention at this point that it had nothing to do with the excessive consumption of alcohol and further my drinking was no more or less prolific than any other 26-year-old British male who has spent 3 years at college. I hope you are not disappointed in me already.

The transplant was necessary because of a little-known disease called Sporadic fulminant non-A non-E hepatitis or, very helpfully, acute liver failure. As I'm sure you know, it's idiopathic. If a fresh faced junior doctor ever looks at a poorly you and says what's ailing you is 'idiopathic' or of 'unknown aetiology' it means, despite the years at medical school and the well-practiced look of concern, he's no idea what's wrong or what's causing it. However, it's probably serious and, in my case, the disease is universally fatal without a replacement organ.

Having established my credentials as a fully qualified liver transplant patient, what gives me the right to start mining a vein as rich as the world of cycling and telling you what I think about it? Good question. I've ridden a bike of one sort or another for most of my life, I've trained and raced in this country and abroad for the last 15 years, I'm a qualified cycling coach and I've won a number of national, European and World titles. This pales into insignificance against the fact I am a club rider, an amateur racing cyclist and a paid-up middle marker. I have felt the sense of achievement at breaking 25 minutes for a '10' and the elation of actually finishing a local road race with the bunch. Equally, I know what it feels like to watch the Sunday club-run ride from you at a pace you can't hold and be beaten by kids and old men. I share the pain, suffering, satisfaction and pleasure with the thousands of cyclists who do this for 'fun' every week. I love it.

I am also one of many who have discovered the unique delights of cycling as a possibly life-saving, certainly life-enhancing, route to physical repair and mental stability. Quite apart from its rehabilitative nature, cycling is a fabulous starting point to meet people from every walk of life. It manages to encompass the arcane and secret. Contrast the coded life of the time trialists meeting early on Sunday mornings at places recorded only in letters and numbers, to perform painful rituals against the clock with the totally accessible, like a kid playing on a BMX on the street.

Most people can ride a bike even if they choose not do it very often and most of us would agree learning to do so is a rite of passage; something we all remember from our childhood. Yes, when cyclists come together it may seem odd they are united by an ability to balance on two wheels, but I have seen 6-year-old kids find common ground with 80-year-old men because they find pleasure in performing the same quirky act.

Something else I've always found fascinating about cycling is that it fits beautifully into the mildly eccentric idea of a proper British day out namely, dressing up in silly clothes and travelling a relatively short distance to drink tea and eat cake. If a village hall is involved, so much the better. This contrasts beautifully with a massive event like the three gruelling weeks in July that is the Tour de France, the

World's biggest annual sporting event, with its multi-million Euro budgets and daily stories of scandal and intrigue. Meanwhile, my fellow transplant riders and I compete in the only cycling event in the world where if you are tested for drugs and proved negative you are likely to be disqualified. The irony is not lost on us.

There may be weighty tomes dedicated to the sociological, psychological and anthropological reasons why people cycle, but I am frankly less interested in these and more interested in the people and experiences my journey through cycling has thrown up along the way. Sometimes these encounters have been in village halls, at other times they have been in towns and cities in Ireland, France, Japan, Hungary, Thailand, Australia and Sweden but they all have the bicycle in common.

Another common ground, particularly when racing, is the satisfaction of shared physical effort. Bike racing against the clock or in a road race is hard work, really hard work. In itself, the process of pushing yourself to your physical limit is not enjoyable for most but I, like many others, have made myself vomit through physically effort in the past. Lovely eh? The exchange of knowing looks, the pats on the back, the excited verbal re-enactment of parts of the race (complete with hand signals) on the other side of the finishing line is all part of the shared experience. I was told once you can't lose a bike race, you can only not win it and most people 'not win it' every week, many 'not win it' ever, but they keep coming back for the satisfaction of trying.

For my part, membership of Transplant Sport UK, the most exclusive sports club in the country that nobody wants to be in, and cycling in particular has undoubtedly contributed to keeping me healthy since my liver transplant. My brother credits cycling with saving his sanity although neither he nor I have anything on paper signed by a psychologist to back this up.

Leave to one side the millions whose principal method of transport is the bike: all those people for whom cycling is a utilitarian method of getting from home to work, you are still left with an enormously rich history full of heroes and villains, triumph and tragedy, skulduggery and honour in equal measures.

Contrasts aplenty. I have been given a unique opportunity by my peculiar set of circumstances to access a world of international cycling that I would not normally have been able to participate in, including the honour of representing my country. Back in the real world of club cycling I'm still trying to beat the hour for a 25-mile time trial and taking a weekly kicking in local road races.

Delivered

I will not dwell too long on my childhood as it is largely irrelevant to the story but it does set my later experiences in context. It will also give you an early opportunity to test your knowledge and assess your attitude to cycling and cyclists generally so I would be grateful for your indulgence for a brief time. I bet you can't wait.

I have to report an entirely unremarkable early life. As a youngster I grew up in various pleasant towns and villages in Cheshire as my father followed his house building job around the North West. We settled in Stockport in 1973 when I was six and I attended the local infant and primary schools there. It was a standard 1970's childhood in a roomy Victorian villa surrounded by go-karts made with pram wheels, endless summers, fishing in the local pool, the Six Million Dollar man and playing on bikes.

Without wishing to alarm you, and do feel free to claim you are unprepared for this; it's time for your first test. You will come across a series of these as you go through this book. If you don't like the suggested answer you should feel free to come up with your own alternative responses or ignore them completely if you choose; it's really none of my business. If you use your felt tip pens to illustrate your answers, make sure you remember to put the tops back on or they'll dry out.

Question 1

You are a 1970's parent and your 8-year-old child has requested you purchase him a Raleigh Chopper, just like the one the big kid down the road has got whose parents have the large house on the corner and the Triumph Dolomite Sprint.

Being a 1970's parent you'd sooner melt your orange Habitat cushion covers or wrestle a Cyber-man bare handed than lash out £36.82 on something that doesn't even look like a bloody bike.

Whilst stubbing out your Embassy Regal, choose the most appropriate alternative response to your child's request from those outlined below.

1. We've already got a bike. Your longhaired layabout brother left it rotting in the garage. It might be a bit big for you but not being able to stand over the crossbar doesn't stop you riding it, just jump off when you want to stop. It was expensive that bike was.

2. Your mother has a perfectly serviceable ex GPO bike her Aunt gave her just after the war. It's hand painted in matt black so the bombers couldn't see it when they flew over. It's got a proper saddle with springs in it and rod brakes, not like those new fangled Japanese cables. Stop moaning, it's not just for girls, it's unisex.

3. Better than a Chopper, I've got one of Eddie Merckx's old racing bikes from the second-hand shop. The frame was broken in a couple of places so we've joined it back together with a couple of bits of broom pole. Don't be stupid; it *doesn't* look like a death trap.

4. I'm not having that ponce from down the road thinking he's better than us. I've bought you a 5-speed Mk2 Raleigh Chopper in electric blue, now get out there and ride it up and down in front of his house until it's dark. I reckon that bloke uses hair spray.

I feel I may have been a little hard on you to start with because, as this is the 1970's not only are all the responses above are appropriate, a whole load of other options are also available to you so we won't keep score on this first one. You could have responded by building your child a go-kart using old prams wheels and rough sawn 3" x 2" timber held together with 6" galvanized nails or bought him an air rifle or sheath knife. It was the 70s; you could do pretty much anything.

My request for a Raleigh Chopper was turned down flat. I had a bike already; it was constructed by an unidentifiable manufacturer, had a single gear and 20 inch wheels. The big kid down the road really did have a Chopper, a rare 5 speed one complete with a gear stick mounted on what passed for a top tube. I recall being so distraught I taped a block of rolled up cardboard to my bike, labelled it 1 to 6, and stuck a pencil in it so I too could change gears. It didn't last very long. A few jumps over a stack of bricks with a plank lent up against them and the makeshift gear lever/pencil combo soon became detached. I consoled myself with the thought that although my bike was tiny and pretty crappy in comparison to the Chopper, it was easier to jump bricks on. I am also pleased to report my loosely assembled cardboard and wooden fake gear shifter left my genitals completely unmutilated. I'm not sure the same can be said of the big kid from up the road. What were they thinking of putting a gear shifter there?

When I wasn't playing on my bike my spare time was spent fishing at the local pond. Much of this was courtesy of my elder brother, Ian, and his friends who tolerated me tagging along with them. Like most kids in those days, I was fuelled by tartrazine-loaded orange squash and the occasional 'curry' made of minced beef, curry powder and some exotic sultanas. None of this did me any harm. Probably.

The 10 year age gap between Ian and I meant one of the fishing trips I was definitely not allowed to go on was an annual jaunt to Bridgnorth in Shropshire to fish the River Severn. Some years later when Dad's peripatetic job made a move to the Midlands necessary, Bridgnorth seemed like an ideal place for the family to head for and so it came to be in 1977, at the age of 10, we moved. I was devastated at the time. I was in my final year of primary school, had made firm friends and was looking forward to going to secondary school with them. Moving to Shropshire, fishing or no fishing, was not part of the plan at all. Eventually I settled into my new school, made new friends, many of whom I am lucky enough to still call friends today and set about the task of being an 80's kid.

The principle means of transport for your typical 80's kid was the 'racer', usually a road going bike of British manufacture with, if you were lucky, ten gears, five sprockets on the rear and double chain rings up front giving you a good selection of gears. My '10 speed' was in actual fact a '5 speed', lacking the double front chain rings. It was a 1970's British Racing Green Dawes inherited from my brother. Despite its antique heritage, in comparison to my friend's bikes, it was light and responsive and came replete with a brown leather Brooks saddle. This pretty much took care of getting me to all the places I shouldn't have been and facilitated all the things I shouldn't have been doing in those years. I commuted on the Dawes to my first job washing up at the Little Chef but it also took care of proper 'bike ride' duties when I was out with my friends polling around the local villages and towns. There was no great organisation to this; we weren't club members or anything, just kids playing on our bikes.

I progressed through secondary school doing the normal mixture of things I both should and shouldn't have done, having some sad but many more happy experiences and being awarded a bunch of pretty average 'O' levels for my troubles. A little later in life, an admissions tutor commented not unkindly or inaccurately, that my CV read like I'd spent more time chasing rugby balls and girls than academic grades. Whilst I'd had little success with either, he was, of course, correct. I'd scraped enough qualifications to go into the Sixth Form of my school and set about a few modest 'A' levels. My small, perfectly insular 1980's world of U2, school boy rugby, bike rides and family continued for another 2 years or so.

The first event to ever make me aware there was more to life than Bono, bikes, sport and girls happened on the evening of June 12th 1985, the day before I was due to take my second 'A' level Geography paper. My Mother had been taken into hospital with chest pains the previous weekend and while Dad and I were awaiting her to be discharged to come back home to look after us again, she died of a massive heart attack. There was no warning, I waited for Dad to come home from his visit to Shrewsbury hospital that evening and he had no choice but to tell me what had happened.

Still in shock, and, even now I struggle to fathom how I did this, I went into school the day after and sat the Geography paper. My education, and that of my brother before me, was top of Mum's agenda and Dad had sold me on the idea she would have wanted me to continue. We were both in shock. Neither of us had a clue what was going on nor have I any idea what I wrote that day, if anything at all. I muddled through in a foggy haze which when I look back now, I can see lasted through my college years. The examining Board and, I suspect, the admission tutors at the colleges I applied to took pity on me and let me continue on my very average academic career.

I completed my surveying degree at a Red Brick college in the North West, worked there for a year or so and then moved to London to pursue Kate, the unfortunate woman who was then the object of my desire. I'd taken the step of inventing some guff about career enhancement and ensuring I'd got a breadth of professional experience more readily available in London to make the whole pursuit thing more palatable in case anybody ever enquired. I don't think anybody ever did. Certainly not Kate. During my stay in London, I became close to her although she made it pretty clear while she enjoyed my company that was about as far it was ever going to go. She was, in fairness, out of my league. She moved in social circles with people whose names were often prefixed with Honourable or Lord.

15

Not tiring of life but definitely tiring of being in London I changed jobs just before Christmas 1992 and returned to my hometown of Bridgnorth. Before I left I threw a little party in the local pub and a good number of the friends I had made locally came along. Most memorably, a guy I'd got to know quite well and his delightful girlfriend Carmel who was from Birmingham. It was the first time I'd met Carmel and it was difficult not to be taken by her. She was lovely and I remember thinking what a perfect couple they made and saw how relaxed people were in their company. I said my goodbyes, sorry to be leaving a place I had grown attached to and the new friends associated with it but excited to be going back home. Anyway, I'd stay in touch, like we all do right? A day or so later, I packed up the Escort with everything I owned, drove home and, as any right minded 26-year-old would do, I got properly tucked into Christmas.

I had a thumping cold and felt bloody awful for the early part of Christmas but with enough Lemsips and Paracetamol I muddled through. Let's face it common colds in winter are hardly revolutionary but I couldn't shake this thing, I was really tired and even a little sick and nauseous. Strange for a cold but I thought little of it, piled down the cold cures and cracked on, as you do. Typical bloke: impassive, I might have had a terrible case of man flu but I didn't like to go on and on and on. And on. About it.

A few weeks into the New Year and the cold had gone but I couldn't help noticing that things weren't quite the right colour, especially me. I was going an unpleasant shade of pale yellow; you could see it in my face and more unsettlingly, the whites of my eyes. I really wasn't feeling very well at all at this point. The thing I remember most clearly was, try as I might, I couldn't get warm. It's hard to describe but it was an internal coldness. I wore as many warm clothes as physically possible and got into scolding hot baths, not at the same time I hasten to add, that would be ridiculous, but nothing would warm me up. It was also impossible not to notice my urine had become very dark and concentrated and my stools were very pale. I later learned this was a symptom of my kidneys trying to do what my damaged liver could not, that is filter the waste products from my blood. Similarly, as I was no longer producing bile in meaningful amounts it was impossible for me to digest anything containing fat so I was suffering appalling indigestion.

Right, off to the doctors then. I suspected I'd managed to get Hepatitis A, a common food and water born virus that effects the liver, unpleasant but usually not very serious. It will clear on its own given time and a fat-free diet. I couldn't imagine where I'd got it from, I hadn't been abroad or drunk contaminated water as far as I knew but I couldn't imagine what else it could be. Perhaps a dodgy curry or something similar.

The local medics ran some tests for the two most common Hepatitis viruses (A and B) and they came back negative. Good news or bad news then? Well, mainly bad on reflection. The doctors were flummoxed and came to the inspired diagnosis of 'yellowness' caused by 'jaundice of the liver and that', although I was initially reassured by the 'probably get better by itself' prognosis. You tend to trust doctors don't you?

All this getting ill with mysterious undiagnosed diseases was inconvenient to say the least. I've always considered being ill a complete waste of time; it stops you from doing things. Even a hefty cold means you can't work, play sport, sleep, eat or drink with any pleasure or at the pace you might want to. This makes me angry and frustrated so I become a typically snot bound ill-tempered male whinger. I'm not remotely stoical, if I'm ill pretty much everybody needs to know. Pathetic isn't it?

January 1993 was coming to a close and I was properly sick. So tired and cold I couldn't get out of bed for more than a few hours. I was off work, which was worrying as I'd started a new job just before Christmas and my employers were getting a little jumpy. I was also very yellow: everything was yellow, apart from those things that should have been yellow. I was changing colour and not in a good way. More blood tests with the local doctors followed but the diagnosis and prognosis remained the same. I was told I would *probably* recover spontaneously within 6 weeks or so. I wasn't convinced and neither was my father. Thankfully, via a contact at his work he knew of a Gastroenterologist in Brocton, Staffordshire, a few miles up the road from us, who had his own private practice. He booked an appointment for me on 11th February. Thanks Dad.

I didn't make it to that appointment. Sorry Dad.

Whilst I was awaiting the appointment with the doctor who, I really hoped, had a clue as to what was going wrong with me, I was pretty worried but was still clinging to the locally delivered prognosis of spontaneous recovery and was wholly unaware of just how parlous my grip on life really was. I certainly had no idea of how critical to life your liver is or, in all honesty, what it does for you. It's a filtration plant for the body amongst other things; it performs hundreds of chemical processes, cleans your blood, makes things you need to digest food and produces a lot of heat in the process. I didn't know it at the time but the fact I felt constantly cold was a reliable symptom that my liver was dying. It's a hardy organ. Under normal circumstances, you can live with only a small part of it working, which is why liver disease, particularly cirrhosis caused by alcohol, is often diagnosed too late to do anything about it. It's the only organ in the body that can regenerate but sometimes it re-grows scar tissue rather than healthy new liver cells, leaving less of it to perform the vital processes for life. Without any liver function at all you'll be dead within a few hours.

On Friday evening, February 5th 1993, I had the crashing realisation I was going to die. I had got to the stage where I was finding it hard to stand; I was becoming delirious and increasingly confused. I'd have been panicking if I had the energy. I didn't know it then but I was already in the first stage of coma. I managed to get to the phone and called my Dad. What else are you supposed to do when you know you're dying? My father's training is in construction rather than medicine so I'm not entirely sure what I was expecting him to do: build me something perhaps? On reflection, an ambulance may have been more appropriate but he'd proved to be a reliable chap in past and I wasn't thinking too clearly. You'll have to cut me some slack on this one.

And that was it. I remember opening the door to Dad a few minutes later and then I hit the deck. Stop. Coma time.

I do have a vague memory of a friend turning up with a cake she had baked for me (mmmm ...cake) but by that stage I was pretty confused and fading out of consciousness so I could have been hallucinating. I also seem to remember a young lady from a fledgling relationship being around but once more, my addled mind could have been making it up. More, much more, on hallucination later.

I have brief memory flashes of the next few hours, a surreal scene of Dad throttling a local doctor, a proponent of the 'spontaneous recovery' prognosis and of being helped into an ambulance in the dark.

The actual series of events was relayed to me later. My father had come around to the house following my call together with Anne, who was later to become my Step Mum, and he had called the local doctors. They turned up and, at my father's insistence, reassessed their 'he'll get better on his own, probably' diagnosis fairly rapidly. He bundle me into the back of the car, held on to me and set Anne off in the direction of Brocton to see if Dr Gibson could squeeze me in. I was delirious by this stage and in a Grade 3 encephalitic coma: I was talking gibberish, shouting, aggressive, confused and belligerent. Much like a normal Friday night to be fair.

It turned out that Dr Gibson could see me. I couldn't see him however and when I got his bill for a consultation some months later he did mentioned he thought it unlikely I'd remember anything about our encounter. He was right but nevertheless, it was the best £70 I've ever spent. The good doctor pretty much figured out what was going on in the first few seconds of our meeting (on reflection, 70 quid seems a bit steep now) and whilst a specific diagnosis could wait, he knew my liver was failing rapidly. He thought an unpleasantly coloured death was a far more likely outcome than a spontaneous recovery.

Dr Gibson 1 v 0 Local doctors

After calling the Staffordshire ambulance service he rang the Liver Unit at the Queen Elizabeth Hospital in Birmingham. He told them to expect a 26-year-old burnt amber-coloured young man who he thought would probably be dead fairly soon without some kind of dramatic intervention.

Don't let anybody tell you the emergency services don't enjoy themselves sometimes. The ambulance arrived and loaded me up together with Dad who was holding me down, or up, as necessary and stopping me from physically abusing the paramedics. They had to cope with the verbal abuse unaided. Anne said she would drive to the hospital. The driver enquired if she knew the way to the Queen Elizabeth Hospital. Quite innocently Anne admitted she didn't but would simply follow the ambulance. The driver advised her that was neither a good idea nor in all probability possible. Had Anne known that our short journey to Birmingham was going to be assisted firstly by a Staffordshire Police Range Rover on the M6 and then two Ford Cosworth Sierras of the West Midlands Force on the Hagley road, she may have revised her journey plan.

My Father tells the story; it's one of his favourites, of a journey carried out at some speed with the Range Rover escorting the ambulance down a short section of the M6 before peeling off at Spaghetti junction. From there the Sierras took the ambulance down the Aston Express Way, through Birmingham city centre and on to the Hagley Road. The police cars were relaying between the lights to stop the traffic and let us through with one car over taking us each time, the officers jamming the car in the junction so the ambulance driver didn't have to slow down. As we rolled into the Queen Elizabeth Hospital, the ambulance stopped and reversed up to the main doors so they could more easily wheel me in when the engine expired with an almighty rattle and a final puff of diesel smoke. I had it in mind the ambulance was a sleek modern yellow paramedic wagon when in fact it was rather more antique. When I first saw it I anticipated the appearance of Kenneth Williams from its rear doors in a white coat mouthing a hearty 'ooooh matron!' at any moment. The ancient vehicle was excellent going forwards but the backwards bit had been simply too much for the old thing. The engine was dead, it's big end destroyed. I however, was still alive and the few minutes saved courtesy of some high speed driving were to prove invaluable. I did mention the emergency services enjoyed themselves sometimes didn't I?

Not that I knew anything about it, but I was admitted into Intensive Care at the Liver Unit and tubed up with an arterial line and bits of monitoring equipment under the supervision of Dr David Mutimer. Back then, Dave was a Senior Registrar in the Liver Unit and that evening he had just come from a squash court. He was straight and direct with my father. Following some pretty rapid blood work, he told him I'd got 48 hours to live, maybe 72 hours if I was lucky, and that a spontaneous recovery was out of the question. It was simple. I'd need a liver transplant, and quickly, otherwise I'd be dead. I'd also need a hole in my head (you can insert your own joke here) as one of the symptoms of the disease is cerebral oedema, a potentially life threatening swelling of the brain. A handy neuro-surgeon was pressed into service; he brought his hand drill with him and popped a metal pressure release valve in my swede. Peep peep!!

I've always been trouble, me. But this was taking the biscuit. I was born 10 years later than my brother. Mum had been told she could never have children. No way. Then Ian turned up. Then Mum was told she definitely would never have any more kids. Then I showed up. My parents were so happy they bought a beagle and Ian decided to call me Duncan: he refused to call me anything else for 2 years. Mum had spent the last 6 weeks of her pregnancy in hospital and I was born rather prematurely. Back in 1967 is was not the done thing for fathers to attend births (they really don't know how lucky they were) and the first thing my Father said when he saw a rather puce me was 'is that the best you can do?' Apparently the woman in the bed next to Mum cried for the next 2 days. So my current yellow period followed my blue tinged beginnings. I'm tempted to offer a prize to anybody who can guess what other colours I've been.

Back in the corridor outside Intensive Care, Dad and Dave Mutimer where getting to know one another in rather difficult circumstances. Dad had a son who was odds-on to expire pretty soon and Dave had lost his squash match.

Occasionally you meet people blessed with great intelligence; sometimes you are lucky enough to encounter charismatic individuals who effortlessly hold your attention. It is rare you meet people who combine both but Dave Mutimer has these qualities in spades. He tells you something, you believe it, it actually makes things very simple and that evening he told Dad that my chances of survival were good if a suitable liver could be found in time. I was fit, young and, unlike many people who are waiting for a transplant, my body had not had time to deteriorate. Mine was an acute illness meaning long-term damage to my other organs was, for the moment at least, unlikely. For the chronically ill it's a hard irony, the shortage of organs available for transplantation means those who really need them are often not strong enough to go through surgery by the time a suitable one becomes available. Many people die while on the waiting list.

My Dad is of the generation that tends to stand when people enter a room. He wouldn't dream of remaining seated whilst somebody was addressing him and would think it odd or slightly rude if the situation were reversed. Dr Mutimer told him this wasn't necessary when he came in to the waiting room and Dad's response was 'I fight better standing up'. I can't be absolutely sure what he meant but it's a very 'Dad' thing to say. It certainly wasn't any kind of threat but putting myself in his position now I am a parent, I understand his urge to fight for me in any way he could: to do anything within his power to help. It must have been appallingly frustrating. It was at this time he suggested they use his liver. He's not stupid; he knew what he was suggesting and the consequences. While his offer might seem ill advised now, he absolutely meant it at the time.

Nowadays, it *is* possible to be a living liver donor under certain circumstances. The small lobe of the organ is removed from the donor and transplanted, with a great deal of success, into the recipient who is often a sibling or child. The transplanted organ grows to a normal size at the same pace as the donor organ recovers and replaces the lost tissue. This takes a great deal of planning, investigation and testing to establish suitability, it is not something that can be done in a hurry and is not without substantial risk. Whatever had infected me had almost completely destroyed my liver in a period of a few weeks and by the time it was removed a piece about the size of a thumbnail was the only bit still working.

NHS Blood and Transplant is a marvellous organisation. Not only do they operate the Organ Donor Register and the Blood Donor Service, one of their many other tasks is the prioritisation of those who are in need of a replacement vital organ. I went to the top of the liver list on admission, an honour of which I was blissfully unaware.

The part of the process that my Dad to this day really struggles with then began. The initial shock of my admission and likely terminal prognosis had sunk in and, such as they were, his thoughts cleared. The realisation that my survival relied absolutely on the death of another did not sit easily with him as he walked the corridors outside the ICU of the liver ward that Friday night.

The Transplant Coordinator appointed to try to find me a liver had a frank discussion with my father. Surprisingly enough her assessment of the situation was that the chances were fair, it was possible a suitable liver could be found within Europe in time. I was a pretty standard if very poorly human specimen (white adult male, Smith, blood type O) the liver just had to be roughly the right size. The tissue typing that is so critical with kidney transplants does not apply to livers meaning that it just needed to physically fit; it could even be cut down if necessary. It was not lost on the Coordinator or Dad that it was a weekend. A dark freezing weekend in early February and that many organs suitable for donation come from people fatally injured in road traffic accidents. Despite every modern safety contrivance on vehicles this type of accident combined with sudden traumatic brain bleeds account for the largest number of organs suitable for transplant. Hard words aren't they? I had the easy job here, I just had to lie there in a coma and not die too quickly. It was everybody else who was running around trying to balance the morality and the logistics of the situation. I didn't even have to say yes or no to the transplant, my father did that for me, I know he did because I've seen his signature on the consent form. He has a very distinctive left handed signature with a whole bunch of middle initials and the only time I've seen one this shaky before was on a particularly big cheque.

As Friday night morphed into Saturday morning some good news appeared on the horizon, as two potential donor livers became available, first from Ireland and then from Germany. Unfortunately, both organs were declined as being unsuitable by the team at the Queen Elizabeth Hospital. There can be numerous reasons for this. Whilst donor organs may appear viable when the unfortunately named Harvesting Team removes them, this view can change depending on a range of tests to determine suitability. I do not know the precise reasons for the organs being declined but I do know it didn't do anything to improve my father's state of mind. Making him and I quote, 'a little jumpy'.

On the same Friday night I was being whizzed down the M6, a very different and entirely tragic set of events was unfolding some miles away in London. A young man, a recent graduate, was travelling in the passenger seat of his friend's car when it was hit from the side by a vehicle that came through a junction without giving way. A weekend in February. A road traffic accident on a freezing dark winter night.

He was fatally injured in the crash that Friday night. His parents arrived from their home in the North West and were told there was no chance that he would recover and was incapable of breathing on his own. It is a mark of his wonderful parents they were not only able to cope with this devastating tragedy but even mention to the team caring for him they had discussed organ donation and if it were possible, his organs should go to help others. There followed urgent phone calls, tests, teams of doctors in helicopters and my Transplant Coordinator having a conversation with Dad. A suitable organ had been found and a retrieval team was on the way on Saturday evening. I would be prepared for surgery and taken down at 6 am on Sunday morning, earlier if necessary as there was nothing to lose. I was pretty much done for, so starting the surgery was risk free. I was going to die anyway.

Most transplant recipients have to go through weeks, months, sometimes years of tests to determine their suitability. Paradoxically, the physical health of a potential recipient is important. If they are unlikely to recover successfully from surgery or the multiple blood vessels or the veins, tubes and arteries are not capable of being cut and sewn together with the 'graft' it is unlikely they will be considered suitable. I by-passed this trauma and the stress of waiting for an organ. There was not much point in giving me a bleeper as I was unable to respond even to 'painful stimuli' as it's known, in simple terms a needle being stuck half an inch into a foot. I guess I must have had an honest, if yellow, face.

By the time I was taken down for surgery on Sunday morning, a big group of friends had joined Dad in the family room. It was the early nineties so they were allowed to fug up the room with cigarette smoke and they did so with great gusto. I was then, and am now, blessed with a big group of friends and I know their presence supported my father greatly. I will always be grateful to them, even though I've never been able to put together a comprehensive list of who was there at what time.

Nine hours later I was wheeled out of surgery and back to the High Dependency Unit (HDU) of E3, the Liver unit at the Queen Elizabeth Hospital. According to my father, even within this short space of time my colour had changed and I was just a touch less yellow – perhaps Lemony or Harvest Gold if you're into match pots. The surgeon who had been good enough to spend eight or so hours of his life up to his elbows in bits of me came into the family room (I presume he'd had a wash) and told Dad and my assembled friends that all had gone well. My liver had been removed without complication and the donor organ had been grafted cleanly. My surgeon is an unassuming man of relatively few words, but his words are worth listening to. When I got the chance some weeks later to meet him he seemed slightly embarrassed when I expressed my awestruck thanks, he was just doing his job. A remarkable job and a remarkable man.

I can't remember anything about being admitted to hospital and had no inkling of what was going on around me during my stay there before the surgery. The lights were most definitely out and nobody, and I mean nobody, was home. I was completely unconscious and unaware. With apologies to Descartes, I didn't think, therefore, I wasn't.

If it isn't a contradiction in terms, I was only aware of an absence of cognisance because I had a dream or an hallucination during my blacked out period. It was extraordinarily vivid and came out of nowhere, like a vignette in a horror film. It appeared with the immediacy of a machine springing to life with the push of a button: from stone cold and inanimate to complete awareness in an instant. I was being held down on my back over an old farmhouse kitchen table. It was dull and cold and outside rain was running down the windows. Hooded and masked vampire-like creatures surrounded the table and they attacked me with their teeth ripping at my throat and chest and in my dream like state, there was nothing I could do to fight back. We've all had those dreams, the ones when you strike out uselessly and without impact or push with your entire might and nothing moves. Despite struggling there was nothing I could do to fend the attack off. I didn't feel any pain but I knew I'd been opened up, my blood drained and my organs removed by these creatures. The last thing I remember is lying on the table, lifting my head up and seeing them walk away into the rain, hooded, carrying parts of me away with them. Then nothing. Back to blackness.

Much later when I'd had the chance to sort out the time line of events and begin to piece together what was real and what was either induced by drugs or my toxin-filled blood, it started to make some sense. I think this frightening vision coincided with the surgery beginning. Although I was totally comatose, the trauma of the anaesthetic, the breathing tubes and the scalpels going into me had almost certainly induced these frightening images.

Although time is a great healer and the impact of that hallucination and the ones that followed it has dissipated, memories of that vivid comatose vision and the emptiness on either side of it remain strong.

You may have gathered a liver transplant is a pretty big and complicated plumbing job. As a full-grown adult human your liver, if you are genetically fortunate and have looked after it, is about the size of a deflated rugby ball. It sits behind your lungs; the large right lobe starts a couple of inches below your right nipple extending to below your rib cage. It narrows towards a blunt point over to the left side of your chest. Attached to it is your gall bladder holding bile

27

produced by the liver ready to be released into your gut to digest fats. You don't really need a gall bladder and during a transplant the recipients is removed and not replaced. Bile from the donor organ drains straight into the gut or duodenum. At least that's what they told me when I asked what the hell they had done with my gall bladder.

The liver filters your blood so a huge amount of the vital red stuff is pumped through it at any one time, it also makes, breaks down and stores pretty much all of the biochemical substances you need to sustain life. Removing a liver without figuring out what happens to the veins and arteries supplying it means a person would pretty soon be in the middle of a very bloody Monty Python sketch and dead a few seconds later. This is why, some days after waking up from surgery, I found a couple of new holes I wasn't expecting. Although this is not the case with all patients, my circulatory system had to be re-routed to by-pass the hole where my liver should have been during the anhepatic (without liver) phase of operation. This explained the scars in my groin and under my left arm where I'd been temporarily re-plumbed.

The one hole I was expecting was in medical terms, a whopper. Twenty six inches in length and known colloquially as a 'Mercedes' it stretches from one side of my abdomen to the other and up to my sternum. It is perhaps unsurprisingly the shape of the Mercedes badge or for those of my generation, the CND symbol like the badge I wore on my blazer in the sixth form. If only Bruce Kent could see me now.

After coming out of hospital years later I would show people, well, let's be honest here, women, my scars claiming I'd been attacked by some knife wielding guys in masks. It's kind of true and also kind of pathetic but by now you are getting a feel for who I am.

One of the many drugs put into my body before the transplant was on clinical trial and known by its developmental tag of FK506, later abbreviated to FK by its friends. Dad had signed up for this on my behalf on the advice of Dr Mutimer figuring it must be good stuff if he recommended it. It wasn't being administered in an attempt to make me better but to see if I had an adverse reaction to it. It is an immunosuppressant drug, given to transplant recipients to stop their natural bodily defence systems from attacking and rejecting the donor organ. In my case the FK was tolerated and did not make me any more ill, which under the circumstances was nigh on impossible anyway. Just as Dave promised it has proved to be an excellent drug.

Transplantation had been revolutionised in the 1980s with the widespread use of a drug called Cyclosporin, originally isolated from a fungus found in Norway in the late 1960s and developed following the discovery of its immunosuppressant effect in 1972. It was the forerunner of many later derivative immunosuppressant drugs but it does have immediately obvious side effects, notably hypertension and accelerated hair growth. The long-term effects of this kind of vital drug therapy go way deeper than a drop of blood pressure and massive eyebrows, entertaining as that might be. Intentionally reducing the efficacy of the human immune system opens a person up to a whole world of nasty stuff, from the avoidable and mildly inconvenient like sunburn, to the potential fatal and less easily sidestepped like cancer and heart disease.

Without the development of these drugs, transplantation as we know it would not be possible and they save and support the lives of hundreds of thousands of people. Clever surgeons in the 60s had worked out the techniques of how organs could be removed and replaced in humans: it was complicated plumbing but it was plumbing all the same. The tricky bit was stopping the recipient from rejecting the carefully grafted organ. It was this, rather than the surgery itself that meant most recipients didn't survive for very long. The drugs are very powerful and the side effects have to be carefully managed. This is accepted on the understanding that the alternatives, chronic long-term illness followed by death or just plain old death at the outset, are infinitely worse.

Back in the HDU that Sunday evening things were looking a little bit brighter, a liver had been found, the surgery had happened and I'd come through it successfully. OK, I had tubes, wires and pinging machines all over the place and I was totally sedated to stop me falling in half should I try to move, but I was alive. Dad's got a picture of me just after the surgery, replete with a breathing tube and pressure cooker valve coming out of my nut like a little chimney. The hospital staff took the picture at his request and Dad claimed later he just wanted a picture of the machines but he got me in it too. You should always include something in a picture for scale and, in these particular circumstances it appeared an amber coloured bloke would do. He tells me he looks at it now and again when he has a bad day; it puts things into perspective for him. It's a useful card to have in the pack and one I played myself from time-to-time when little annoyances encroach into life.

There was still a long way to go in my recovery and although the success rate for liver transplant operations at the Queen Elizabeth Hospital was pretty good even back then, I was not yet assured of sustainable reanimation. Put it this way, in medical speak, success in transplantation is measured by reference to a 1 year survival rate, being how many recipients live for 1 year following the surgery. Fair enough, but it doesn't exactly inspire a lot of confidence does it? I can't see the marketing people for the world's leading consumer brands jumping on that one as a way to sell their products. 'Might last a year' doesn't have a great ring to it.

I was still away with the fairies but the plumbers had done their job and they handed me back over to the routine maintenance team. The next thing for everybody other than me to worry about was the dreaded rejection. Bless them; they were already working on that.

If you've ever been unfortunate enough to spend time in hospital you will know it's a scary place. Nights in hospital are even worse because the night staff try to kill you. It's not true of course but everybody thinks it when they're in there. You can't help it. Intensive Care or High Dependence is singularly the most disorientating experience a person can have, as it appears *everyone* is trying to kill you. There is no natural light so artificial lights are on 24 hours a day and your senses start to play games with you. Sometimes you can see and sometimes you can't. You can hear voices and machines and sometimes you can feel yourself being handled. Eventually your senses become a little more reliable as the drugs reduce and you start to heal. Often, one's hearing returns first and you pick up familiar voices. This return to sentience took a few days for me. They keep liver transplant patients sedated for quite some time as, crudely put, they cut you in half, move everything to one side, remove, replace, repack and stitch you back together. Having you thrashing about as soon as you come out of surgery and before the healing process has begun would not be a great idea. I'm pretty sure I'd have been thrashing about given the opportunity and indeed, a little while later, thrashing and shouting became one of my favourite things.

Following the vivid imagery during the surgery, I had returned to an empty state of complete blackness making it difficult to pinpoint exactly when sounds and shapes started to filter back into my brain through my fully functioning ears and short-sighted eyes. The medical notes from my time in High Dependence indicated that by the Tuesday following the surgery on Sunday morning I was starting to get pretty agitated. The sedation, the immunosuppression, the intravenous antibiotics and the toxins that still filled my body combined to induce the most horrific hallucinations you can image. In fact, I hope you can't imagine them. I didn't believe that I could. To this day it upsets me greatly that my mind was capable of generating the thoughts and images that flashed in and out of my semi-consciousness over the next few days. I can see little point in upsetting you with graphic descriptions of what I conjured up, suffice to say the more gory ones involved have various body parts either attached or removed. More upsetting still that I was involved in the death of others or watched helplessly as people were attacked and killed. It was truly terrifying.

At one point I believed three hospital staff were under my bed drinking cans of beer. They were young and antipodean, two Australians and one who kept reminded me he was a Kiwi. Every time they needed to get out to take a leak they simply squeezed my arm to let me know I needed to move out of the way. This happened about every 15 minutes in a curiously identical rhythm to the inflation of the automatic blood pressure monitoring cuff around my arm. Odd that. Apparently me trying to lift myself up to let the guys out by levering myself up on the machines surrounding me was not doing a great deal to promote the healing process but I wasn't to know that at the time. The under-the-bed antipodean medical team also had to fight off a woman who was trying to stick infected needles into me from under the bed. They won. Thanks lads, but I did have to throw some pretty nifty moves myself to stay out of her way although this was completely misinterpreted in my medical notes as seemingly aimless 'thrashing about'. If only they knew the truth.

As I physically recovered in the HDU and the amount of drugs was reduced, I started to override the ventilator and breathe for myself. This was no great feat on my part. After some time with a machine breathing for you, if you can't start doing it again yourself you are pretty much stuck there for good. Dave Mutimer couldn't take me off the ventilator himself; he needed a consultant anaesthetist to do that unless there was some kind of crisis and only then could he take matters into his own hands. No anaesthetist could be found but as luck would have it, entirely coincidentally, right then, there was an unspecified crisis. Again, odd. The breathing tubes came out and up I came out of the medically induced state of partial paralysis and very much back to life, if not to reality.

My cheese was still completely off my cracker. I can remember having a throat as dry as a desert, a symptom of having tubes down my neck for days and being allowed to have some ice to suck to relieve it. Sometime later they tried to make me eat cauliflower cheese, my first solid meal for a couple of weeks although I would sooner have had the 'under the bed needle woman' back. I can't stand cauliflower cheese.

I do remember Dad coming into see me. I was convinced Dad had died of a heart attack during my illness so I can't even begin to explain how happy I was to see him. By now, Thursday following the surgery on Sunday, I was sufficiently cognisant to understand I was hallucinating but not able to distinguish what was real and what was a product of my fevered mind, I just hoped to hell Dad was really there. My confusion and fear was increased because I'm short sighted and wear either contact lenses or glasses, without these all I could see were blurred shapes and images. I couldn't bring anything into focus making distinguishing between what was real and what was fantasy even more problematic. I have it in mind when a bunch of doctors were surrounding my bed at one point I was loaned a pair of large comedy glasses and they all started to tell me how much I looked like Ian MaCaskill, the BBC weatherman. I really hope this was a figment of my fevered imagination or if it wasn't, nobody had a camera.

Following a conversation with Dr Mutimer, it had been agreed Dad should tell me I'd had a liver transplant as soon as practical and this he did. It was a shock to hear but it had sunk in over my time in hospital that something pretty significant had happened. I couldn't really process the information but I do remember him putting some normal sized glasses on me and telling me I'd be absolutely fine, that all the tubes and bags would be removed and I'd have to take some drugs but they were small tablets and nothing to worry about.

Then, I think, he left quickly with tears in his eyes. If there were, that's twice in my life I've seen him shed tears, the other time being when my Mum died. He's not unfeeling; far from it and as far as I know he's not a Vulcan is Dad. He's just tough and he's been through a few things in his life and doesn't show his feelings easily sometimes.

This was apparently the second time Dad had tried to get this information over to me but at the first attempt I was still having more regular florid hallucinations. At that particular time I was working on the basis my limbs had been removed systematically and they were coming back for the rest of me when it suited them. I distinctly remember a phrase I used during a conversation with him. Thankfully Dad doesn't remember this so it may have been in my head rather than audible but I asked him to 'push the button'. I'm not sure what or where the button was but I do know that I'd asked him to end my life. I recall looking down and seeing wires and tubes all over my chest and trying to pull them out, I was struggling and fighting. I pulled out whatever I could get my hands on, relaxed my body and waited to die. I do not know whether the relaxation was of my own doing or more likely involved another hit of the suppressant drugs, but either way it had the inevitable effect on my bowels. It was with a feeling of embarrassment and frustration that I soon realised I was not dead and that no buttons had been pressed. Real or not, it has remained with me to this day that I had asked him to help end my life and it does not make me proud.

I was moved out of the HDU and onto the ward the following day, the Friday following surgery on the previous Sunday. I can't really remember too well the move itself, but after a week flat on my back, I couldn't walk anywhere. It's amazing how quickly your muscles lose strength.

I got particularly upset at one point because I didn't know where I was, what day it was or what time it was. I was completely disorientated and demanded to see a newspaper. I must have got the whole 'proof of life' deal a little confused, you know, when they send a picture of a snatch victim through to the family with a copy of the Daily Kidnap to demonstrate currency. I was convinced that seeing a newspaper would prove something although I hadn't really thought through what that might be. I was becoming pretty agitated so they brought me a copy of a local paper to calm me down. I couldn't really read it because I couldn't focus and even if I could I had no idea what date I'd come in to hospital so its currency was irrelevant. The only fact I was able to glean from the paper was the WI jumble sale in Harbourne had been cancelled; a singularly unhelpful piece of information.

I was now sufficiently aware to know I was finding the catheter upsetting. I think it's fair to say nobody has a tube up their willy for longer than absolutely necessary. Well, perhaps some people do but I presume there are specialist magazines and websites for those folk and personally I do not number among their subscribers. I asked a male staff nurse who was later introduced to me as Dave Allison, my Post Transplant Co-ordinator, to get the thing out of me quick. Please. He said he would but did I realise this would mean I'd have to walk to the toilet myself? Yes of course I'd walk to the toilet, in fact, I'd done it loads of times before and considered myself something of an expert. Dutifully, he screwed his eyes up and I screwed up mine and he pulled the little plastic tube out. Totally painless and a total relief. A few seconds later I discovered why he had his eyes screwed up when in one swift movement he deftly removed the 6 inch square of sticking plaster securing the catheter and covering my entire pubic region. Despite the painkillers, that did smart a bit.

A minute or so later I was trying to pick myself up off the floor after trying inexpertly to walk to the toilet and finding my claim of being an expert in this field was a wild and unsupportable exaggeration. I had no discernable leg strength at all. I perceived some knowing looks as I was helped back to my bed and I think one of the nurses asked if I wanted to see another newspaper. That evening, as the more unpleasant of the hallucinations became less frequent my mind conjured up an image of a close friend visiting me and bringing me a toy fishing kit including a small rod, line and a plastic float and a police outfit complete with badge, little gun, a whistle and plastic handcuffs. Laughably ridiculous I know but I'd got used to the kind of nonsense my brain could generate with help of hallucinogenic drugs. I've still got the toys now. Thanks Siv. He later told me if he'd bought something serious I'd have known how desperate the whole situation was and he didn't want to further alarm me further.

My brother came to see me the next day. I was still hooked up to some pretty serious substances but my new liver was working hard to remove the toxins my old liver had been unable to process. He had phoned the ward in the morning, asked if it was appropriate to come in and was told it was but he should expect to find me in a very confused state. My brother's response intimated it would be unwise to expect any great improvement from that position and my current state was likely to be as good as it was going to get. By the time Ian arrived, I was on a medical ship in the tropics with sun blazing through the high portholes and the white-coated stewards going about their daily duties. I was so pleased to see him I didn't dare ask how he'd managed to get on the boat in case he and it disappeared. I do recall asking who was paying for the cruise and the treatment and he told me it was the remnants of the NHS. Bloody good of them I thought.

That Saturday evening on the ward the last hallucination visited me. With my glasses off, I squinted up at the ever present red night-lights on the ceiling. A neon sign, a cowboy hat with 'Jesus Burgers', in red and green letters appeared in front of me. Odd, but not scary. Not as scary as 'under the bed needle woman' or the cauliflower cheese anyway

My head continued to clear over the next few days and I began to get a grip on what had happened to me. There were still gaps, gaps I'd fill in later and gaps that remain unfilled, but reality was filtering back in to my world. A procession of friends came to see me for which I was enormously grateful. I told one friend about my experience with the antipodean team and was so convincing of their existence he repeated the story to others as being factual. I was questioned about them months after coming out of hospital by which time I had realised it was a fantasy. He's no fool and it shows just how powerfully convincing and utterly realistic those hallucinations were.

On the ward my muscle strength was returning, there was physiotherapy, some exercises involving a static bike and some sit ups. I had made the decision to walk to my daily chest x-ray appointment using the two sets of stairs to get me down to the first floor. I do recall expressing concern to the radiographer during one of these visits about my repeated exposure to radiation. He looked at me incredulously and mentioned I might have other things to worry about right now.

I was starting to interact more lucidly with the staff on the Liver Unit. Some of them still viewed me with caution, most probably embarrassed by their misinterpretation of my seemingly wild thrashings and grabbings. They were all staff nurses, sisters or doctors as there were no junior staff working on the unit. One of the staff nurses looked strangely familiar although I didn't think anything of it as I was still pretty hazy with the drugs. She came to see me whilst my Dad and Anne were visiting and asked if I recognised her. Well I did, sort of, but was that because I'd seen her on the ward, did we know each other whilst we were at school together or something? How bizarre that would be. Then it dawned on me. She was the daughter of the landlord of my local pub in Bridgnorth right? Wrong.

She was in actual fact Carmel, my London based friend's girlfriend, who I had met a few weeks earlier at my leaving party. This rather threw me. I was still pretty fuzzy from the pain killers and other drugs and was trying to come to terms with the enormity of what had happened over the last couple of weeks so I was unsure whether I was dreaming this or not. If I wasn't hallucinating, it was a pretty cruel trick as Dad and Anne were in on it too. But it was indeed

Carmel and when they had first realised the connection, Dave Mutimer and Dad had agreed it was probably sensible to tell me so I didn't drop a sprocket when I first saw her. They were concerned if I saw or thought I saw somebody I recognised from my London days I would think I was hallucinating and or crackers. I mean, why would my friend's girlfriend from London be wandering around a hospital ward in Birmingham dressed as a staff nurse? Please don't try to answer that. To avoid this they told me as soon as they judged I was sufficiently compos mentis to take in the unlikely coincidence.

I would never criticise them for it but at that particular moment it just added to a whole pile of stuff I was trying to come to terms with. My bagging area was very much full of unidentified items, not least the fact that I was pretty much dead a few days back and had gone through a fundamental physical and psychological trauma.

Carmel looked after me during my stay on the ward and did so with the professional care, patience and skill exhibited by all of the staff on that unit. She also brought with it a warm heart and never had I needed that so much. Yeah, I know I was a 26-year-old adult, a big tough lad and very lucky to be alive but, like many of us brave heroes, I wanted my Mum and unfortunately she couldn't make it. This wonderful Staff nurse stepped into the breach with the added touch of having taken the trouble to introduce herself to me *before* I got ill. That's some kind of forward planning in my book and not something you'd normally expect on the NHS. Discounting the fortuitous timing of my phone call to Dad, the fact Dr Gibson was available that Friday evening or that a suitable donor organ had been found so quickly, the appearance of Carmel was the first extraordinary coincidence to reveal itself. It was not to be the last and by no means was it the most unsettling.

Re-livered

Some of my fellow patients on E3 Liver unit were there following general liver surgery. Others were awaiting treatment, assessment or hepatic prodding of some kind but the majority were recovering from transplant surgery. Most of them had been through a pretty comprehensive pre-transplant programme having been tested to ensure their suitability for surgery. They had gone through, for want of a better phrase, some awareness training. They had some idea of what to expect when they came around from the anaesthetic, what the tubes and wires were doing, how disorientating the HDU would be and where to expect to find holes in their bodies. They were the regulars in this particular local and knew the drill on the ward. I, as the new boy, did not.

I started to get to know the doctors fairly quickly as I was, it appeared, a bit of a minor celebrity in the crazy rock and roll world of liver transplantation. News of my thrashing around in intensive care had spread widely and I was apprehensively eyed up by many of the staff who kept me at arm's length. A nurse later told me I'd got it into my head I was ill because I had too much blood in my body. I'd made a grab for a small pair of scissors in her top pocket to let some blood out of my arm and got pretty aggressive when I couldn't get hold of them. There have been very few diagnoses of 'too much blood' since doctors of yore put their leeches away but I was totally convinced of it at the time and pretty angry they hadn't spotted it. Accordingly they gave me an appropriate amount of distance, preventing a repeat of the rather unfortunate 'grabbing and trying to throttle and/or stab' thing.

The doctors kept asking me what my name was. I was pretty much okay on this one although I had rather hoped Dad might have told them if they'd really wanted to know. Then they got tricky on me. "Where are you?" they asked. "What has happened to you?" Frankly, I was disappointed. As taxpayers we spend millions on training

39

these people and they didn't know who I was, where I was or what had happened to me. Shameful. I was relieved to find out later they had all this information to hand. It turns out they were just checking whether I was still doing the Lucy in the Sky with Diamonds shuffle or not.

There was the bizarre ritual of an en masse daily weigh-in where we were lined up and took turns to sit in a chair whilst our weight was announced to an expectant crowd of patients. I can't recall if there was any applause. There followed breakfast, a ward round visit by a group of doctors, lunch and visitors. This was interspersed with visits to other exciting parts of the hospital for x-rays, scans and physiotherapy. The day finished off with dinner, coffee and mints, and more visitors. I made the coffee and mints bit up but the rest of it is true. It was like the worst holiday camp ever. There then followed what was to become the nightly, universally unsuccessful, battle to get some sleep. The back of the bed was permanently elevated so it was difficult to lie sideways. When I did manage it I pulled the drip out of one arm or the other depending on which way I rolled. This pleased nobody. Finally, when I did lie briefly on my side without leaking drugs, it felt like all my organs had made a tidal journey to the lower most part of my abdomen. That was distinctly unnerving so I righted myself and prayed nothing had fallen off. Or in. I entertained myself one sleepless night by eating two large bags of wine gums sending my blood sugar reading bonkers in the morning. The staff were remarkably tolerant: I'd have thrown me out by now.

I do remember one of the surgeons talking to me about the need for a biopsy. This spooked me a bit. I was unclear on an awful lot of things including what had caused my liver failure but I didn't think it was cancer. It was probably naïve of me but I'd always assumed biopsies were performed on tumour tissue to determine malignancy but in my case, he explained, they were going to take a piece of liver tissue to determine the degree of rejection. I'd been taking the new wonder drug, FK506, to prevent my body from rejecting the new organ but I was told some level of acute rejection was to be expected and this needed to be controlled. Great. So, my poorly ass had been dug out of the fire at considerable trouble and expenses, not to mention my donor's death, and it could all be back to whatever exists on the other side of square one if rejection couldn't be adequately controlled.

I was visited by a recently transplanted fellow of a similar age to me, Andy, who had been in the Navy until his diagnosis of Wilson's disease, a genetic condition where copper accumulates in tissues and can lead to liver damage. In his case his liver had failed in a similar time frame to mine although this is uncommon and Wilson's disease can usually be successfully treated without such drastic measures. He'd had two transplants, the second after 3 weeks in intensive care fighting rejection. He described his condition rather stoically as 'sore'.

Immunosuppression therapy had moved a distance from the early days of a handful of steroids and a hope for the best approach. The place it had moved to was a handful of FK506 and hope for the best approach. The reasons why some patients reject so aggressively it cannot be controlled, while others seem to tolerate a new organ with a relatively low level of drug therapy, are still not understood. Not by a long way. If you ask, they'll mutter something about the whole thing being idiopathic.

Whilst I was worrying about how I was going to handle the rejection issue, I should have been worrying about the more immediate problem of how they were going to get a piece of liver tissue out of me. I still hadn't really twigged when a young lady from the pathology department appeared. Perhaps I should say arrived rather than appeared as she was very real and not a product on my mind. She had with her a canister full of dry ice and a tray full of needles and other sharp looking accoutrements in sterile packaging. What they were about to do still hadn't sunk in when they ask me to lie on my side, breath out and practice holding my breath for as long as possible. Carmel was looking after me,

41

holding my hand in fact and telling me how brave I was being. Brave? What was there to be brave about? Who cares, I was having my hand held by an attractive young lady and things were looking up.

What was happening sunk in in a very real and literal sense a few seconds later when they put a needle the size of the inside of a Biro through my ribs and into my new liver to remove a core of tissue. The pained look on the face of the lady from the pathology lab pretty much summed up the shock I felt at being well and truly lanced. I'm sure she had chosen the pathology laboratory over a clinical role precisely so she didn't have to watch people being surgically stabbed. It had all been a ruse, a comforting hand to keep me still so the doctor had less chance of sticking the needle into my lungs. I rubbed my side, pouted and sulked like a kid whose Mum had taken him to the doctor for his first inoculation. Oh, the betrayal.

I'm a bit of a veteran of biopsies now. I once heard of a young doctor doing his first liver biopsy getting a piece of liver and some kidney: an offal kebab if you will. I personally have had a doctor miss my liver although she said it was okay, they could have another go through the same hole. Every now and again, they still try to pull the whole student doctor thing on me. The conversation goes like this.

Young doctor: "Biopsy time, Mr Smith."
Mr Smith: "Have you done this before?"
Young doctor: "I'm a fully qualified doctor, Mr Smith."
Mr Smith: "That, with all due respect, is not the answer to the question I asked, young man"
Young doctor: "Ermmm, well "
Mr Smith: "Nurse! This man's going to stab me!"

It's not necessarily a painful process and they do give you some local anaesthetic to make boring through the ribs bit less uncomfortable, but it is wholly unpleasant having a needle that big driven into the core of you. The breathing exercise and the reason you have to hold your breath during the procedure is to make your lungs as small as possible. This reduces the risk of puncturing them with the needle. If you hear a noise like you've got a flat tyre you're up Shit Creek without a paddle. Or a boat.

To add to the experience, you have to spend the next 8 hours flat on your back with a blood pressure cuff on to monitor if you're bleeding internally. My advice, if you are ever unfortunate enough to need one of these, is to have it done during the day as the theatre will be better staffed in case you bleed. And get a pretty/handsome staff nurse to hold your hand. You might as well and it makes the thing entirely more bearable. You may also like to keep a puncture repair kit to hand. Oh, and go for a pee first.

Later that day the surgeon returned. Good news! I had moderate-to-acute rejection. Good news? Apparently yes. No rejection would be deeply worrying and indicate whilst my new liver might be fine, the rest of my body could be totally screwed. Acute rejection at some level is the standard bodily response following a transplant and a single episode of it can normally be successfully controlled. Multiple episodes become more problematic but it was too early to tell if that was going to happen to me. So with a wing and a prayer he gave me a handful, yes a handful, of Prednisolone, a steroid that stuck me to the ceiling for the rest of the night. The final bit of excellent news was that they'd do another biopsy in a few days to see if the steroid sandwich had worked. Goody, something else to look forward to then.

Gradually, the IV antibiotics were removed and replaced with oral ones, pain killers were reduced, anti-fungal syringes (relax, no needles, just syringes) in the mouth stopped and things began to get a little less strange. The next biopsy came and went a few days later and the result showed the rejection was resolving. Another quarter pound bag of Prednisolone would not be required. This was an enormous relief as I really did not fancy repeating the last few weeks anytime soon.

43

As something approaching normality returned I realised I needed a few things. Firstly, some fresh air, but also probably more importantly for those around me, a shave and a bath. I had spent so long in hospital that the people looking after me had thought I was a beardy where in truth I'd just not been able to shave for the best part of 3 weeks. Adding to this my great, and very direct, friend Dave had told me I smelled like a kebab and I should do something about that as soon as possible. I suddenly felt a need to get clean, get my teeth clean and to remove the brown iodine stains around the scars on my abdomen and my legs. All part of the process of getting better. I asked if I could go outside and they reluctantly said I could, provided somebody accompanied me. Dad and I went into a little paved garden area outside the canteen on the ground floor and we sat down on a wooden bench. It was cold but bright and dry and I could feel a breeze on my face and see unfiltered daylight. It went a long way to proving I was real, awake and alive. Never had a mixture of chip fat and fag smoke smelled so good.

Two eminent medics, Professor McMaster, a surgeon, and Professor Elwyn Elias, a physician, had established the Liver Unit in Birmingham in the early 1980s, and had developed it into the largest transplant unit of its type in Europe. The former occasionally led the ward round surrounded by a team of younger doctors who hung onto his every word and it was he and his entourage who came to see me on Thursday morning. I clearly remember him asking me the normal who? what? and where? questions which, despite his god-like status in the medical world, he seemed disappointingly unable to work out for himself. I must have answered to his satisfaction as his next question was to a young Sikh doctor standing next to him, "what shall we do with Mr Smith now?" McMaster peered over his glasses awaiting a response. The gaze of the other doctors fell upon the young Sikh and they all moved back a pace in case a hole should appear beneath him. I held my breath and felt a genuine need to help him out with an answer despite being the least qualified to do so.

"Send him home?" replied the doctor, almost apologetically.

"Home?" queried McMaster, "Eleven days following fulminant liver failure and you want to send him home?"

The young doctors move another pace back. This was bad. Very bad. The floor was cracking.

"Just for the weekend, perhaps?"

The eyes of the assembled mass turned back towards McMaster to watch him deliver the killer blow from behind their clipboards. He turned to them all.

"Views?"

Silence.

"Hmmm?"

The tension was unbearable.

McMaster relieved all our suffering at this point by saying that a weekend at home was a good strategy provided nothing untoward happened between now and Friday afternoon. I was to be back in hospital by 9am on Monday morning otherwise he'd come and get me himself and neither of us wanted that to happen did we? We certainly did not, no indeed. I'm not sure who was happier and more relieved, the young Sikh doctor or me.

Friday came around, I'd sat on the wonderful weigh-in chair, 'bloods' had been done and remarkably, my liver function was now pretty close to normal. An ultrasound scan had indicated there was some bruising to my new liver but that was resolving. For my own part, despite being told by one doctor I looked like I'd fold in half with a good sneeze, I was feeling relatively sprightly.

Anybody who has spent time in hospital will tell you there are two different kinds of sprightly, the hospital one and the real world one. In hospital it's abnormally warm, the floors are even and without carpet. You are not expected to walk very far if at all, and you only have to navigate stairs if you choose to do so. There is somebody feeding you,

45

watering you, monitoring you and watching your every move and, at times, movement, if you get my meaning. Also, you are hopefully getting better and after a week or so on the ward they begin to move you further from the nurse's station and slide in other people who are more ill making you feel pretty chipper, relatively speaking.

I will let go a secret here. This is important for anybody spending time in hospital. Take sweets, a really good selection of sweets. And get a bowl, a big one. That way, as you become less of a celebrity and are moved further away from the nurse's station, you have the means to attract medical staff towards you. It's much like hanging out a net containing nuts for the birds. It works, I promise, and as you improve and get better, the company and conversation of these universally wonderful people becomes a vital part of your rehabilitation. Not that I'm competitive or anything but something of a confectionary based Cold War developed between me and the lad from Manchester in the bed opposite. We had completely cleaned out the WVS shop on the ground floor a few times during attempts at total sweetie dominance. It was a way to pass the time and we developed a real sense of camaraderie. I'll come back to the important concept of shared suffering later on, in a rather different context.

Dad drove me home. It was a short journey that took a long time. I felt like I was being shaken to pieces. The 26 miles from Birmingham to Bridgnorth is a journey I've done thousands of times for work, hospital and pleasure but that one was the most uncomfortable and worrying. I was delighted to get out but as soon as I'd left its confines I realised access to immediate medical support of limitless potential was further away than I might like. The fact that things could go critically wrong pretty quickly at that stage in the transplant process was not lost on me. Should some kind of infection get hold, I was unlikely to be able to fight it off bearing in mind the immunosuppresant effect of the steroids and the FK506. Hospital may not have been great but in my predicament it was safe.

The first night back at home was a worrying one and I had to recalibrate my 'sprightly' meter on a minute-by-minute basis. Home in this particular instance was not my house but Anne's farm where Dad was now living. An unfamiliar place to me, not odd, just not my home. Dad slept in a single bed next to me on the first night and whilst I didn't hallucinate I did have some very strange dreams. I also slept properly for the first time in a few weeks. A deep sleep uninterrupted by night-lights, staff, general hospital noise or other patients.

I woke up not knowing where I was but we've all done that from time to time right? I was up early on Saturday morning; I went downstairs and sat in the enormous living room of the farmhouse. The room is the same size as a small house itself with large patio doors, a whole wall of glass in fact, facing out over the fields. I remember sitting and looking out as the morning drifted in. It wasn't much of a morning, no magnificent sunrise clearing the low-lying mist but never had I been so relieved to see daylight emerge. The time during my illness, the coma and my stay in hospital had been characterized by a seemingly inescapable stone cold darkness. This weak February light was the closest thing to heaven I believe I will ever experience and I sobbed for a couple of hours just looking out across the half-lit Shropshire fields. I can't tell you exactly why I was crying but I guess I was totally overwhelmed by my recent experiences. Being out of hospital, away from a controlled clinical environment and back in the real world with cups of tea and warm kitchens, put a different perspective on what had happened. It made the whole thing very real.

Just to make absolutely sure I'd got the crying thing sorted, I got up really early on Sunday morning and did it again. This time Anne's Labrador–Collie cross, Emma, snuck out of the kitchen and came to see what all the fuss was about. I'd been advised by the hospital to stay well away from animals, as my immune system was so low, but nobody had told her that. Emma had a lovely gentle disposition, was knocking on a bit and, dare I say, carrying a pound or two more than might be ideal. I don't know if she knew I was upset or not very well, but when she came over and lay across my bare feet I was not about to move her out of the way. She was a great comfort.

Over the weekend, the District Nurse turned up at the farm complete with instructions to re-dress my primary abdominal wound. The hospital had applied three long broad strips of tape, big plasters in essence, over the Mercedes scar and similar material on the wounds in my armpit and groin. My head scar had been covered with a smaller plaster over the stitches. Whilst the hospital had access to dressings ideal for the job the District Nurse only had access to cotton wool and surgical tape but she had lashings of it. By the time she'd finished, I look like an infant school Father Christmas art project complete with cotton wool pom pom taped to the side of my head at a jaunty angle. It was less neat than the hospital job but functional. It made up for its slightly unprofessional appearance by having top-notch comedy value. She came, she saw, she totally taped me up in cotton wool. I returned to the hospital on Monday morning as instructed and after convincing them it was, in actual fact me and not Santa or the marshmallow man, I was reinstalled in a bed. I couldn't even see the nurse's station now. There weren't enough sweets in the world to get anybody's attention from there. A staff nurse appeared and started to take my decorations down, redressing me with the more utilitarian hospital supplied sticky bandages. Twelfth Night, I suppose.

And with that my rather dramatic stay in hospital came to a close. Wednesday 24th February saw me discharged and sent home to return regularly as an outpatient and on occasion to be re-admitted for further pokings and proddings.

I cut off the plastic wrist tag with a pair of scissors (R. Smith DOB 23/4/67. Liver fulminant) and threw it in the bin.

Back to Life

My next visit to hospital was a dual-purpose one to see my surgeon in clinic and to visit Dave Allison, my Post-Transplant Coordinator (PTC). I needed to have my stitches removed and to discover a little more of what life as a liver transplant recipient might be like. You'll remember Dave, he's the sticking plaster removal expert: him of the screwed-up eyes. I remembered him too and a fine fellow he turned out to be as his help in those early days was invaluable. It is sad his role is no longer funded in the modern NHS as he filled in a lot of information gaps that appeared between the time pressed surgeons and medics.

I wanted to thank my surgeon for his time and trouble that he shrugged off as being nothing more than doing his job. I was also interested to receive an update on how the team was getting on in isolating the disease that had struck me down. Disappointingly, little progress had been made. Primarily because nobody was looking. It's a rare disease but the second most common cause of acute liver failure following paracetamol overdose. It might be a virus, it might not be, and whilst research into the various types of hepatitis viruses goes on worldwide it turned out holding my breath for a result on my specific case would lead to asphyxiation. I didn't really fancy another blue period.

Dave was waiting for me in an anteroom next to where I met the surgeon. Three separate sutures held the three long scars that made up the Mercedes on my abdomen together, not visible on the surface of my skin. They joined the epidermal level whilst the surface skin was stuck together with the famous sticky plaster stuff. Nowadays they use staples: sounds awful. The long stitches were secured at either end by a small plastic ball threaded and knotted to prevent them from disappearing inside me inadvertently. He informed me they were simply removed by being pulled through in an entirely painless process he himself would carry out. It was very much an, "I know kids, let's do the show HERE!" approach. I lay down on the table; Dave put some latex gloves on, wound the end of the first stitch around his fingers, screwed up his eyes and pulled hard. I'd seen that face before, it was his 'this is going to hurt you more than me' face although this time I'm not sure it worked quite how he had anticipated. He'd cut the blood supply to his fingers off by the time he'd removed the third one. The other stitches in my groin and armpit had been removed on the ward, including the one from my little bit of brain surgery.

Physically I was healing pretty quickly, the steroids were removed from my diet of drugs and the dose of FK506 was brought down gradually. At high doses it has an impact on your kidney function which is unfortunate as it is used very effectively with kidney transplants. It's also a neurotoxin meaning in practical terms it gives you the shakes. Not great for a surveyor when you are trying to use a pen to draw or write, so I was pleased these effects faded as the dose was reduced.

Whilst the doses of drugs were being changed and balanced the hospital were regularly checking up on how my liver was working and were keeping a close eye on whether I was suffering from any rejection. The principal test used to monitor liver function is a suite of blood chemistry levels analysed from a standard blood test. There are all sorts of different enzymes in liver cells that perform the huge amount of chemical processes carried out in there. If they can be detected in your blood at higher than normal levels it means something is attacking the cells and damaging your liver leading to the release of these enzymes into your blood stream. My blood chemistry returned to normal very quickly after the transplant indicating a good match and that rejection was being well controlled. All good news.

I started to re-integrate myself into the real world back at Anne's farm although I was still advised not to drive for at least 6 weeks. A seat belt suddenly snapping on across my chest and abdomen might have caused some damage should a crash occur. I'd been advised to get active as quickly as reasonably possible with the physiotherapy I had received in hospital starting the process off. At first, walking up a set of carpeted stairs took some effort, but within a couple of days a walk of a few hundred yards over the rough farm drive was manageable.

Email wasn't widely available in 1993 and the Internet was still in early development, so I took a little time to write to a few people to let them know what had happened. Kate was top of the list to be advised. She rang a few days later and I ran her through the whole affair.

Dave had set me a little test. Before I started to do any more demanding physical exercise I had to stand on the back step of the house, jump off and land two footed. How hard could that be? Very, as it turned out. Not exactly bungee jumping I know but the first time I stood and looked over this modest precipice I retreated from it. I felt like the jump would shake me up inside and there was a good chance I would fall to bits. A few days later I managed to take the leap of faith and landed in one piece. I was beginning to feel the need to get back to taking exercise that was more vigorous than double-footed 6" step jumping or rough farm path walking. I could also feel a pressing need to get back to what I considered to be normal. I wanted to get back to work and far more importantly to friends, family and sport as quickly as I could in part to prove to the outside world there was nothing to see here and all was well. Nobody from the outside world was watching of course: those close to me were interested in my progress because they cared about me. They weren't monitoring me with a normal-o-meter.

The end of March was coming up, I was 5 weeks out of hospital, physically recovering quickly, and to all intents and purposes I was 'better'. It was fairly straight forward, I'd been ill, had some treatment and got better. I didn't perceive there was anything worth dwelling on or anything particularly to deal with: it was time to press on with this whole life thing. It was all very admirable and stoic but I had stored up a few things in the back of my mind that I was going to have to deal with sooner or later. I chose later or better still, not at all. And press on I did. I was proud of fact

51

I'd come out of hospital quicker than anyone previously with my condition although my naturally competitive spirit does not stretch to wanting to have another go at that particular record now it's been beaten. I returned to full time work on the 1st April 1993, about 7 weeks after the transplant, commuting from Bridgnorth into the Black Country and resuming my career, such as it was, as an unenthusiastic Chartered Surveyor.

A few weeks later I went out and bought a bike. Oh yes, a bike, and although I didn't know it then, this was to change my life fundamentally for the better. One of the reasons for my return to Shropshire, so rudely interrupted by liver failure, had been to join in the mountain biking scene my friends were enjoying. Whilst in London I'd run, gone swimming and over trained with pointless exercises in the local gym. Post-transplant, running was out of the question. Firstly, I'm rubbish at it but more importantly any attempt at even the mildest jog resulted in an off-putting 'loose' feeling. Candidly, a disturbing sloshing noise from ones insides is not an attractive accompaniment to a jog in the park. I had returned to the swimming pool once after I'd tried myself out in the bath to ensure I wouldn't leak. No really, I did. That visit had resulted in some very odd looks from the lifeguards and had scared some small children. On reflection, perhaps saying "shark!" whilst winking and pointing at the scar as I walked past had not been such a big hit.

I'd spoken to Dave Allison at length about how soon I could return to sport and he generally advised caution and a slow re-introduction commenting that the 22 mile sponsored walk in May my friends had thoughtfully entered me into would be frankly 'taking the piss'. Further, rugby was out of the question. A transplanted liver hangs a little lower in the abdomen and protrudes probably an inch or more below the rib cage, it is deep set, but a big hit or repeated big hits could cause problems. On top of that, no company was going to cover me, a club, a referee or anybody else with meaningful insurance. I hasten to add, this is no great loss to the world of rugby. I was never any good but I wanted to get back to team sports. Ask anybody who has ever played for a team or club, anywhere, at any level, at any sport, and they will tell you why. So a bike seemed like a good idea. No shaking about on a bike you see, it's all nice and smooth.

The embryonic mountain bike scene was kicking off in a big way and many of my friends were knocking about on 1st generation mountain bikes like the Clockwork Orange, the Orange P7, the Specialized Stump Jumper or Rockhopper and the Muddy Fox. It was all very exciting and pioneering. One more adventurous mate had a GT RTS, an early full suspension bike using, if I remember correctly, elastomer based rear suspension and a lurid pair of gold Rockshox on the front. It probably provided 30mm of suspension and weighed enough to have its own gravitational field: you could see light bending around it as it got up to speed. Having said that, it did have an excellent pilot so it went down hill using 'route 1' very effectively leaving riders of rigid bikes way behind, irrespective of their handling skills.

My budget wouldn't stretch to anything as fancy as the Orange I had set my heart on so it was off to Halfords for me. I walked out a couple of hours later with a 21" Raleigh Apex in all its glorious purpleness. The lack of any meaningful advice in the shop meant I had picked a frame size identical to that of my previous bike, the 5-speed Dawes 'racing' bike of my 80's youth handed down to me by my brother. It fitted me, I think, so logically the same size in a mountain bike would do the trick. It was £375 and a lot of money for what, at that time, was described as entry-level mountain bike but it was very purple so clearly worth the money. Moreover, it had 21 gears, three chainrings at the front, seven on the back and a rudimentary damping system on the handlebars called a 'flex stem'. The fact you don't see these around anymore is testament to its effectiveness but it was funky at the time. After a period of wearing-in, or perhaps more appropriately wearing-out, the 'flex stem' meant I had the only bike around with a prototype yaw control system.

These days, the bike is the cheap and easy bit, it's the bike specific shoes, helmets, clothes, sunglasses, tools and associated equipment that cost the real money. Back then, in 1993, these things hardly existed so with a pair of weight training gloves, some Rayban Aviators, football shorts, baseball boots and a yellow Ocean Pacific T shirt I set off on my maiden voyage. I looked fantastic as I'm sure you can imagine. I hadn't ridden a bike for some time, although what they say is true, it's as easy as falling off a log. Or something like that. It took me a while to get used to gears as the shifters where now mounted on the handlebars rather than on the downtube like my old Dawes racer but they moved satisfyingly and accurately when I clicked the switches. I headed off towards one of the many country lanes we are blessed with in and around Bridgnorth and rode out towards the golf club with a broadening smile on my face.

It was a euphoric feeling and I recalled a quote I thought was attributed to Albert Einstein. He reportedly wrote his faith in humanity was restored whenever he saw a grown man riding a bike. I was very much getting to grips with that sentiment as I headed into the countryside.

As part of my slapdash and shoddy research for this book I thought I'd better check the provenance of Albert's quote and I came across something very similar by H.G Wells. He said 'when I see an adult on a bicycle, I do not despair for the future of the human race'. Who actually said what is immaterial really, which is a good job because I was getting bored, but the sentiment of both statements runs true. If you ride, you'll know it is an indescribable feeling of freedom and fun that, however often you do it, never dissipates. It's also mildly eccentric, faintly ridiculous and very British in my mind. You're already dressed up and heading somewhere, you just need sandwiches or tea and cake.

I suspect neither Albert nor 'H.G' had been hit squarely in the chest by a ball hooked viciously off the 18th hole at Bridgnorth golf club when they put pen to paper but that's what happened to me. There was a rustling of tree branches, the briefest of whooshing noises and then a painful thump. It didn't take me off the bike but it did wind me, hitting me above the sternum just north of the surgical scar. I came to a halt, got off the bike and pulled up my T-shirt to inspect the damage. A cartoon-style egg shaped lump beginning to appear. The golfers arrived in search of the ball. It just so happened one of my friend's fathers was amongst them although it was his playing partner who'd got the problem with the hook. He looked at the scarred mess that was my abdomen, pointed and asked if he was responsible for it. I reassured him he was only down for the egg-shaped bit, the rest of it was my look out.

It was just one of those things and he was more shaken than I was after he'd been filled in on recent history. After a few minutes of sitting down outside the clubhouse, nerves had been largely restored and the conversation could return to whether he needed to drop a ball and play three off the tee. Frankly, trying to play the ball from where it landed was not in my best interest.

An eventful first ride of maybe 5 flat miles on smooth tarmaced lanes and, with the exception of the golf ball incident, pretty successful. At least it proved my lungs and legs still worked. I was confident that with some practice and training I could go further and faster, although that big chainring on the front was always going to be reserved for rolling down big smooth hills.

I started to go out for little rides, at first by myself, just to see how far I could go and still have a reasonable expectation of getting home in one piece. Along the way I learned a few valuable lessons. The first was that 5 flat miles on a reasonably equipped mountain bike is not a great challenge for most people, even ones with new livers. A 5 mile walk pushing a mountain bike with a flat tyre is. Note to self, must take spare inner tube, tyre levers and a pump next time. I also learned, with a mixture of joy and terror that a mountain bike really was equipped to be ridden off road over rough terrain. I could go places you wouldn't dream of taking a road bike like my hand-me-down Dawes racer. Big tyres and sturdy wheels meant bridle paths, old railway tracks, footpaths and the like all become manageable. Damn it, it was almost like the bike was designed for it. Oh yes, it was designed for it. Unfortunately, I wasn't. My reasoning that riding a bike would be less hard on my recently reconstructed body than running was looking increasingly shaky by the minute, although as I continued to heal I was gaining in confidence. Had the confidence been shared by a similar increase in my ability to handle the bike then all may have remained well but the two were badly mismatched. My first major 'off' saw me lying on my back in the local woods, my fall softened by a patch of stinging nettles.

If you've ever done this, you will understand the process of events. It goes in phases thus:

The 'weeeeee, look at me bombing down this hill' phase.

Here, all is well with the world, the dappled sunlight is your friend; the birds are chirping their approval and the bunnies applaud as they marvel at your progress. The world is yours, all things are possible and your status as a fat-tyred hero is as assured as attention of the world's most glamorous women.

Nothing could possibly go wrong.

The 'what the fu....?' phase.

This second stage is a rapid transition out of this fantasy world and back to a more fragile reality. You are wrenched back to the real world at the same speed your handlebars are wrenched from your hands and you are launched unceremoniously from your machine. However, in my considerable experience of these events it's rare you are launched cleanly. Commonly your legs become entangled in

56

the bike and, wherever you are going next, the bike is coming with you.

As you, the world, and your treasured bike all turn upside down you are ready to enter the final phase.

The 'Christ that hurt but I'm still alive' phase.

Yes, there's a little pain, some de-entanglement and a brief visual inspection to ensure your body parts are still attached. Personally, I like to add a wholly unscientific cursory internal assessment to my post-crash checklist but unless you've got any new bits you should feel free to skip this. It's likely you will have sprung a few leaks and you will be covered in chain oil. This is nothing beside the mocking laughter of your riding companions who will be just able to enquire as to your well-being whilst drawing sufficient breath to continue laughing. Nevertheless you will almost always be ready to continue your journey within a few minutes at a more sedate and less confident pace.

There is a fourth stage sometimes, perhaps involving the emergency services or as was in my case here, the startling realisation the nettles had set about their work with painful efficiency. I shouldn't have worried, my body was fully protected by football shorts and an Ocean Pacific T shirt. I had a sturdy bandana protecting my head. What could possibly go wrong?

A few days after this, I was back in the Liver unit as an outpatient for a routine blood test and a chat with Dave Mutimer. A call from the Dave Allison came through the following day at work which I took with some trepidation. I clearly recall being told, 'my blood results were not all we might have hoped for at this stage'. The reality of my situation suddenly came crashing back on me with the transplant unit statistics at the front of my mind. It was only 7 months or so after the transplant but it's amazing how quickly after a trauma you revert to the unthinking 'it will never happen to me' mentality. Just like an incurable random disease without known cause would never happen to me, neither would any kind of post-transplant complication. Those, like unexplained diseases, were the business of others, not me. The statistics told me that 90% of people survive liver transplant surgery, 70% survive for 12 months. 60% survive… I stopped reading at this point. Lies, damned lies and statistics.

I had to get back into hospital in the morning and was told I should prepare myself for an ultrasound scan, a biopsy and more blood tests. When I asked the obvious question, he sensibly said he didn't know what the problem was but it could be a range of things, that I was not to worry and we'd deal with it, whatever it was. He went on to say a dodgy set of results was not uncommon by any means at this early stage of the process. Okay, great, but my overriding fear at the time was the disease that had so nearly killed me had come back for a second go. I didn't sleep much that night.

I had overheard conversations in out-patients about second transplants, further surgery, battles with rejection that lasted for months and then resulted in another transplant or death. My journey through the transplantation process had avoided the usual preamble but it looked like I was going to be caught up in the post-transplant experience just like everybody else. Dave had asked if I'd maybe been over doing it a bit. My blood pressure was way up. Maybe the mountain biking, the couple of pints of beer, the new girlfriend and the speedy return to work had been pushing it a bit. Well, maybe a lot.

Back to E3, back to Carmel, who I felt like I had let down by being re-admitted. Back in front of another biopsy trolley compete with dry ice and lots of pained worried expressions. A brand new plastic wrist tag was attached and I was back in the hospital machine. Bloods first. The phlebotomists at the Queen Elizabeth Hospital can get a needle into your arm and the blood out without you even realising it's been done. You hear "sharp scratch", the phrase that has replaced the wholly more amusing "little prick", as the needle goes in and before you know it it's all over and your blood is off to the lab. If I may make so bold as to dole out a little advice here, be aware that doctors often can't do this without inflicting a deal of pain on you. If you have no choice but to let a doctor get a needle into you, try to find one who works with the elderly or with kids as their veins are smaller and they are more skilled at the process. If only a junior doctor is available you may as well put the needle in yourself. Nurses are better than doctors but phlebotomists, who do nothing other than take blood, are the best. I recommend them very highly.

The ultrasound scan was next as once the biopsy is done you're on your back for 8 hours so it was off to the X-ray department. This is not part of the Liver Unit and is shared by the rest of the hospital. You see some things here. Please trust me and give yourself a good chance of never seeing the inside of one. Don't drink or eat too much and don't smoke. Really, don't.

Whilst you are sitting and waiting for your turn with a Deli counter style raffle ticket in your hand and your arse hanging out of the back of a surgical gown, your fellow waiters are arranged around you. Some are in beds and wheelchairs full of tubes or are drinking litres of water at the behest of the radiographer so they can get better shots of your bladder, etc. My experience of having many of these scans is that the process itself is painless but the terrified looks on the faces of the people waiting for a scan after being told they have 'a mass', is not. It is a relief to get out of the waiting area, in to the darkened room with the machine and the doctors and away from the worried people and their scared other halves. You can normally tap the radiographer up for some information once the scanning process is completed. On this particular occasion he indicated he could see nothing abnormal other than that I'd ignored the request to fast for 12 hours and that I'd had eaten a sandwich. Cheese and tomato by the looks of things. These guys are really funny.

The biopsy came next. I assumed the position; everybody else assumed their worried looks. The doctor ("Yes, Mr Smith, I've done loads of these before') percussed my abdomen with his fingers and the back of his hand until there was a big dull blood-filled thudding noise indicating he'd located the large lobe of my liver. Bit of Novocain in the ribs, bit of a cut with a scalpel and whack, in went the big bore needle. Not too bad this time and no 'pssssss…' noise. Excellent. On went the automatic blood pressure cuff and I settled down for 8 hours bed rest as it dawned on me that in all the excitement I'd forgotten to go for a pee. Again.

By this time, Dave Mutimer had come to see me as my blood results were back. He told me my blood chemistry had returned to near normal in the short time between the test in outpatients and the test done this morning. It was just some kind of blip that had resolved itself and could have been a bit of anything – an infection, a spot of rejection perhaps. No further treatment was necessary right now, I could go home after the allotted bed rest and he'd see me in clinic in a couple of weeks. Greatly relieved, I took the opportunity to ask him a couple of questions that had been on my mind. First and foremost, what were the chances of the disease that had destroyed my liver in first place returning? What, realistically, was my life expectancy and, critically, could I have beer every now and again?

Dave explained the nature of the disease as being just what it said it was, sporadic. It occurred without rhyme or reason across a broad cross-section of people; men, women, children, across all ages without an identified common denominator. Neither it seemed was there any correlation in lifestyle, travel, food, work or anything else. As far as they could tell it was entirely random in whom it chose to infect. He further explained the common assumption that it was caused by some kind of virus, but no carrying agent had been identified meaning if it was indeed a virus, it must somehow have cleared the body spontaneously. Example; if a transplant is performed on a patient whose liver has been damaged by a known strain of viral hepatitis (A, B, C, etc) and that virus has not been removed from the body with treatment, it is more than likely the new liver will become re-infected with the same disease. Dave Mutimer told me this had only ever been recorded once in his knowledge in a patient with the same condition as me and that she had died almost immediately after the surgery. He went on to explain there had never been two cases of the disease occurring in the same family, that it could not be transmitted from one human to another and that the likelihood of it recurring in me was no greater than it randomly occurring in anybody else. So, broadly speaking, good news.

Dave was in full flow by now. I guess he could be fairly sure I was as compos mentis as I was ever going to get and that I was capable of taking some information in and retaining it. There was little chance of him morphing into a green and purple penguin on a cruise liner in the tropics this time. He basically told me to stop looking for signs my liver was going to fail, typically dark urine, pale stools or yellowing of the eyes. Any kind of changes in my blood chemistry would be picked up by tests long before I could spot the physical symptomatic signs should anything interrupt my liver function. Anyway, this wasn't going to happen and I should work on the basis of a normal life expectancy. At that time a good number of liver transplant recipients had been living normally for 20+ years. After twenty years they didn't know what the long term prognosis was. They hadn't been doing them in any quantity for that long but they had no reason to believe they were all going to start dropping dead anytime soon.

Much of his confidence in my potential longevity came from my young age, 26, and from the speed the disease progressed. I had avoided the effects of the strain on other vital organs from being exposed to a long-term chronic illness. I'd gone from being fit and healthy to deaths door and back again in 6 weeks. I should crack on with work and having family if that's what I so desired. Basically, get on with living my life, stay fit, look after myself and not constantly worry about my liver. The beer question remained unanswered and was, of course, entirely inconsequential within the context of the conversation. Anyway, I'd made my own rules up on that one on the basis that seeking forgiveness is often easier than seeking permission. So, healthy blood chemistry restored and armed with some reassuring advice from Dave I was out of the Queen Elizabeth Hospital and on my way back home again to pick the nettles out of my bike.

Bank owes you £50

The routine visits to the Queen Elizabeth Hospital started to become less frequent. Beginning with a weekly trip, then bi-weekly and then monthly. For the most part my blood tests remained normal and stable which allowed me to start pushing the whole transplant experience to the back of my mind and get on with my second chance at life. This was made easier by my rapid return to health. I guess if you lose a leg or an arm, you heal but the wound is obvious both to you and those around you. There remains a visible sign of injury. It's different with a transplant, I had a few cracking scars yes, but meeting me for the first time you would never be able to spot my exotic medical history. Also, I *was* better wasn't I? I knew somebody must have died and donated the organ that was now keeping me alive and I'd have to deal with that at some stage but it wasn't in the forefront of my mind then.

In the months immediately following the transplant there were a few pleasant duties to perform. A note to the excellent Dr Gibson of Brockton to say thanks and pay his bill. A bottle of Scotch to the Staffordshire ambulance station whose drivers had destroyed Bluebell's engine on the run into Birmingham. Also a big cheque, literally and figuratively, went to the Liver Unit as a result of me and a group of friends doing the ill-advised Bridgnorth sponsored walk in May of 1993. The July of that year saw me fulfil one of my proudest duties and be Best Man to yet another Dave, a very close friend from my school days who had basically ordered the visiting schedule for me during my convalescence. He'd been in the hospital throughout my stay, quietly making sure everybody was looked after, including my father.

Cycling had by now become an essential part of my physical rehabilitation and certainly the place where I found solace and peace when on my own. Conversely it was where I had most fun when out with the increasingly large group of cycling friends. It wasn't becoming excessive, not like now,

I'm completely addicted now. Back then it was just a social thing, I could take it or leave it, I could give up easily if I wanted to. Probably.

Over the next year or so my drive to be Richie Normal rather than Richie the Liver Transplant Bloke meant I changed jobs and went to work in Birmingham and got married to a young woman who had been a long-term friend in May of 1994. I won't bore you with the details, I promised this was going to be about cycling and transplants not domestic issues and it is fully my intention to stick to that. On reflection, it would have been better for me and everybody around me if the transition to Richie Normal had not sidestepped the vital 'Richie Striving for Normality at a Responsible Pace Fully Recognising Recent Life Events' phase.

Back on the cycling front a small piece of good fortune, much in a 'Bank owes you £50 or it's your birthday, collect £10 from each player' style, had winged its way from London. A company I had worked for briefly had gone bust owing me some salary and the receivers had sent me a cheque for £800. Now then, you've managed to plough your way through my story this far (congratulations) so you may think you deserve a little light relief. Not so. Its exam time again. Don't worry, it's multiple choice and you don't have to use diagrams to illustrate your answer unless you really want to. Please read the question carefully and mark only one answer. If you change your mind that's fine but you've not been paying attention.

Question 2

A young man unexpectedly receives a cheque for £800. He is newly married and saving for a house. He has changed jobs recently and whilst he is not in debt money is tight. He has no savings to speak of, no pension, life insurance or common sense and, having recently had a life saving liver transplant, could pop off at any stage. He is a keen cyclist. What should he do with the money?

1. It's obvious. £800 is a substantial sum of money in those circumstances. A wise approach would be to put the money in a building society account to significantly increase the small amount saved towards a deposit for a house. Anything other would be foolish.

2. Hmmm. Sounds like he's had a pretty rough time recently and whilst it might be prudent to save the money maybe a well-earned break with his wife would be a good idea. Yes, a lovely holiday seems entirely appropriate as it would give them time to relax and recharge their batteries.

3. Spend the money on a new 'Clockwork' Orange mountain bike advertised in that mountain biking magazine and get some SPD pedals for it too. And shoes. Get proper cycling shoes. And some other bike stuff.

I won't insult you further by giving you the answer.

So, the Clockwork Orange came to pass and what a machine it was. It was a rigid steel framed bike equipped with STX RC Shimano componentry and the most fantastic hand built wheels – double butted spokes on super-light Mavic 217 rims. The finishing kit, handlebars, stem and seat post were all Orange branded and were lightweight aluminium. It weighed half as much as the purple Raleigh and as will become increasingly clear, bike weight is an important topic to be debated amongst weight weenie cyclists whenever possible. It was cutting edge at the time and remains a modern day classic if you can find a decent one.

I also managed to squeeze in some Shimano SPD pedals and some shoes into the deal. For those unfamiliar with this weird mix of initials and brand names, this combination allows you to affix your feet directly to the pedals by way of a small metal cleat attached to the sole of the shoe. It increases the efficiency of power transfer to the pedals and helps you control the bike better when riding tricky off-road sections. Equally importantly it opens a whole new world of falling-off-while-attached-to-the-bike comedy moments as you forget that you and the machine are now one. If you are going to do this, make it worthwhile by trying to find an appreciative audience. My first SPD-related collapse was in my garage and whilst painful went undocumented, until now.

Critically, the bike was smaller than the Raleigh, a 19" frame as opposed to 21", it fitted better and was easier to handle. Whilst it took me some time to get used to a bike without yaw control, I was not missing the Flex Stem™ and could now begin to turn corners when they occurred rather than a couple of minutes beforehand. It took some of the excitement out of riding but it meant my collarbones were more likely to remain intact. The Clockwork revolutionised my riding. It was a proper bike and while the Raleigh had done its job of introducing me and I suspect many others to the joys of riding off road, it was not in the same class.

Any serious rider will tell you can buy a thing colloquially known as a BSO (Bike Shaped Object) for very little money. They look like a bike from a distance but, get close to one, try to pick it up and, if you're really adventurous, try to ride it but do so at your own risk. You will find it a difficult, uncomfortable and unrewarding experience and one you are unlikely to repeat. Not that I'm suggesting the Raleigh was one of these, far from it, the BSO will be poorly constructed with cheap materials and simply will not last long enough to get worn out. These are the things that populate people's sheds all over this country and although they make bike ownership statistics look great, they rarely get used. They are in technical terms, crap. Because of its butted steel construction and super-stiff light wheels, my new bike would jump and spring forwards. You know how puppies just want to be your mate and think everything is brilliant!? It felt like that.

You couldn't help but ride it quickly and it made me realise that I'd got hold of a bike that was much better than its rider. It also dawned on me there was a yawning gap in my fitness. If I was going to get maximum enjoyment out of my new found toy I was going to have to get properly fit. Bike fit. Now, how the hell do you do that?

These were the young heady days of mountain biking in Britain. Those of you involved at the time will remember, though not fondly I suspect, the cantilever brakes that represented a gentle step-up in power from the systems used on road and cyclocross bikes. Imagine, if you can, the stopping power of sausage meat brake blocks on full-fat buttered wheel rims and you will get a feel for their efficacy. Anything resembling a spot of rain or dirt and you'd be better off using your feet. Similarly, most bikes were equipped with rigid steel or aluminium forks meaning your arms and upper body took something of a beating when riding over anything other than a smooth, hard surface. Suspension forks were becoming more widely available allowing faster more comfortable and controlled riding but in the early days they were heavy, unreliable and offered relatively little in the form of travel.

Early trips to Shropshire's finest mountain bike spots, the Long Mynd, the Wrekin, the Brown Clee and the Mortimer Forest, were supplemented by our use of a seemingly endless supply of less demanding local trails. Footpaths linking bridleways to an old railway track and bits of the local lanes were pressed into action. Weekend rides were becoming longer and harder and week night rides when light allowed it in the spring and summer, were getting faster and more challenging.

One of my favourite incidents during these miles of off road riding involves my friend Mark, a seasoned and naturally talented bike handler learned from years of riding on the road. One evening we headed towards the wonderfully named Frog Mill trail, a short lanes ride away from home. The route to the old mill pond involved a very quick rolling descent over a well grazed field which we all knew contained one three foot deep hole with sheer sides: too small to ride through and too big to go over. Problem with this particular hole was that it moved: it was never in the same place. How it moved I couldn't say, probably something to do with the Cycling Gods, but move it definitely did. Mark found it this time, his front wheel dropping into it before he had time to adjust his line. He had managed to scrub some speed off with his sausage meat brake blocks but the momentum ensured, whilst his front wheel was very definitely stopped, he and rest of bike continued upwards. As his back wheel rose into the air for some reason, possibly comedic intuition or more likely his inability to get unclipped from his pedals, he continued to pedal. This achieved nothing other than blurringly quick unresisted leg speed and uselessly spinning back wheel. He came to rest with his forehead on the ground and the entire bike at 90 degrees to ground level. There he remained there until he was gently toppled over like the controlled demolition of a tower block. This is the only time I have seen a 'head plant' of this nature and I feel happier now it has been recorded for posterity.

My beloved Orange had had its own transplant and was now resplendent with a pair of RC35 Pace suspension forks and later V brakes. Wow, didn't they make a difference. I could now steer the bike *and* stop. Wonders would never cease. The improvement in bike technology was another mismatch with the skill of the rider, the physical evidence of that being the chainring marks tattooed into my right calf and the bits of the Long Mynd I carry with me in my left hip. Still, no broken bones so far and I'd become fit enough to at least ride the bike for 4 or 5 hours when called to do so without too much discomfort and without keeping my riding mates waiting.

'Can you smell sheep shit?' said Alex. We were back in Bridgnorth, showered and sitting in the pub after a day on the Brown Clee. 'I can smell sheep shit, are you sure you can't smell sheep shit?' We assured Alex that we couldn't smell sheep shit and, although sheep and their shit had surrounded us all day, both the bikes and us were now thoroughly cleaned, presentable and fragrant. After a few more pints of high calorie muscle relaxant, he'd pretty much asked everybody in the pub if they smelled sheep shit when a sizeable lump of the stuff dropped out of his nose and onto the bar. I think I stopped laughing after I had walked home that evening, only to start laughing again first thing in the morning.

One of the great things about mountain biking certainly more so than riding on the road, is that it's pretty accessible and enjoyable in all weathers. Even in ice and snow. In fact inclement weather can enhance the whole experience provided you are properly equipped and are prepared to get wet and muddy. My great friend Barry and I went out for such a trip during a Christmas break: as much to get the mince pies and beer off us and get some fresh air into our lungs as anything else.

We headed out on a local trail towards a marvellous single-track route that followed a stream known locally as Ned's Lane. It was properly snowy, a good 6 or 8 inches lying on the ground, freezing cold but with a bright blue sky. A stunning, clear winter day. The road and lanes were pretty treacherous and although we were well away from road traffic the conditions dictated the going was slow and hard but we were well kitted and warm. Helmets remained an optional extra but an option we had both failed to exercise at that time. Relieved the long slog along the lanes was over we arrived at the wooded entrance to Ned's Lane. Surrounded by snow-laden conifers we set off at a pace and unusually for me I was at the front. I should have realised something was up. Barry is a far superior bike handler than me so under normal circumstances I would have, and should have, been behind him watching and following his line. This time I was ploughing my own furrow and blasted around a bermed corner halfway down the trail. The inevitable happened of course and I catapulted myself over the handlebars and up into the air landing upside down suspended in a thick snow covered conifer. Barry was not far behind me and as he rode past, concentrating on the trail and not taking his eyes off it for a second, he simply wished me a Happy Christmas. It struck me later that the District Nurse had once decorated me and now I'd become part of the decorations myself.

A bit odd that

Looking back, it's easy to pin point when I realised I was going to have to deal with significant peripheral issues that surrounded my illness and recovery. As much as I would have liked it to be, my illness was not one which I had spontaneously recovered from with the help of some antibiotics. And whilst I had needed the help of a good surgeon he hadn't just whipped a chunk out of me that wasn't working, he'd also replaced it with something that did. That something had come from another person and I needed to recognise and deal with that, even if it was for no better reason than my continued good mental health. What better place for this kind of epiphany than Pizza Express in Berkeley Square? Look, you've made it this far, do try and keep up.

In outpatients, Dave Mutimer had asked me if I would talk to someone who had just had a transplant, as had been done for me when I was on the ward. The young man I visited had not suffered from the same condition as me but the decline in his liver function had been rapid. Apparently he'd had a number of surgical interventions during childhood, having stents and shunts put into his liver to improve the flow of blood and keep it working as well as possible. Eventually, his liver could take no more and had begun to fail. He'd come into hospital in the knowledge a transplant would be necessary if he was to live and fortunately for him, one had been found in time.

He was 18 and had been studying for his A' levels throughout his illness. I didn't hesitate in agreeing to talk to this chap. Dave had asked for one thing and I had found Andy's visit of comfort, apart from hearing about the whole double transplant thing of course. He was on the same ward, E3 with his parents at his bedside and had recently had a tracheotomy. It was difficult to hear what he was saying.

I turned the bravado knob up to 11, introduced myself to his folks and sat down next to his bed, close enough to hear him talk. It brought back a lot of memories

71

for me, most of them pretty unsettling but I remember asking him how he was doing. I could have answered this for myself but you've got to start somewhere. He'd had a tracheotomy, a liver transplant and was fighting a case of shingles so, "bloody awful" was the only truthful answer. Unsurprisingly, he looked ill but he was clearly very scared as well, terrified in fact. I got closer to hear him a little better and he asked me if I could smell it?

"Can I smell it?" I said in reply, thinking I had misheard him.

"Yeah", he said, "the petrol."

I said I couldn't, I couldn't smell anything stronger than antiseptic and the normal odours of the hospital ward.

"How can you not smell it? I'm covered in it." he said.

I carried on the conversation and he told me last night the staff had covered him in petrol and were standing around his bed flicking cigarette lighters off and on, laughing while they did it. This man was going through exactly the same process of hallucination as I had. He had spent the night and much of the day in the belief he was being tortured and under the perceived threat of being burned alive. It wasn't real, but he believed it to be so it was very real to him. I spoke to him and tried to convince him this was not the case although his belief was unshakeable and I spoke to the staff. There seemed little point in upsetting his parents as there was nothing they could do to make it better for him.

I went home, thought about it, bunked some time off work and went to see him again the next day. He looked the same, still gravely ill, no great surprise there and I spoke to him again. He had no recollection of our meeting the day before but this time the petrol hallucination had subsided only to be replaced with another one. Now he was convinced he had a mouth complete with teeth in his armpit and every time a thermometer was put under his arm to take his temperature, he thought the mouth was chewing it up and the mercury was heading towards his heart. I was unable to reassure him that this wasn't the case and that thermometers in any case no longer contained mercury. All I could do was pat his arm and talk to him although there was just as much chance I was creating another hallucination rather than helping him.

I couldn't get through to him on any meaningful level. I was at least able to demonstrate to his parents when the throat and abdomen scars had healed, when the shingles had got better, when rejection had been addressed and when his head started to clear there was light at the end of the tunnel. That was the easy bit, I could just stand there saying very little but still show them this transplant thing worked and the suffering was both temporary and worth it. It made me reflect on my own circumstances. I'd spent more time than was good for me resenting the fact I'd been hit by an unexplained illness rather than celebrating being saved by unbelievable timing and a hefty dose of good fortune. I was going to have to rethink my position on this one.

In April 1995, I was asked to talk at a transplant symposium in the Midlands to a mix of people with an interest in transplantation although the event was targeted at medical professionals involved in broader donor issues. One of the aims was to raise awareness amongst hospital staff of how the logistics of donation work in an attempt to increase the supply of donor organs. I said my piece, ran through my experiences and talked about how they should stop forcing people to eat cauliflower cheese. I pleaded that they looked for a way to reduce the incidence of post-transplant hallucinations, a subject close to my heart. Following the various talks, there were workshops. No tools, no overalls and no oil.

We were put into mixed groups, recipients, nurses, medical specialists and members of donor families, and given a topic to discuss. I don't recall the subject of our discussion but I do remember talking to the mother of a child who had died following an asthma attack at 7 years of age and had donated his organs. It was pretty harrowing for all concerned and the discussion was becoming a group therapy session that I really didn't feel qualified to be involved in. This woman had clearly been through the most awful tragedy and was becoming increasingly agitated and aggressive. Her ire was most definitely focused on me.

She wanted two things from me. First, she wanted me to tell her how grateful I was, implying that I should be grateful to her directly for the decisions she had made. Secondly, in a state of some agitation, she wanted me to tell her I didn't consider myself to be normal. Her view seemed to be that having a transplant put you into some kind of mid ground between chronic illness and disability: a sort of partially crippled purgatory. It is not in my nature to back away from a discussion, debate, argument and/or a punch up should it become necessary, but I wasn't going to pursue this one any further out of deference to her situation. I told her I thought I was entirely normal as calmly as I could, made my excuses and moved away.

Normal? Of course I considered myself to be normal. How much more normal can you get than a white, middle class, married Chartered Surveyor from Shropshire? I'd been ill, I'd had some surgery and now I was better.

Well, yes, but it's not *quite* as simple as that. My continued existence involved the death of another person and the feelings of their family and friends were pertinent. There's an inescapable link, a different link depending on the circumstances of the transplant and the donor of course, but a very definite link all the same. The woman came to see me briefly later during the day. I had tried to keep out of her way but she tracked me down and continued in a similar vein. This time she was talking specifically about my donor and she extracted a promise from me that I would contact my donor family. It was not something I had considered before; I was preoccupied with dealing with the illness and the aftermath. My difficulties at coming to terms with being ill were still overriding any thoughts about any bigger picture.

I was pretty upset by the whole thing with the worse bit being at least one person out there considered me to be abnormal. Despite my indignation, a promise is a promise and I spoke to my Transplant Coordinator at the Queen Elizabeth Hospital and asked how I go about contacting my donor family. It transpired there is a strict protocol of how this can happen and understandably so. Donations come about in many ways and contact between donor families and recipients is not always possible or, for numerous reasons, advisable. Donors or their families are not able to put conditions upon where an organ goes or who gets it. The decision is a clinical one unhampered by considerations of the relative worthiness of a recipient.

The act of organ donation is the pinnacle of altruism, a demonstration of the human spirit at its very best: generosity for the good of an often unknown other. It has to be considered by the donor before death, meaning they have to confront their own mortality and then supported and confirmed by their next of kin at the most difficult of times. I am totally in awe of people who are able to do this, every single one of the 18 million or so of them who are on the organ donor register in the UK.

Donor families do not have an automatic right to know where the donated organs have gone, they cannot be traced or tracked and the decision about whether contact is made is entirely down to the recipient. Like I said, pure altruism. If and when contact is established it is by letter. The recipient writes a letter and sends it to the Transplant Coordinator who reads it and considers its suitability not, thankfully, its grammar or spelling. You don't get it back marked with red pen. If suitable, the letter is then sent to the donor's Transplant Coordinator who reads it, undoubtedly raises an eyebrow at the dreadful spelling and, once more, considers its suitability in the light of the circumstances of the donation. If all is well, then and only then, does it get sent to the donor family.

I wrote a letter introducing myself, explaining my circumstances, a little about my background and family and expressed my appreciation of the decisions they had taken. Appreciation. See what I mean? Thanks. Cheers. Grateful. It doesn't do it justice. It doesn't even come close. Dad had written a brief note at the time of the transplant some 4 years ago but had not sent it at my request, he had very sensibly kept it and we sent that note with mine.

In May 1995 I got two letters back, one from my donor's father and one from his mother. They told me a little about my donor, his background and his family. They were beautifully written, descriptive and full of love. The recipients of his other organs had contacted them sooner and I had been the last. Hospital staff had told them his liver had gone to a young man in a critical condition and that it had saved a life, until then they had had no further information about me.

Sometimes the correspondence stops after the initial contact but in other cases it continues. This is entirely down to the parties involved although it is always carried out through the coordinators for the protection of all. The relationship between donor family and recipient is a rare one, perhaps not unique but nevertheless still largely unprecedented. There are no well-established rules or social norms around the relationship so it's important, particularly in the early stages, a sensible mediator is in place. The Transplant Coordinators perform this role.

Meanwhile, back on the ranch, it was 1996 and my first child, Charlie had been born in May of that year. I was delighted to see him but I felt the burden of parental responsibility very heavily. My father had been with me through every step of my life and together with Mum, they had frozen their toes standing beside all manner of rugby, football, hockey and cricket pitches as much as they had boiled inside sports halls, swimming pools, tennis courts and the like. My concern was that I would not be around long enough to do this for Charlie.

I had continued the correspondence with my donor family and we had begun writing to each other on a reasonably regular basis, exchanging letters once every few months. They were pleased to hear about Charlie's arrival and I took great pleasure in updating them on his exploits as he grew.

We were getting to know each other better and it was clear my donor's father and mother were lovely people who expressed themselves beautifully and always with great care for my feelings. I tried to do the same in return. It was very easy to write the letters from my side, I had a young family, work, friends and sport: the stuff that everyday life is made of. I was acutely aware my donor could not have any of these things and that I was corresponding with his parents. Despite this they never made me feel awkward or uncomfortable about giving them updates and news. I looked forward to writing and receiving the letters.

One of the rules of exchanging letters via the coordinators is you only use first names and don't put your address, phone numbers or e-mail contact details on any of the correspondence. This stops any inappropriate intended or unintended contact. All the same, as our relationship grew we had established a lot of common ground and it seemed inequitable and simply a little rude that I couldn't let them know where I lived, even in general terms. Think about it, when you meet somebody face-to-face for the first time in a social context if you're British you'll go directly for the safe ground of weather and geography. You ask your new acquaintance where they live and find your closest contact to the place; lived there, been there, family lived there, heard of it, never heard of it, in descending order. Remove the weather and geography and some important context is lacking. Added to this despite being Cheshire born, Shropshire had been my home county since I was 10 and I was proud of my town. I wanted to tell them about my home. Simply overcome I thought, rather than doing the whole formal letter writing thing and putting my full address in the top right hand corner, I'll just put Shropshire and the date. A full address would never get past the coordinators anyway. Over the next few letters my donor family and I surreptitiously exchanged a little geography until they knew I lived in Bridgnorth and I knew they lived in a town close to where I had gone to college and close to where I had first met Kate. It was hard not to draw a parallel with Carmel's appearance on the ward a few years back. The incidence of extraordinary coincidences was, well, extraordinary. Try saying that quickly. To add further to the puzzle, the letters were beautifully written and conveyed much empathy and emotion in relatively few words. They were the kind of letters you might see published in the memoirs of somebody famous: not a footballer but a diplomat perhaps. Somebody who might move in the same kind of circles as Kate and her family.

Kate and I still saw each other on a reasonably regular basis, she was working in the West End of London for a firm of property investment agents and I was in London on a weekly basis continuing my wholly unenthusiastic career as a surveyor, now working for Barclays Bank. Kate and her boyfriend had come to my wedding a few years earlier and they were still together. Over the years we had become very firm friends although time and distance made it difficult to see as much of each other as we might like. Our relationship was entirely platonic, just in case you were wondering.

In early March 1997, Kate and I met up for lunch in Berkeley Square and we began where we left off last time, exchanging news and views of family, work and friends. I mentioned the exchange of letters with my donor family and the seemingly unlikely coincidence that the family were in the same region as Kate's home. The conversation came back around to my donor family and she asked if I knew my donors name and of course I did, so I told her. Then she asked for the names of his parents and the date of transplant. Again, I reminded her. Suddenly the blood drained from her face and she went very white. Kate went quiet and looked down at the floor for long enough for me to become concerned about her well-being. When she eventually looked up she told me she knew my donor family, more to the point they had been next-door neighbours in the late 1960 and early 70s and they now lived within 150 yards of each other. Her parents had comforted my donor's parents over the weekend of his death. This meant I had lived a few streets away from my donor during my time at college.

We both sat there completely stunned. The information was too much for either of us to take in and it's difficult to come up with words to describe the feelings of that particular moment. We finished off our lunch as best we could but it was, of course, impossible to talk about anything other than this truly remarkable revelation. I felt poll-axed by the discovery.

I was numb sitting on the tube and then the train out of Euston station. Just how unlikely this set of circumstances was started to sink in when I got home that evening. I didn't tell my wife, I couldn't, as I didn't know what to say or where to start. The only time I'd felt this coshed before was back at Anne's house soon after the surgery. The mixture of an 8 hour anaesthetic, drugs, toxins and shock had left me unable to answer simple questions like "do you want a cup of tea?" I didn't know, I couldn't come up with an answer; I couldn't even respond or speak. My father, Anne, my wife and my brother all realised there was something amiss and tried to get through. All I could manage was a kind of shrug and a bit of a non-committal hand waving gesture when they asked what was wrong. Perhaps unsurprisingly it was Dad who managed to get through to me first and I explained the circumstances as best I could. I stumbled through it but I got it out. Dad, didn't get it. At least, if he did he played it down a lot for my benefit. Unusual he thought, yes, but just one of those things he said. One of those *another* things more like, how many more of these phenomenally unlikely incidents were going to occur I wondered? I spoke to my Transplant Coordinator and she kindly took hold of the situation. She could see I was struggling and thought it might be a good idea for me to see a psychologist. A woman who specialised in counselling parents who had lost a child whom she rated very highly, agreed to see me at short notice.

Under normal circumstances I may have questioned the need for this but I was sure I needed some help to get things into context and maybe provide a few answers. I didn't know what to expect but I was relieved to be going to see somebody who might be able to tell me how and why all these things might be connected and what it all meant. On my own I couldn't find an explanation for this other than just a series of coincidences. The odds were millions to one against it. I was, if you recall, offered unsuitable organs from Germany and Ireland, I was on top of the critical list that covered the whole of Europe. What are the chances of my life-saving donor once living within 100 yards of me?

The psychologist sat me down and asked me how she could help. Oh I see, this was going to be tricky was it? It took me a few minutes to formulate my thoughts but when I did manage to speak the first words out of my mouth were about my Mum. For the next hour or so I recounted the bit of my life story from the death of my Mum until present day and the discovery of the links and identity of my donor family. I didn't expect to start talking about Mum; I expected to start talking about transplants but it's just what came out. Over a period of time with this kind lady, who wasn't remotely tea and sympathy, but empathetic, direct and very helpful, it became clear that she didn't have an answer to my question. I don't think anybody has a direct answer to the question, if you've got one I'd love to hear it. I don't believe it was fate or predestination and under no circumstances would I ever believe I had been saved by some higher authority or for some cause. My unusual circumstance just being 'one of those things' wasn't a very satisfying answer but that's what it appeared to be.

She pointed out the reoccurring pattern in my life, in particular, the trauma of my Mum's death followed by the unseemly rush to finish of my exams and get to college four months later. This was subsequently repeated with my rush back to work after the transplant and the rush to get married so quickly. I had conveniently pushed anything I didn't like the look of into a lockable cupboard space in my mind and cracked on with life without ever thinking that I might have to deal with any of these issues. The discovery of the links with my donor had opened the cupboard door and chucked the contents around a bit. When I could see the pattern of my life and better understand the mental processes that led me to feel the way I did, I felt reassured, just as I did when I found out more about the process of organ transplantation. Having the facts helped a lot. No answer to the impossible question but an understanding of the ramifications of my journey at least. It didn't take too long for my head to come back together although I was now careful not to rush back into everyday life without checking in with myself to see if I was wholly missing the point. Missing the point was one of the few things I had become expert at.

I've struggled a few times since. I've become a little depressed at times, but that initial essential consultation taught me to recognise the symptoms and do something about it before I found myself in La La Land.

Amongst the flurry of letters around that time, one arrived from the Liver Unit I wasn't expecting. It was thin so I knew it didn't contain further correspondence from my donor family. After a routine clinic visit they had taken to contacting us patients only if something was wrong. If you got a call the day after, you were straight back in with a needle between your ribs, a few days later and they probably wanted to re-test you and have a think. This letter was out of sync. Maybe they thought I'd sprung a mental leak and wanted me to see the psychologist again. Panic over, it was just another routine appointment letter.

Don't let me con you in to thinking that I'm anything other than chicken. I still hated waiting for the call, getting the letters and, most of all, going back into clinic. Of course, I'd take a deep breath at the door of out-patients, stand up straight, march in and order a table for two (non-smoking) or something. Bravado to cover up the fear. They'd smile (they knew, they knew) and ask me to take a seat. During one visit to the phlebotomist when I was wound up tighter than a watch spring, I even asked her what my blood looked like while she was taking some out of my arm. "Red" she said. I should have guessed. Instead of sitting down that day I'd had a walk around outpatients trying to

81

look sprightly and not remotely ill, peering at leaflets about other interesting liver diseases I might contract or examining the massive cardboard cheques. This time I saw a poster titled 'The World Transplant Games, Manchester 1995'. It was partially obscured and had other notes pinned over it. It was an old poster, the date having long since passed but it looked interesting all the same. There are Games are there? What type of Games? I moved a few notes regarding patient transfers and how to queue for blood tests and read a little more.

Apparently the World Transplant Games had been held every 2 years since 1978. Ross Taylor, an eminent transplant surgeon, had the idea of increasing awareness of transplantation and organ donation and promoting physical exercise as a means to a healthier life for recipients. Back then it was really the kidney transplant games, there weren't many other transplant patients around, certainly few capable of running, jumping, swimming or heaven forbid riding, but there were a growing number of kidney transplant recipients. Ross is no longer with us although, I'm proud to say, I did have the chance to sit down and talk to him over lunch once. He was another one of those men who held your attention for all the right reasons. The world could do with more Ross Taylors. He was even kind enough not to mention the T-shirt I was wearing which stated, ironically I hope, "The liver is evil and must be punished".

Some further investigation revealed there was also a British Games held every year and each hospital transplant unit entered a team. This was proper stuff, a full athletics and swimming calendar, racquet sports even cycling. Cycling? Yes, cycling. But it was road cycling, not my type of fat-tyred 'hang 5 dude' mountain biking. I didn't really know much about this kind of racing other than what I'd learned back when I was playing around with my school mates on bikes in the 80s. I did know it was very different. Different equipment, different style, different terrain. Why on earth would you want to spend your time mixing it with traffic when you could stick to woods and hills and mountains? I read it again just to make really sure and yes, road cycling it was. It seemed a little odd as almost everybody had access to a mountain bike by now and surely it made more sense to race on those?

With this sense of frustration came a mild sense of relief. This wasn't for me anyway; I was a dyed in the wool mountain biker and wouldn't countenance engaging in this ridiculous skinny-tyred nonsense. Also, if I didn't enter, I couldn't lose could I? Risk and stress free, see? It was a perfect excuse not to have to test myself against people who had been through the same thing. I could continue to use the excuse of being prevented from playing sport by my tragic and unfortunate circumstances. Sob. Poor me. Banned (effectively) from rugby, not by a lack of talent or courage, but by the insurers. Damn them, damn them I say.

Conveniently, the inexcusable exclusion of mountain biking from the games also ensured that I was not involving myself with others who'd had a transplant who were clearly not normal at least according to some. So, within a few seconds of discovering there was a set of national and international games for people who'd had life supporting organ transplants I'd dismissed them because they didn't involve the particular branch of sport that interested me.

It must seem ridiculous, particularly after the revelations about the circumstances of the transplant, that I was reluctant to involve myself with others who'd had similar experiences but it was true all the same.

The path to enlightenment

The realisation that one bike isn't enough comes quickly to people who take cycling even remotely seriously. If they choose to compete, one genuinely isn't enough. But I would say that wouldn't I? Helpfully, there is a well-established formula for determining the optimum number of bikes to own. Relying on the incontrovertible laws of nature removes much stress and worry. The easily solvable equation is: –

$$n + 1$$

Let n = the current number of bikes in your ownership.

The Orange was becoming very well used. Brake blocks, chains, cogs, wheels, tyres all had to be replaced at regular intervals after being trailed through muddy gravel. We were convinced the old railway track that connected together so many of the paths and bridleways in the area was regularly re-supplied with Shimano paste. This being an abrasive product formulated specifically to grind down and erode products made by the Japanese component manufacturer. It was very effective too and combined with multiple washings and rebuilds of hubs and headsets and the like, the bike was wearing out. If you're a cyclist you will have already formulated various solutions to this conundrum and you shouldn't be too hard on yourself. It's part of your programming.

If you can't come up with anything try using the formula above. Use diagrams to help illustrate your answer if you want.

For the non-cyclists, think for a minute and you'll manage to come up with loads of ways of preventing the bike from wearing out so quickly. Such as, don't ride in the wet then, stick to the lanes, look after it better, ride it less often and, you've got a car, use that instead. You will also be thinking that at £800 it should last forever anyway and further, not long ago, you bought a car for less than that. Don't be too hard on yourself: it's part of your programming too.

My solution was brilliant. What I'd do is, get an old road bike, something like the Dawes I had years ago. I'd build it up from a box of old bits; it would be a project, a creation of my own. It would be cheap, as it didn't have to be flash like the mountain bike. I could ride it on the lanes in secret during the winter months when the weather was foul and the trails were too muddy and impassable. It would save the wear and tear on the Orange. It would certainly make me fitter and leaner as everybody knows roadies are skinny blokes with shaved legs. A flawless plan I'm sure you will agree.

I'm not quite sure when the modulation of excuses against reasoning employed in *most* of my major decisions and *all* of my major purchases reached its optimum peak but, what had begun as a 'box of bits' project started to morph quite early on. The principal is an extension of the logic I have seen used to justify all kinds of expenditure and has two basic threads, thus. If you buy something cheaply, perhaps in a sale, for, say £75 as opposed to the full price of, let's say £100 you have, through your own diligence and skill saved £25. The item you have bought was an unavoidable and essential purchase and consequently the £25 you have saved is, in effect, free money and yours to do with as you see fit. Well done you. Or me.

The second strand is only marginally more complex and involves the value for money principle. Don't buy two cheap things that won't last as long, look as good or be as satisfying to use when the purchase of one more expensive thing is clearly a better idea. Just buy the more expensive item in the first place and you're helping everybody out there. To do anything other would be reckless and unwise.

Killer blow time. What about this Transplant Games thing? It's a road based competition. I'd never know if I was fast enough to compete without having a go on a proper road bike so I'd need something much more reliable and race worthy than anything I could knock together from a box of bits. Until I trained for a while on adequate equipment my ability would remain untested.

I had no real intention of doing any such thing of course. It was a contrivance, a massive bloody fib, an excuse to allow a guilt-free purchase of a new bike using a noble and worthy cause I had not the slightest intention of engaging in. Oh how you must hate me now! I've let you down; I've let my family down, but most importantly (adopts gravely concerned look and lowers voice). I've let myself down.

I also conveniently ignored the fact the racing in the Games was mass-start road racing and therefore even if times of past events were available they would be irrelevant and entirely dependent upon the profile of the course. Even if I did get hold of the times – I still couldn't test my fitness against riders who competed in the Games unless I actually raced against them. If I'd bothered to do a little research or looked for this information beforehand it would have put a major dent in my logic, blowing my reasoning out of the water. So I didn't look. Simple.

Bike shop visit then. I'd played with a modern road bike in the local mountain bike emporium. It looked incongruous amongst all the big-tubed, fat-tyred machines but it was a fascinating bit of kit. Most interestingly, the gear shifting mechanisms were now installed, like a mountain bike, on the handlebars and incorporated with the brake levers. On my old Dawes you had to take your hand off the bars and use a lever on the downtube to change gears. Having said that, the Huret derailleur gears on the Dawes had jammed up years before, effectively making it a single speed bike, but the theory is sound. On top of this, you no longer had to deploy the black art of friction shifting to switch between cogs, the new levers were indexed so one click, one accurate shift. Bonus.

Having convinced myself that life as we know it would be wholly unsatisfying without a new bike, I set about my research with diligent vigour. George Bush *had* now invented e-mail but was still working on the Internet, so this involved much reading of road cycling magazines; most notably the long running Cycling Weekly, known universally as 'The Comic'. Like now, there was little meaningful crossover between mountain biking and road cycling publications so it was all very new for me. Much like there is no meaningful cross over between mountain bikers and road riders, both parties thinking the other is crazy and wasting their time. They are both right of course.

In late spring of 1997, this is how a blue and yellow custom built Reynolds 653 racing bike with 8-speed Campagnolo Athena componentry came about. As I write this, I'm getting the same tingle of excitement I got when I first saw this thing of beauty. I am also hiding behind my virtual sofa and peeking over to look at the expression on your face. If you're a cyclist, you're smiling, maybe thinking you had something similar a few years back. If you're not, you're scowling at me and thinking, "I could have bought a car for the amount he paid for that!" I shall dip back below my virtual sofa and pretend the Daleks are coming for me.

It cost £1100 so it would have been a rubbish car. It actually cost a little more by the time it had been equipped with a suitable pair of pedals, a bottle cage and a computer. That, admittedly, is a very expensive box of bits. I quickly realised I'd need a number of other bits of peripheral cycling equipment in order to get full use and enjoyment from my new purchase and this would mean further expenditure. It was true. The bike is the cheap bit. In order to make the whole experience comfortable and safe I'd need to accessorise. This would mean more 'extras'. Oh, and I'd need to maintain the bike properly and find a way of recording the valuable time spent training.

This realisation started my collection of road cycling accoutrements, much of it expensive rubbish. Certain items are essential; others only clutter up the garage. I see no reason why you should waste your time and money should you choose to take to the roads when I have done much of the job for you. Consequently some of the bits that might feature in your consideration and the pitfalls that go with them are set out below.

Tools

The amateur racing cyclist needs to have a selection of tools to perform routine bicycle maintenance tasks at home. My tool kit has evolved over years from my father's. It included ancient wood working tools and adjustable spanners that are so old they won't adjust to metric sizes out of principle. It contains some useful specialist tools for getting cogs off and bottom brackets out although anything of quality has been borrowed from my friends. If anything needs doing I invite them around to borrow their tools back for a few minutes whilst they are working on my bike. I ply them with tea, food and, if necessary, alcohol on completion of the work.

I learned the hard way. My kit does no longer contain the two most dangerous tools a cyclist can own. First, the hammer. A hammer has no place anywhere near a bike. Particularly one that is made predominantly out of carbon. Giving things 'a little tap' to help them move will undoubtedly result in an expensive trip to the bike shop, possibly to buy a new bike. I have discovered that attaching a tool, often a long handled pedal spanner, to an immovable nut and giving it 'a little tap' is also ill advised. An unsuccessful 'little tap' that causes no collateral damage will undoubtedly be followed-up with a more robust tap. Then a bloody good belt. It is entirely possible the spanner will become detached and fire itself off into a treasured bike or expensive set of wheels with a terrifying 'thunk'. Additionally, the hammer is likely to recoil and hit you squarely between the eyes. I managed to lose 15 minutes of my life that way. The last thing I heard was the dull thud of ball pain hammer on skull. My metalwork teacher would not have been proud of me.

Secondly, a spoke key. Spoke keys are designed to be used by professional magicians trained in the dark arts of wheel building and should not be touched by the amateur.

Superficially, it may seem that a slightly loose spoke can simply be 'tweaked' a little to restore the tension. This usually means the opposing spoke now also needs a little adjustment too. The tweaking continues until rather than having a wheel with a loose spoke, you have something looking like a metal taco crisp and a bill for a new wheel. It has, in effect, been tweaked to death. When you take the wheel into the bike shop to see if it can be rescued, take the spoke key in with you and donate it to them.

I was once in my local bike shop, Fred Williams Cycles in Wolverhampton, when a gentleman came in with a self taco'd wheel and asked if they had anything similar in stock. 'No' was the simple answer, they had nothing even remotely like that in stock. They *did* have something much rounder that would probably work better.

Workstand

A simple device allowing you to work on the bike at eye level, crushing the top tube with the clamping device in the process. Working on a bike whilst it's standing on the floor presents some difficulties, not least because the interesting, dangerous and expensive bits are less accessible. Raised up, it allows you to do more damage more efficiently. Better sight of the damage you have caused also means it is easier to explain your foolishness to the mechanic in the bikes shop when you inevitably take it in for repair.

Working on the bike at ground level also risks damaging your back and/or knees whilst being bent over. A decent work stand allows you to replace back damage with back of the head damage as you stand up under the bloody thing and cave your swede in.

In my house at least it is traditional to hop around swearing after this has happened and is another good reason not to have a hammer where it can easily be reached.

Spare bits box

After you have been riding for a little while and have accumulated a number of bikes you will also have gathered a good selection of part worn, obsolete or broken bike bits. These should be retained for a future 'something'. I've never quite worked out what the 'something' is because I can't recall actually ever finding a use for a part worn 7 speed mountain bike cassette or a single road pedal (the bearings went in the right one) but, hey, you never know. One day I might need to help out a one-legged retro mountain biker with a well-worn chain who needs a left-sided road pedal I suppose. He could have a set of squeaky old 'V' brakes too and any kind of bike computer wheel magnet he could dream of. I've got thousands.

I think my hoarding is motivated by meanness. Subconsciously I work on the basis the componentry was expensive to buy, so even when properly knackered and useless it must still be worth something. It's not of course, but you never know when a broken seat stem might come in handy do you?

Like everybody else, I keep my unused spares like cables and bar tape in the obligatory tartan shortbread biscuit tin but I leave my expensive mistakes, like the numerous carbon water bottle holders, on display in the spare bits box as a reminder of my foolishness.

Clip-on aero bars

For those who don't own a time trial bike, these are a set of extension bars that can be attached to a normal pair of drop handlebars turning your bike into a wind cheating aero machine at the drop of a torque wrench. I have some because it's not always possible to take two bikes when travelling to transplant events where there is both a road race and a time trial. Although not ideal, clip-on bars do help in these circumstances. They also came in handy at my one and only attempt at a 100 mile time trial where I knew trying to sit on my time trial bike for 5 hours would mean I was likely to spend the rest of my life on my hands and knees eating from a dog bowl. I have seen people finish time trials using these with one arm in the air above their heads and the other nearly touching the front wheel because they have not put them on tight enough and they have revolved around the bars in opposite directions. This is very funny and I'd like to thank them for entertaining us all but, in truth, it's not very aerodynamic.

If you decide to attach these to your bike and have carbon handlebars you will be faced with one of cycling's newer dichotomies. Do I tighten them up enough to stop them moving and wait for the tell-tale cracking of carbon sound or do I run the risk of having two useless spare bits of metal dangling from my bike? Tricky, and I wouldn't claim to know what the answer is: possibly invest in a torque wrench or a new bike. There's a useful formula for this you know?

Computer

The vast majority of cyclists use a little bike-mounted computer to record time, distance and speed and indeed I had one fitted to my new bike. They can either be for casual interest or for recording manually in a training diary to keep a check on progress. You might think this is the antithesis of what cycling is all about, man and a simple machine out there against the elements, judging pace and effort by reference to the tides, prevailing wind direction and the amount of porridge consumed that morning, but I fear you may be wrong.

Although not readily available at the time I bought the 653, nowadays, the next step up from this is downloading your heart rate or power output data from racing and training directly on to a laptop. This produces a series of indecipherable lines, graphs and bar charts to scare the living daylights out of you. At one level these are no more than expensive toys producing lovely coloured shapes on your computer but, at another, they can provide you with useful data to improve your performance. This assumes you can interpret the data and turn it into a training plan of course.

You don't need a computer to tell you you need to ride much faster: your mates will do that for you but it's unlikely the computer will laugh whilst telling you this.

The latest advance combines all the earlier benefits of cycling related electronic wizardry and adds GPS functionality and the ability to download the information not only to your computer but also to social networking sites. This means you can invite your friends and contacts to look at the details of your ride give them a comprehensive picture of your biometrics. This way they will all know, in graphic techno-colour, if you are in the least bit under trained, fat, slow or lost. A good reading of the data may also show where you have crashed meaning your club mates don't have to wheedle the information out of you to nominate you for the clubs 'falling off' award. The wonders of modern technology, eh?

From the first ride the new bike was a revelation. Anyone who switches between a mountain bike and a road machine will tell you the difference is like getting out of a tractor and into an F1 car. Okay, you might not want to ride it off anything higher than a kerbstone but on a reasonable piece of tarmac it will fly along with a minimum amount of effort.

The bike was beautifully built and handled like a dream, you could put it into corners, crank it right over and it would sail through. The mountain bike had taught me something about distributing body weight (of which I had ample) to get through tight lines quickly and with handling like this, riding felt effortless. I started to understand what this road cycling thing might be all about.

You could cover huge distances in relative comfort. The stories my father's generation told about riding to the coast and back in a day and round trips of 120 miles or more while youth hostelling seemed less like old man nonsense and more like real possibilities. I wasn't covering this kind of distance but I could see how it was certainly possible on such machinery. But it wasn't an instant and complete conversion. I was still riding my mountain bike, still enjoying the pleasures of off-road riding, still upgrading suspension forks, this time to Pace RC 36's and other bits and pieces, but cycling on the road was seductive. I was so enamoured with my recent purchase I thought the eternal n + 1 formula could be suspended. Temporarily. Sometimes the mountain bike was pressed into service for training rides so my shiny new road bike didn't get dirty. Oh how things change. I felt like my strength and fitness were coming on although I had nothing empirical to judge this against, just a gut feeling and a slightly looser waistband.

My discovery of the transplant games had sowed a seed and I'd had to consider the possibility of riding in them as part of the subterfuge to support the purchase of the new road bike. Casually I made a call to the hospital to understand how teams for the British Games were formed. I wanted to understand what the qualifying conditions were, where they trained and what kind of people were engaged in it. Apparently it was open to anybody who had received a life supporting organ transplant; primarily these were kidney patients who were the most numerous. The reason for this is simple. If your kidneys fail you can, as I'm sure you know, we kept alive by dialysis, a process that filters your blood and mechanically replaces your kidney function. It's not great; it's tiresome, time consuming, limiting and I'm told you feel pretty crap most of the time because your blood is either too dirty or too clean. However, you can survive like this long term. With the other most common transplants, hearts and livers, you get one quickly or you tend not to need one at all. Also it's a numbers game. Most cadaveric donors have two available kidneys and most recipients only need one. You can survive quite happily on one well-functioning kidney and many people do this without ever knowing it.

It turned out that there were no qualifying times or selection criteria for teams for the British Games. If you'd had a life supporting organ transplant you could enter and give it a go. In Birmingham, if you had not previously competed, they stuck you in the B team, so you'd do less damage and off you'd go. All of the teams were heavy on runners, swimmers and racquets players. Cycling sounded like a poorer cousin and as it happened the Birmingham team didn't have a cyclist representing them at that moment. Hmmm, food for the thinkings, as a Russian friend of mine once said.

The next British Games were to be held in August 1997, in Liverpool, with the cycling event being held in Birkenhead Park. I figured I better get on with it even if it did mean mixing it up with other transplantees. They were turning out to be surprisingly normal.

Birmingham B

I secured a berth in the Birmingham B team on the basis I would just do the bike race. I didn't enter the rest of the games either socially or sportingly; I wasn't asked for any reasons why not so I didn't have to offer any explanations. So, it appeared I had entered my first bike race.

I had to set about training properly because even with my limited knowledge of road riding I knew there was a whole world of difference between polling about with your mates on a mountain bike and racing. Some of the differences are blindingly obvious, equipment for one but I'd got that covered.

With mountain bikes you often ride with a group of friends but when riding off road you tend to give each other a fair bit of room. There's a good chance one of you is going to have to hit the eject button at some stage. You also need to pick lines that are appropriate to the terrain; the ability to do this well is one of the things that separates a good rider from a novice. Finding the quickest line usually involves flicking the bike around, lifting the front or back wheels to reposition them, dropping off ledges or avoiding obstacles like rocks and logs. Occasionally making violent switches in direction and speed is necessary. This is the complete antithesis of riding on the road. There are good reasons why you see groups of road riders in close formation travelling at speed and you'll see this perfectly illustrated if you've ever watched an event like the Tour de France on the television. Violent switching manoeuvres are not encouraged.

I did a little research and discovered the greatest opposing force you have to overcome when riding a bike, any bike, is wind resistance. You have to push your way through the air when you pedal forwards. Go ride into a head wind and you'll see how hard it is. If you are immediately behind another rider they have already done part of the job by punching a hole in the air. Riding behind somebody doing this is called 'drafting'. It is a fundamental principle in many types of bike racing. The ability to draft another rider, and to ride well enough to allow a rider to draft you, is a skill all competitive cyclists must develop. Even if you only ever race on your own against the clock you will almost certainly train in a bunch or peloton with other riders. Very simply, it takes 20% to 30% less effort when riding directly behind somebody on the road or a track, but to feel the benefit you have to be no more than a metre from the back wheel of the rider in front, preferably less. Any more than this and you might as well be a mile behind. It requires a little courage, confidence in the people you are riding with and a good deal of practice. In a group of riders, so long as most are prepared to take a turn at the front, a pleasingly speedy pace can be held with minimal shared effort. It is a great example of the effectiveness of teamwork in cycling. Two weaker riders will easily be able to outpace a solo rider over anything more than a mile or so by sharing the workload. There are more unwritten rules and etiquette to group riding than you can imagine. A breech of these can mean you have a lonely 50-mile ride home on your own: often in the rain, but we'll come to that later. The principle is fine. The practice part is rather more difficult.

Any erratic or unpredictable riding in a bunch and there is a good chance the whole lot will come down, particularly if the culprit is near the front. Even one novice rider in an experienced bunch can wreak havoc as all the other riders will be nervous and leaving bigger gaps than they normally would. I know this because I've been involved in a few crashes, seen a lot of near misses and if pushed, I'd have to admit to causing a few wobbles myself. Crashes on the road are expensive, painful and not the best way to make new friends.

Most commonly, riders new to bunch riding leave too much of a gap because they are understandably worried about being in very close proximity to others: they may have grasped the principle of drafting but executing the technique is a different matter. This disrupts the group as leaving holes means some riders are not getting the benefit of the shelter from the rider in front. Filling these holes and making up little gaps consumes energy you don't really want to waste and in my experience, makes people rather touchy.

Traditionally, the novice rider is schooled in the practice of bunch riding by his new found mates by being roundly abused. Commonly he won't actually know he's doing anything wrong because he doesn't know what right looks like. Furthermore, established cycling etiquette requires that rather than actually being advised where he is going wrong, he must attempt to interpret the abuse and use trial and error until he gets it right. If he is lucky, he may be advised to 'tighten up' or 'close the gap', although he will have no idea what this means of course. There may be some mumbling or pointing but more often single expletives are employed; tosser, pillock, dick and the like.

Most likely he will then find himself on his own out of the back of the bunch wondering what the hell he's done wrong. The friendly people he'd met at the start of the ride now seem to think he's Satan himself. The bunch will then continue on its way discussing in great detail what the new rider should have been doing and how he should have done it. He will have done the unthinkable and departed from cycling etiquette in some way. The cycling equivalent of turning up at a new golf club in jeans and cowboy boots and asking to borrow somebody's bats for the day. They will not of course be so rude as to tell him what sacred unwritten rule he has transgressed, as that would also be an unforgivable breech of etiquette.

This old-school process: the absorption of bunch riding skills by a 3 to 5-year period of osmosis, guess work and systematic abuse means that in the past, many potential club riders have been put off cycling for life. It can be a hard and long apprenticeship. It's another reason why there are so many bikes in sheds rather than on the roads.

In relatively recent times, as cycling has expanded as a sport, it has become more accessible and there is less of this 'I learned the hard way, so can you matey' mentality and thank goodness for that. Cycling clubs still tend to have traditions and secret rules but the influx of younger riders and more women and, it should be said, the positive influence of British Cycling, the sport's governing body, has gone a long way to change things for the better. You can now join a club and be successfully coached in the art of group riding in a traffic-free environment, on a tennis court or a playground. All you need is half a dozen riders, some cones, a competent coach and the basics can be learned in a few hours. It's far more humane, safer and means more people will ride their bikes rather than use them to hang garden tools on. Some clubs have access to tracks and circuits and it's great to see youngsters riding at speed quite safely leaning on each other's shoulders or gently bumping off each other as their bike handling skills develop. Fair enough, most people also bump off the ground once or twice as well, but it's better done on a tennis court at slow speed in front of your mates than on a main road in front of a car.

For me, I didn't have time to practice the art of bunch riding, I was racing in a few months and although I wasn't a member of a cycling club I'd watched the Tour de France on the telly. How hard can it be? Anyway, part of the reason for just dropping into the Games for the bike race was that if I made a complete arse of myself only my wife and father would see me do it. Nobody else knew me and I could just fade away behind my big new Oakley sunglasses (good sports eye wear is available from other reputable manufacturers) and never be seen again. I could even fake a puncture or something. You know, robbed of maiden victory by an unfortunate mechanical incident that definitely wasn't my fault. At this stage I didn't even know there *was* a secret code and etiquette of road cycling let alone how to go about unlocking it. I'd just have to make it up as I went along.

Training began in earnest in the early summer of 1997. From my reading I gathered in order to get great race fitness you needed to build up your training from long rides carried out over the winter months. Right, well, I didn't really have that as such but I'd been riding the mountain bike and that would have to do. I wasn't unfit although sadly I wasn't unfat either and those roadie guys looked pretty

100

skinny to me. Again, not too much I could do about that in the time available. I wasn't obese; I was just carrying a couple of spare puddings with me that's all. I put that down to the medication. Probably.

I devised a rudimentary training plan, nothing comprehensively written down or anything crazy like that, just a rough idea of what hard efforts might look and feel like. I had a hazy understanding of what interval training on a bike might be and I knew I'd need to rest and recover.

I'm sure somebody somewhere is doing, or has done, a thesis on the effects of immunosuppressant drugs on recovery after exercise, but at the time I figured a day off riding after battering myself into the ground was probably a good idea. I can see the sports scientists cringing as I write.

I bought myself an early model Polar heart rate monitor and started to learn the basics of how to use it: how to judge the levels at which I could sustain hard efforts and for how long I could hold them. I recall riding hard up a hill close to my home thinking, "This is quick, there's no way people are going to be racing faster than this, not even the pro's, it is just too painful to sustain." I was wrong of course. Not a bit wrong but like really, really wrong.

I found the discipline of the training regime; the prospect of the race and the focus on a new objective a real help in coming to terms with my illness, the transplant itself and the series of coincidences I had uncovered. The hard physical effort of training was also a big help in relieving the stresses and strains of everyday life, family and work. It was a much needed tonic. I had started to reposition the training from an optional activity to an essential part of my life. I wasn't obsessional to the point of over training, I'm too lazy for that, but it was important to me I got my training sessions in. People who train regularly may be familiar with the guilty twinges associated with a missed session when you know your competitors and club mates are out there getting some in.

The day of the race arrived and I packed up the car with my bike and kit and set off.

I hadn't told anybody I was riding. I wanted to give it the best go I could and it would seem I was actually looking forward to it. Nervous certainly but with healthy anticipation rather than fear.

I was far too self-conscious to wear a proper tight-fitting cycling jersey. Even though I had a long-sleeved yellow Cannondale top I used for mountain biking that would do the trick, I would definitely look like I was trying too hard in that; so my old loose-fitting, long-sleeved Quiksilver t-shirt would have to do. Also, rules is rules and I needed to wear a helmet for the race. I had started to use a helmet for mountain biking at the time Charlie was born on the basis that a Dad with a mashed head was not going to be much use to him. Unfortunately, it had a peak, which as any self-respecting roadie will tell you, is a complete no-no for racing on the road and a glaring breech of etiquette.

More people started to arrive at the venue; other riders, supporters, organisers and officials, some of them in blazers with British Cycling Federation (BCF) written on the badges. I went to find out where I had to sign on. I knew you had to do this because I'd seen them do it in the Tour de France. You'd walk up onto raised dais; sign your name with a big marker pen so everybody could see you were up for another gruelling day in the mountains. You'd turn to take the applause and adulation of crowd, wave and smile and off you'd go.

Here it was actually a rickety old table in a pavilion that smelled of Deep Heat but, hey, you've got to start somewhere. I had a moment of blind panic when I thought I was going to be asked for my race licence which, of course, I didn't have. I was handed some numbers and told where to position them on my jersey. I pinned them onto my t-shirt and set off for a look around the course. The park was used a lot for bike racing and you could see why: a broad flat well surfaced tarmac path with no obstacles to crash into. It broke onto a road section that was closed for the race then back into the park via a set of rather splendid ornate gates.

A few minutes later I found myself on the start line with forty or so other riders in BCF skinsuits and cycling jerseys with their club names printed on them amongst a wonderful array of top quality racing bikes. There were also a few people with less spectacular bikes and kit who positioned themselves to the rear. There was clearly a pecking order I was ignoring and it looked as though I was down at the golf club in my cowboy boots again.

So there I was, a mountain biker on a road bike with some numbers on my back and a heart rate monitor strapped around my chest. One of the guys looked at my pride and joy and asked, "Is that yours?" The implication being that, looking like I did, I'd probably borrowed it for the day. When I told him it was, he looked back at me and genuinely and without irony, nodded wishing me good luck.

Back in 1997, the bike race at the Games consisted of a single 10k mass start circuit race of 5 laps and on that sunny late summer evening, it started with a loud whistle blast. It went off like a rocket. 10kms is much too short for a bike race but back then it seemed like it was going to be 9.5km too long for me. The guys in front tore off down the road whilst I was still trying to get my right foot clipped into my pedal. Riders who had positioned themselves behind me were starting to go past. I managed to get clipped in and put in an almighty effort to get back to the main bunch of riders. I got there just as they slowed a little for the first corner and immediately started to drift off the back again as they accelerated out of it. Another chase and brief glance down made me think I'd attached a rev counter to my bike rather than a heart rate monitor. 186 bpm, 188 bpm, higher than I'd seen the thing go before by a long way. My mouth was bone dry. I'd have loved to suck on a bloody ice cube now. I was gulping down air for all I was worth but it didn't seem these guys were really trying very hard, they all looked pretty relaxed. I was lucky, the pace slowed down a touch, at least enough for me to hang on in there. I hadn't thought about tactics, drafting or anything else, I was just concentrating on trying to stay with these riders for as long as possible without expiring.

By the time the fourth lap commenced, a number of riders had broken away at the front and there was no way, no way in this world, I had the energy to chase after them. They were off in the distance and I was left with a smaller bunch who I thought I might be able to finish with. Wrong. Some of them were quite old, you know, maybe in their fifties and we all know old blokes are rubbish right? Wrong again. They rode away too and I was left with a few riders who were still riding as fast as I was able. As the first few crossed the line I was still half a lap behind, then the next small group went over. To my surprise we passed a few of the others who had broken away early on and were now suffering as much, if not more, than me. I launched everything I had left, which was not much, as we got towards the line and I managed to gain a few more places. Once again, I glanced down at the heart rate monitor and saw 192 bpm flash up. Bloody hell.

As soon as I'd gone over the line the dry-mouthed feeling of pain and physical exertion dropped away as quickly as it had come on at the start of the race. I was left with a feeling of exhilaration and puppy-like excitement. I presume it was adrenalin mixed with a sense of achievement at actually finishing, but the overriding feeling was one of satisfaction at having completed something worthwhile without disgracing myself. The guy who had asked me about the provenance of my bike rode over, patting me on the back as he went past and saying well done. "Thanks, and you." I said, "But I was rubbish, you guys were miles ahead.". He seemed to imply I might have 'got' something but then we were both still rolling around on our bikes so I didn't really catch what he said. I certainly didn't have it in me to ride after him to seek clarification.

I did another lap of the circuit just to soak in the whole experience a little more and then went to find Dad and my wife. I was still gabbling and they were still listening as a modest crowd was gathering. A podium was brought out and the medal presentations began. The chap who I'd spoken to earlier was called up. Dave Sykes had won the gold medal in his age category; he walked over, shook hands with the local dignitary, got onto the top step and received his medal. "...and the silver medal goes to...Richard Smith of the Birmingham B team". Some mistake surely, I didn't go over that line second, 22nd maybe but not second. I walked towards the podium and asked if they were sure. Yep, they were. The winner said, "I said you'd got something didn't I?" Indeed he had.

Something else I'd completely neglected to research properly was the age categorisation of the race. Had I looked I would have discovered I just made it into the youngest age bracket and it just so happened, it was the least populated. Many people who have a transplant are, it has to be said, a little older than me. I was 26 when I had mine, and most of the bike racers were older, some of them quite a lot older, and clearly quite a lot better too. Nevertheless, transplant statistics meant I had come second in my age group and I had a little medal to prove it. I stood on the podium with the winner whilst Stephen Belcher was awarded the bronze medal, we all shook hands again and stepped down to allow the presentation for the older guys to go ahead. There were some grey hairs, a few wizened faces but lots of lean, tanned muscular clean-shaven legs amongst them.

I got chatting to my new-found podium mates. The winner had won a few of these races before, a seasoned rider of some years and a kidney transplant patient. He told me I should be going to Australia. Strange I thought, I've only just met the guy, he's beaten me, now he's suggesting I deport myself to the colonies. Bit rough that. Turns out the next World Transplant Games were being held in Sydney that September and, at least is his estimation, I was good enough to go and compete. Logistics, selection criteria and preparation all made this impossible of course but it was nice to be thought of as being sufficiently able. I asked him if he had ridden in the World Games before and he said he had. I was impressed. I asked if he'd ever won anything there and said not but he'd had a good bunch finish in the Games in Manchester in 1995 and was hoping to get onto the podium in Sydney. I remained impressed. Stephen was a heart transplant patient. Wow, now that *was* impressive, I'd just seen what my heart had been doing a few moments ago and that was the one I was born with. To get on a bike and race it like he had after a heart transplant clearly took some balls. He told me it was okay, although his transplanted heart took a little longer to react to the stimulus his brain was telling his legs to output. Human turbo lag if you will.

With another big smile, he said he'd see me at the rest of the Games and asked if I was going to the party tonight. It was with some regret I made my excuses. He looked slightly surprised and, dare I say, a little disappointed. Why would I not want to stay for the rest of the fun? Good question. I didn't really have an answer for that one but I was going to have a good look at my reasons. I travelled home, delighted, surprised and very definitely inspired to do more of this stuff.

The socks of death

The local paper published a tiny piece on my result, just a little paragraph on the bottom of the back page. Honour had been served and in a small way the purpose of the Games had been achieved. They existed to promote awareness of organ donation and transplantation issues, so publicity of a positive kind that helped persuade people to sign up to the organ donor register was a good thing. My little second place and correspondingly little article were unlikely to have people rushing to sign the register in droves but it was a start.

I realised that if I wanted to be competitive, let alone ever win anything on a bike, I was going to have to make a substantial step up in terms of performance. This meant harder and better targeted training, but at least I'd put down a marker. I had completed one bike race even though my second place felt like a rather hollow victory. Twenty or more riders had crossed the line in front of me.

The British Transplant Games are an annual event held in different cities around the country and the 1998 event was scheduled for Belfast. I had established that having a target to train for suited me – it kept me on track and out of trouble. I began to focus on what I would need to do to ensure I gave myself a good chance of winning.

The games events usually started on a Thursday evening with the bike race and opening ceremony and continued until the Sunday night when a gala dinner was held. Broadly speaking, you hit things with bats on Friday, splashed about in the pool on Saturday and had a run around on Sunday. There, that's upset pretty much everyone.

I was still unsure I wanted to get involved in the totality of this movement; it felt like it might be a massive group therapy session. Having said that, the guys I had met at the race seemed pretty cool and I wanted to give the experience another go. My reluctance to immerse myself fully in the whole Games scene could legitimately be interpreted as me struggling to come to terms with the rapidity of my transplant. There was never the slightest doubt in my mind the transplant was absolutely necessary for my survival but I was far from ready to embrace it. I know that because of the nature of the disease its effects were not reversible with any other kind of treatment so it had to happen for me to live. This didn't automatically mean I felt compelled to spend my time with others who found themselves in similar circumstances.

If my condition had been more accurately diagnosed before that dash down the M6, I would most likely have been referred to a local hospital without the specialist knowledge and treatment capabilities of the Queen Elizabeth Hospital. It is entirely possible I would have died while they figured out what to do with me, or a precious day or two would have been wasted limiting the time to locate a suitable organ. In many ways I was grateful for missing out on this period. I can only imagine how awful the wait for a suitable organ is.

Your declining health is monitored and balanced against the likelihood of you continuing to be strong enough to go through the surgery. You get a bleeper and off you go to wait. There are false alarms of course, for example, where a prospective donor organ doesn't materialise. On top of all of that, the fear of the surgery and the prospect of what life may be like on the other side of it, juggling rejection and the like, must constantly prey on your mind. I'd missed out this phase.

The choices had been taken away from me. It was another one of my favourite risk-free non-decisions. I could whine about how unfair my illness was and how none of it was my fault. I didn't even have to make the decision about receiving a transplanted organ; my father had done that for me. It's an unattractive, petulant and adolescent attitude.

Missing the pre-transplant phase had saved me from the stress of the wait and fear of the outcome. It also meant I hadn't had the opportunity to consider my fate before the operation or to talk to anybody about what it might actually be like. If ever there is a right time to talk to a medical

108

professional schooled in psychology, a doctor of the mind, then that was it.

Post-transplant counselling had consisted of a single visit from the hospital Chaplain who kindly sat and talked with me for a while. The conversation with her on the ward centred on whether or not I was married? (no), had a girlfriend? (unsure), err…partner? (nope). Did I have anyone special in my life? (too complicated). She was trying to tell me that in her experience people in my position usually suffered a major confidence blow and this could have a significant impact on relationships. Her line of gentle questioning led me to interpret that this applied to the limited sphere of personal relationships with a sexual element. Of course, it applies more broadly to all relationships with workmates, family, friends, the lady in W.H. Smiths, everybody.

For a long time I felt I had to 'confess' I'd had a transplant. Like my existence was a subterfuge: I was only in front of them because of smoke and mirrors, a creation of clever surgeons and powerful drugs. I felt people had a right to know who they were dealing with. The transplant was defining me and maybe I wasn't 'normal' after all. Maybe the woman at the symposium had a point? Looking back now I can see this was the crisis of confidence the Chaplain was talking about. My self-perception and ability to interact with the world at an appropriate level had taken a knock.

Cycling had become my therapy and, to my eternal delight, my brother, Ian, had decided to do some mountain biking. He bought an equivalent to my Raleigh Apex: only without yaw control. It was a Diamond Back and putting my rapidly developing bike snobbery to one side, was an entirely serviceable bike much like the Apex had been. Ian came over and we set off for our first ride together on the Brown Clee: the highest hill in Shropshire and the site of some excellent but much underused mountain biking trails.

Ian was still something of a novice. He looked as incongruous on a mountain bike as I did when I was out on my road bike in my virtual jeans and cowboy boots. He'd not yet acquired the array of bits and bobs that add a little comfort or control like clipless pedals, cycling shorts or a jacket. It wasn't too cold or damp, so his white squash trainers, tracksuit bottoms and rainproof walking jacket were doing the job. He had complemented his makeshift cycling garb with a pair of white sports socks pulled high up over his ankles and onto his calves. Lovely.

It was a testing ride for Ian over what is some pretty challenging terrain for a novice. We had climbed to the summit and then started a series of descents, the first being a technical, steep piece of single track that he managed quite well. By God, he was starting to get the hang of this. A bit.

The next downhill section was a broad banana-shaped fire road, the width of a dual carriageway but with deep tractor ruts made more pronounced by years of having water run through them. You had to ride either in a rut or along the ridge of one, there was no other way down. On either side, the road dropped away quite steeply into wooded areas. I once saw a friend of mine, Alex, you remember Alex, the guy with the sheep shit up his nose, descend this part of the Clee on a borrowed rigid Orange P7 at a ridiculously fast pace. The bike was bucking around and trying to throw him off but he managed to hold it together all the way to the bottom. I congratulated him on his performance only to be told the thing was so unstable he didn't dare take his hands off the bars to apply the brakes. He was just hanging on waiting to crash but, well, missed, I suppose.

I reached the gate at the bottom of the relatively short section and looked back up to check on Ian's progress. Initially slow and awkward was the answer but he was gathering speed. Quite a lot of speed at quite an alarming rate. He was 'Alexing' this but without the same level of skill or, as it turned out, luck. Unable to navigate the gentle corner, he was now travelling at right angles to the rutted surface rather than parallel to it. He was riding it in much the same way as a roller coaster, repeatedly creeping to the crest of a rise before hurtling down the other side. The last I saw of him was as he headed toward the wooded area at the side of the track via the final naturally ramped embankment. Hitting it at some speed he was propelled skywards and began to break out of earth's atmosphere. The bike appeared in the air, wheels up, indicating it was now upside down and separation had occurred. The long white socks appeared soon after indicating that he was also upside down and no longer connected to the bike in any meaningful way. There was an enormous crashing noise as he came back from the stratosphere and unseen by me, hit the ground. Startled wildlife scattered in every direction, birds took to flight and small mammals ran for their very lives. With the exception of the crashing noise, the whole episode had happened in complete silence, as it appeared Ian had become entirely resigned to his fate during his journey as passenger rather than a pilot. He emerged from the woods a couple of minutes later, remounted and gingerly continued his journey at a more sedate pace until he reached me at the gate. My laughter was uncontrollable. It was then and remains now, one of the funniest things I have ever seen on a bike. Ian was covered in a fair selection of vegetation with leaves, twigs and moss sticking out the vents in his helmet and covering his makeshift cycling clothes. It was at this stage he uttered the timeless line, "I appear to have lost control of my machine." Indeed he had *completely* lost control of his machine. Later on, he firmly laid the blame for his misfortune on the long white 'socks of death'. There was no attempt at explaining quite why the socks were responsible for the crash but they have never seen the light of day since.

My winter training for the Belfast Games became a little more systematic and I started to use the heart rate monitor properly, making the most of the data I'd gathered from my first, and so far only, race. I bought a turbo trainer. For those who are unfamiliar, a torture device on which you can affix your bike by the back wheel and train statically indoors when it's too dark or cold outside. These are appalling implements that should be banned by all liberal countries as an affront to human rights. They are the only

111

known apparatus capable of removing the soul from a human body. Look long enough at somebody using one of these things, look really closely, and you will see them become gradually translucent, hollowed out as their life-force drains from them. They should be classed in the same category as cluster munitions in my view. All right I'm exaggerating, but only a bit. Anybody who has spent time on these infernal contraptions whilst staring at the garage door and getting their iPod cables tangled up with their towel will tell you. They are only to be used in the most desperate of circumstances.

Rollers are another indoor training device in a similar category but as the bike is free floating, it relies on constant tiny adjustments in balance by the rider to stay upright. This replaces the boredom of using a turbo by adding a massive dollop of danger to training inside. The flimsy excuse used by their proponents to justify their existence is that they help you improve your balance. Do they hell; I can balance perfectly well on a bike, thank you very much, I learned to do it when I was 6-years-old and I cannot see any possible reason for learning to balance on these death traps. Just for the record, if one practiced long enough to stand on marbles and was prepared to invest the time in recovering from the injuries sustained whilst doing it, would that improve balance too? I suppose it might, but surely it would only be useful when practicing for the World Standing on Marbles Championship. But we're not, and neither is anybody else to my knowledge, so we're unlikely to do it.

Track riders use rollers for warming up and cooling down between relatively short events, heats and Omnium races. This is because they don't know any better and do not realise they would be far better off using a turbo trainer, substantially reducing the risk of injury from falling off. I have seen youth riders balancing on these things no-handed and pedalling with one leg but, as we will discover later, youth riders are pretty tricky individuals many of whom are in league with the Devil. I have seen them do things on a

112

bike I can only assume involves the use of supernatural powers because they appear impossible to mortals. I have also seen senior riders so badly injured from falling off rollers that they have missed part of the racing season.

The winter of 1997/8 consisted of mountain bike rides, long lonesome road rides, and soul sucking turbo-training sessions. I was analysing my recovery times with the heart rate monitor and recording my average speed and mileage with a little bike computer when I was out on the road. I was starting to take my riding a little more seriously and enjoying it too. I invested in some new wheels, better tyres and some new pedals. I even started wearing a few bits and bobs associated with road cycling. Not so anybody would really notice, just short white socks and a short-sleeved racing jersey.

As winter turned to spring I realised it was time. It was time to be honest about how I really felt even if I found the strange stirrings unsettling. Perhaps I'd always known deep down inside. I also knew if I told Dad he'd be shocked and upset. However he always had my best interests at heart and he wouldn't want me to be unhappy. In time he'd come to understand. Yes, I was going to shave my legs.

Most people who race or spend a lot of time riding on the road will, at some stage, get this urge. If you watch the big international bike races or Olympic track races on the telly you will see perfectly former specimens of man and womanhood with tanned, toned, beautifully smooth, shaven legs. Watch closely as they climb Alpine passes in the summer heat haze or as they accelerate out of their starting blocks on the boards of the velodrome. More toned lean muscle is on display than you can shake a stick at. But why do they do it?

It feels like exam time again. No cheating. Graph paper has not been supplied because you don't need it.

Question 3

You are chatting to a friend who knows you are a keen cyclist. He mentions while you appear normally hirsute on your top half, your legs show no sign of hair whatsoever. After a while, when he has stopped laughing and pointing, he asks you what ludicrous explanation you can proffer for doing something so seemingly bizarre?

From the four alternative explanations set out below, indicate which response most accurately reflects your reasons.

1. "I know it's a bit well, girlie, but it makes me more aerodynamic by allowing the air to flow cleanly over my legs increasing my maximal speed. I have sacrificed my leg hair on the altar of speed and efficiency".

2. "It makes it easier to apply creams and more comfortable for my sports masseur when having a post-event rub down to promote recovery following hard training or racing. This, and for this reason alone, have I taken to the depilatory cream".

3. "Should I be unfortunate enough to crash, hair can be ripped out by contact with the road surface making an injury worse than it need be. It stops me from getting road rash and helps the healing processes. A hardened road man such as me can't afford to be off the bike for long. Therefore, I whipped out the depilator".

4. "Alright, everybody else I ride with does it and it shows off my leg muscles. I had to balance the stick I was getting from them for being hairy against my non-cycling mates taking the piss for being 'girlie'. I figured I'd be wearing long trousers most of the time

with you lot and thought you probably wouldn't notice anyway".

4 is of course the correct answer and don't let anybody tell you otherwise. Hair would totally ruin the look. It's all part of the 'form'. All those hard hours in the gym and on the road to shape those athletic limbs would be wasted if nobody could see them under a matt of wiry hair. So we shave it off. It's true, there is no reason other than vanity for cyclists shaving their legs.

Cycling is one of the few non-specialist environments where men with shaved legs feel comfortable getting together and slapping each other on the bum whilst wearing skin-tight clothing. You can even throw in a mention of chain whips, big rings and skin suits too if you like, nobody will bat an eyelid. The Police will only turn up if drugs are involved. Notwithstanding this, you should be careful when having 'leg shaving-bum slapping-big ring-lyrca wearing' conversations. These are entirely acceptable when surrounded exclusively by fellow cyclists. They understand the references and will empathise with your inability to shave around your ankles without nicking yourself. When not surrounded by others of our ilk, you may find the piano stops and everybody looks and stares. Be a good cyclist and always be aware of your surroundings and any potential hazards.

If it helps to dispel a few myths, the aerodynamic properties of shaven limbs have been tested in wind tunnels and proven to make no difference at all. Some have gone so far as to suggest it actually increases wind resistance. The massage excuse is quite a good one but then any athlete who has regular treatment would also shave their legs too. And they don't. 99.9% of the cyclists I ride with are teachers, factory workers, accountants and the like and although they'd like to have a massage on a weekly basis, time and cost make this impossible. Once or twice a year as a treat maybe but usually no more than that.

Road rash? Not according to Sister Green at my local casualty unit and she's been picking bits of gravel out of me since I was 10. Hair growth back through a wound after shaving can actually increase rather than lessen the chance of developing an infection but it's pretty marginal. You should try not to fall off anyway, at least that's what Sister Green keeps telling me.

If you *are* going to take the plunge, take a little advice from somebody who has been there, done that and then gone to the doctor for antibiotics to treat a horrendous case of folliculitis. Twice.

Do

Use a new razor, one specifically designed for shaving legs, as ladies do.
Get a pink one; go on, you might as well.
Trim the matting off first with some clippers or you'll be there forever.
Use shaving foam, not soap.
Stand in the bath and have the shower hose handy.
Have plasters and antiseptic standing by.
Remember, seeking forgiveness is easier than seeking permission.
Exfoliate with an exfoliater thing you can get from the chemists. Get a pink one.
Put some post-shave moisturiser on your legs when you've finished.
Ask your GP to prescribe Flucloxacillin, a very effective antibiotic for soft-tissue infections such as folliculitis.

Don't

Moan to me when you've cut your ankles.
Tell anybody you're doing it, or have done it, that isn't intimately involved with cycling.

116

Be surprised if it feels really odd when you put your trousers on or get into bed after you've done it for the first time.
Expect sympathy for any blood loss.
Tell your wife, partner or significant other before you do it.
Finish a race behind somebody who hasn't shaved his or her legs. It makes you look like a pillock.
Use depilatory cream from unreliable sources unless you're tired of having skin on your legs.
Get any funny ideas about wearing tights or stockings.

My shaven-legged training was somewhat interrupted in the late spring by a 'deranged' set of blood results, yes, that's what they called them, 'deranged'. Also, my blood pressure had shot up, most probably due to the immunosuppression. I was prescribed a slow release anti-hypertension drug called Adalat 'Retard'. So there I was then, half shaven, deranged and retarded, back in outpatients talking to a Registrar who looked like he was 12-years-old.

Dave Mutimer was still looking after me but assigned more junior doctors to perform the routine check-ups. This young fellow fancied sticking a needle between my ribs and digging a bit of liver out. Not a popular choice of treatment option in my book so I politely declined his invitation until Dave pulled rank. He explained that they couldn't tell what the problem was by the liver function tests alone and needed to get some liver tissue under the microscope for a proper look. After some discussion, Dave confirmed it would indeed be appropriate if the tissue came from *my* liver rather than *his*, as I had sarcastically suggested. I had to be re-admitted to hospital, this time to a specific biopsy suite for the test.

My father and I had attended a celebration of the 1000th liver transplant in March of 1995 (the operation had actually been done in November 1994). The number of successful transplant patients was growing (more than 300 per year in Birmingham alone). Hence Dave Mutimer's time being better spent looking after those people who really needed his skills and the creation of a specialist needle-through-the-ribs unit.

The things that were of particular concern to me now were, broadly in order of importance, how quickly I could resume training after the biopsy and whether I could still get a medical certificate to allow me to compete in Belfast. Further, would the deranged blood results affect my performance and, what the hell was wrong with me anyway?

They told me to take it easy as they didn't know what the cause was yet but signed the certificate anyway as the blood results showed some 'grumbling' rather than anything too awful.

You may recall I got a bit of a deserved reputation for kicking off during my initial time in hospital and this time, although not stuffed full of drugs and toxins I was again labelled as an awkward patient by the Staff nurse in charge of the biopsy suite. My awkwardness arose from my inability to stop bleeding all over the floor and passing out after she'd had three goes at getting a needle into my vein. One attempt pierced straight through the vein and out the other side. I'm not bragging, but you could hit the vein in my right arm blindfolded with a dart from the other side of a room: how she missed it that many times I will never know, nobody else ever has. Not even a junior doctor.

The biopsy came and went relatively smoothly and off they went to the pathology lab with the liver tissue. I was expecting the result to come straight back whilst I was enjoying eight hours flat on my back berating myself for not going to the toilet beforehand. It didn't, it was routine now and the results would be available for my next clinic visit.

Despite a fairly solid promise that a first-hand examination of my liver tissue would tell the doctors what was going on, it didn't yield anything conclusive. They thought it might be grumbling rejection, 'a bit of hepatitis' whatever that might mean or something, well, 'idiopathic'. Nevertheless, I got another sweetie bag full of steroids and a 6-week reappointment at outpatients.

I had the medical form signed and an all clear to carry on training, well, I assumed it was an all-clear. Anyway, like I said, it's sometimes easier to seek forgiveness than permission. Despite an uncomfortable few weeks of waiting and worrying, the grumbling had either begun to resolve itself or the Prednisolone had worked. Either way, things were on the mend.

Belfast

I knew Belfast was important. It was a chance to try myself out against the same riders as last year for one thing. It was also the qualifying event for the next World Transplant Games. Originally these had been scheduled for Holland but now moved to Budapest, Hungary for financial reasons. Winning in Ireland should mean an automatic invitation to the Great Britain team and I definitely wanted some of that.

I was proud to be representing my hospital, the Queen Elizabeth Hospital, and Birmingham; I was working in the city and it was where my life was saved. I held it in great affection but representing my country was the real dream. I know it sounds trite, anybody would find that easy to say in the same circumstances, but it was an opportunity that I very much wanted a shot at. It would mean spending time with a lot of other transplant patients, potentially thousands of them, but previous experiences had indicated these gatherings were far from the mass group therapy sessions I had initially feared.

On arrival in Ireland for the Games I found the race circuit in Belfast was around Donegal Square, in front of the Town Hall in fact, right in the middle of the city. It simply could not have been any better. The street had been barriered off and people were lining up behind them. I'd seen things like this before for 'proper' bike races but never expected to be in this kind of environment myself. It was a real criterium course of 1km in length meaning 10 laps of a very tight circuit with right angle bends. Perfect.

Dad and Anne had taken the scenic route, driving over from Britain, taking the ferry from Stranraer, and I had flown over from Birmingham. My wife had stayed at home with Charlie and was, in any event, now pregnant with our second child. Looking back at the pictures I can see that 2 months of steroids had put some weight on me. I'm not going to get away with that am I? I'll rephrase. I'd eaten way too much over the past couple of months, my appetite stimulated by the steroids and I was a bit fat.

I saw some familiar faces from the previous year but others were absent, sadly this is something you have to become accustomed to attending the Games on a regular basis. Transplant recipients get ill from time to time and most, thankfully, recover but others do not. One of the new faces, if a slightly wrinkled one was Wes Clayton, a former Tour of Britain rider. Wes had got a year or two on him and like me he'd had a liver transplant but he was a top class rider in his day and still looking dangerous and lean now. Dave Sykes, the rider who had won last year in my age category was also there together with a pretty large group of other competitors.

The racing was frantic, particularly with the tight course and the rapid corners but the surface was good allowing some pretty hairy speeds to be reached. There was a bit of barging and some pushing and shoving. Clashes of hands, shoulders and wheels are not unusual in criterium races but it was a new experience for me and unnerving to say the least. A couple of breaks went away but I managed to hold my nerve and the bunch pulled them back. I was trying to keep track of my rivals, the winner of last year's race in particular, but the speed and number of riders made that a real challenge. I saw Wes Clayton make a break and dart clear on his own. Like the top class rider he was, the turbo boost seemed to come from nowhere and before we knew it he was on the other side of the road, head down and out of saddle powering to get a gap and prevent anybody from following his wheel. It was a textbook perfect attack by Wes, despite my gut reaction and desire to not let him get away I couldn't get across to him. I couldn't match his speed. In truth I didn't need to try. Wes was in an older age category to me and, in order to stand a chance of getting selected for the British team I needed to win in my age group, the overall race being secondary. Wes had gone on the penultimate lap and I saw him cross the line in front on me. I could sense that Wes's attack and the increase in speed that came with it had shelled out a few more riders from the group but I didn't know where last year's winner was. He was, like an experienced rider should be in those circumstances, right behind me, using my effort as I made a hole in air, drafting me and saving his energy for the sprint. His tactical savvy: my tactical ineptitude. I saw the line and launched what you might charitably call a sprint. I was out of the saddle giving everything I could just like I'd practiced on the roads at home hundreds of times. I could sense a rider coming off my rear wheel and moving up, gaining on me, I could see him next to me now and we both went over the line together.

I had absolutely loved the race, even the bumping and barging, but in the excitement, I'd momentarily forgotten that a win in my category would put me in with a shout at selection for the World Games. We all warmed down, riding another couple of laps and soaking up the atmosphere of the race and the applause of the people who were watching. It was just like, you know, a proper bike race and everything! There were a few slaps and pats on the back and some 'well dones'. I went over to shake Wes's hand to congratulate him on his win. He had a broad genuine smile on his face which was, of course, entirely understandable because of his victory: as I got to know Wes a little better, I understood the smile was pretty much permanent. What a warm-hearted likeable man he turned out to be. I went to talk to Dad and Anne and they seem to think I'd won. Wes had definitely gone over the line first but they thought I'd just pipped Dave Sykes the winner of last year's race. I wasn't so sure. I really didn't know whether I'd beaten him or not and, when chatting to him, he seemed convinced he'd got it. He was the senior rider. I was not about to argue with him and left it in the hands of the judges. Unusually, they asked us. He claimed the victory and I said I couldn't honestly say but would respect their decision.

I was delighted when they awarded me the win. Dave, as was his right, protested: he honestly thought he'd won and in truth it was entirely possible he had. There was no photo finish equipment on the line; we'd had to rely on the judge's recall. There was a brief discussion on calling a dead heat and awarding two gold medals but that again was dismissed.

So there I was, on the top of a podium, in the magnificent surroundings of Belfast Town Hall, being awarded a gold medal and being crowned in our own exclusive little category, a national cycling champion. Bloody hell.

It's unusual for blokes to talk to each other in a urinal – It's bad form. But on this occasion my peeing companion looked out of the corner of his eye and in a full on 'Norn Iron' accent said, "I won a lot of money on you tonight so I did". Apparently a good proportion of the crowd had been studying the form of the riders as we warmed up and a decent amount of money had exchanged hands. It made a certain amount of sense. The quality of the racing had been pretty good but perhaps not good enough to produce quite the amount of noise coming from the crowd.

Later on, as we enjoyed the fabulous hospitality and wonderful surroundings, I was fielding questions about what I was doing for the rest of the games. The answer? Going home. This wouldn't really cut it anymore.

The organisers are happy for people to come and go in this way but it did seem increasing disingenuous to only come for the bit I was interested in trying to win. It was partly defeating the object of the exercise to raise awareness of organ donation and transplantation. I needed to get around to watching the other sports and meeting more of my fellow transplantees. Maybe they weren't so scary after all: my experience of being there so far was that there was a lot of talking about cycling and not that much about transplantation. These were seriously competitive events for dedicated athletes (who happened to have had a transplant).

There was a good deal of local fuss when I got back home. The two local papers had reports and pictures and there was I, sharing the back page of the Shropshire Star with Pierre Van Hooijdonk, the footballer. I can't recall why I was sharing the back page with him and I've often wondered if he was thinking the same thing: I knew who he was but I'm pretty sure he'd never heard of me. I got a call from a local cycling journalist asking if he could do a little article on me for the same paper and, of course, I agreed. The whole point of the Games is to raise awareness so with that as a justification, I didn't feel particularly self-conscious about the publicity. I personally had nothing to hide and was becoming more comfortable with my situation. Perhaps not quite ready to embrace it but heading in that direction.

The article led to a call from Dave Poulter, the Chairman of the Telford-based Wrekinsport cycling club, and an invitation to go and meet some of the guys on one of their Sunday rides. It made sense; I needed to join a club to improve my riding. I wanted it to be a Shropshire-based club and it seemed every other male I knew was called Dave. I thought I might as well continue the theme.

To reward the 653 I bought some rather snazzy Campagnolo carbon Record gear and brake levers and my local bike shop hand built me some beautiful wheels with Campag Record hubs and Mavic Open Pro rims laced with double butted Sapim spokes. I appreciate that to a non-cyclist that probably sounds like something from the menu of an over-priced restaurant. I hope those riders of a certain vintage will be gently nodding their approval as they read the Carte d'or.

Riding with a group means you have to take responsibility for looking after yourself as well as possible. It's not reasonable or fair to depend on your club mates for assistance without making an effort yourself. So, it was time to stock up on those essential little bits of equipment you need to take with you when you ride. You also need a few things to stop you freezing to death in February and to get you home in case of an emergency.

It's amazing what you can fit into the voluminous pockets of a cycling jersey and with the knowledge that some inaugural club rides were coming up, I set about filling them. Once again, I went through a learning process. My stupidity, and that of others, is documented below.

Arm warmers

These are fleece-lined tubes of water repellent material you put on your arms giving your jersey some temporary sleeves when it's a bit chilly. Ideal for rides where temperatures can change from boiling hot to freezing cold without warning i.e. any British season. Useful because they can be taken off or put on during a ride. Some riders casually remove them whilst riding no-handed, folding them neatly and putting them away in a back pocket. I've tried this. It's difficult to be precise about the order of events that followed but I had to grab the bars to steady myself after half removing the first one. The trailing bit of arm warmer got caught in the front wheel stopping it and launching me over the handlebars. In fairness, it did remove the arm warmer but it also nearly removed my arm.

In light of my experience described above, it's fair to say I am not an arm warmer expert, should there be such a thing. All the same, I refuse to believe I am the only person who has punched himself in the face while putting them on. I pull them up my arms as far as I can, my fingers slip off them and whack, once more I have clobbered myself in the mush. Classy.

Arm warmers also come in handy for cleaning things in an emergency. They can be redeemable after being used for certain emergencies, but not all. Need I say more?

Finally, they come in a range of colours to nearly match your club kit. Only those with great patience and money to burn should consider buying white ones.

Multi-tools

A pocket-sized foldable tool including a range of hex keys, screwdrivers and at least one thing for which the purpose is completely unidentifiable. These are supposedly useful for making minor adjustment to a bike when away from the garage or workshop, although it's unlikely the multi-tool will contain the actual tool required.

I think it would be useful to have a tool for getting stones out of horses hooves as cycling is the only time I encounter horses. No, I've never seen one with a stone in its shoe, but it's possible I will. It would be a shame if after a lifetime of carrying a Swiss Army penknife and never once bumping into a horse in need, I should be ill equipped when I eventually do.

Multi-tools must not be placed in your hand luggage when travelling abroad. My plea to airport security that it was unlikely I would be able to take the plane to bits, even if I was motivated to do so, fell on deaf ears. I further explained that most of the tools didn't even fit my bike so I felt sure it wouldn't work on an Airbus 320. I personally didn't think the full body cavity search was necessary. I would advise caution on the tone you adopt with these people unless you too want to hear the tell-tale snap of latex gloves.

Mini-pump

A pocket-sized pump to inflate a replaced or repaired inner tube following a puncture. Carried either in a rear jersey pocket or strapped to the frame. It is very unlikely a pocket carried mini-pump will work. By their nature they are tiny and although the manufacturers often claim 100 psi is attainable it will be dark by the time it is achieved. Possibly twice. It is equally unlikely a frame mounted mini-pump will serve any better. They do work, but rarely do they stay attached to the frame long enough to find out. More likely it will have fallen off and been flattened by a car somewhere without you noticing.

In the unlikely event that your mini-pump does work, it will allow you to get 40 psi in the tyre for about 20 minutes work: just about enough to get you home if you are careful. If you are lucky, somebody in the group will have the foresight to take a proper-sized frame-mounted pump with them and will let you use it.

A pump of any kind is completely useless without a couple of tyre levers and some spare tubes of course. Even better if the tubes are compatible with the wheels.

Take care if you are purchasing a mini-pump whilst abroad. A girlfriend of mine, a fluent Italian speaker, went into a bike shop in Sardinia whilst cycling there sure in the knowledge anything 'small' is suffixed with 'ino'. Consequently, her request for a 'pumpino' seemed entirely appropriate to her but caused a certain amount of comment in the shop. In the local dialect, a 'pumpino' is a completely different kind of blowing up altogether.

Gilet

A phenomenally useful piece of clothing either on its own or coupled with arm warmers. Basically a sleeveless jacket that goes a long way to keeping you warm by blocking the wind and cold off your chest while riding on cooler days. Small enough to roll up and stuff in a pocket if it warms up, they also provide any extra storage when your jersey is full of arm warmers, mini-pumps and other miscellaneous tools.

As with arm warmers, many riders slip these on and off whilst on the move. I don and remove my gilet with the same dexterous touch I employ with arm warmers now. I stop. Get off. Fold it up. Put it in my pocket. And continue. It is possible to constrict your movement with the ruthless efficiency of a straightjacket playing with these on the move. The consequences of doing this are inevitable.

I splashed out on an expensive gilet recently. In fact I've got loads, I like them that much. The latest one includes a small zip pocket on the front to put keys in. I found this works best when the zip is done up. Should anybody find my house keys, anywhere by a roadside in Shropshire, there is a small reward for their return.

Glasses

Covering your eyes is vital when riding. Grit, stones and all sorts of things can be thrown up from the road surface and, more importantly, you wouldn't look very cool without them would you? I was determined some time ago to be *forced* into buying some glasses from a very well-known and expensive eyewear manufacturer. No other company made them with the interchangeable yellow 'light enhancing' lens I required. I was devastated to discover on a visit to my local bike shop that another company did in fact make these and they were 15 quid rather than the £100 or so I was banking on spending. I was gutted: my excuse had gone and I had to settle for the perfectly serviceable pair of cheaper ones. It took me over 2 years of abuse to accidentally break them allowing me to purchase what I really wanted in the first place.

Sunglasses are even more vital if you are a youth or junior rider and should be worn at all times, irrespective of light (or dark) conditions, either to prevent getting annoying particles in your eyes or to avoid being recognised out in lycra by your mates, perhaps? I turned up at the track once on a Winter's evening to find what looked disturbingly like a midget Roy Orbison convention.

Phone

Take a smartphone with you if you can. When you break down you are unlikely to be able to get a signal to call in air support but you might as well have something to play with whilst you are waiting for help.

Helmet

Tricky. There are two sides to this argument within the ranks of cyclists and, as I may have mentioned before, until the birth of my first child I didn't wear one at all. After Charlie arrived I wore one for mountain biking as I thought there was a greater chance of me caving my head in or, if I was riding alone, getting knocked out and stuck in the woods somewhere.

In contrast, I knew I was perfectly well-protected riding on the road with a traditional cotton casquette protecting my bonce because I turned it backwards. 'What could possibly go wrong riding at 60kph on a rock hard surface surrounded by cars and lorries?' being the slightly suspect thought process that separated my on-road and off-road riding attire.

On my first Majorcan training camp I wore one because it's the (hardly ever enforced) law you must ride with a lid in Spain. I spent some time chatting to a First Responder paramedic who, in non-hysterical terms, explained why he used one and why on balance he thought it was a good idea. I've used one ever since.

I think you have a duty to the people you ride with to take what precautions you can to ensure, if you should be unfortunate enough to have an accident, they don't have to deal with an injury that could have been lessened by your choice of headgear. At best, this will stop the ride being delayed and, at worse, might save them from some images they'd sooner not have in their still intact heads.

I find the reasoning that helmets give a false sense of security preposterous: the consequences of crashing on a road bike at speed can be severe and even in a relatively minor scrape you are going to lose some skin from your hands, arms and legs. In a high-speed incident it's possible you will not only be relieved of skin, you are also likely to break bones and damage other stuff needed to function properly. All cyclists know this and accept the risk: I find the prospect of this knowledge being diluted in any way by having a piece of polystyrene strapped to your head, frankly ridiculous.

Taking on the World

After a bit of a break from the bike immediately following the British Games, preparation for what might come next started in earnest in the Autumn of 1998. I can be precise on dates because I had started to keep a training diary to track my progress. The first entry on the 4th October 1998 identifies my weight as being 'too much' in block capitals. Useful. In actual fact, I weighed over 13 and a half stone and that *is* too much for a bike rider of 6ft in height.

Unfortunately, I'm only 5'10 making it much worse. I was going to have to do something about my weight; actually I still need to do something about it.

I was doing a pretty healthy mix of gym work, soul-hollowing turbo training sessions, mountain bike trips and lengthy road rides. My fitness was coming on but I really needed to make the jump from being a reasonably fit bloke with a bike to being a cyclist. It's a big leap and, if you recall, the path to enlightenment is fraught with danger including verbal and physical abuse.

All things liver related seemed to be stable, my blood tests were coming back normal allowing me to train as fully as possible but work was becoming pretty intense. I'd been promoted (I know, I've never been able to work it out either) and consequently I was spending more time in London. We'd bought a new house in preparation for the arrival of our second child and there were a good number of pushes and pulls on my time. I think many mature amateur cyclists who race find this. Something always has to give, either work, family or training time, it's just not possible to fit it all in. Most riders, certainly including me, have to do a minimum of 5 or 6 hours of training a week just to be rubbish.

I was waiting for a letter from the Great Britain team management to drop through my door. It didn't happen. Through speaking to riders at the Belfast Games I knew that selection for the GB team, based on the results of the games, had begun. I had chatted to two team members, both experienced riders who had represented GB at previous events, about the process. It transpired that both had been selected for other events, racquet sports specifically, and had decided to enter the bike race while they were there. There was no cycling team as such, just a collection of individuals riding in marginal time rather than as a specific focus of their sporting endeavours. Cycling was considered very much a minor sport by the management and within the team: an add-on that some competitors would do as a secondary event.

I was a little disappointed and worried. I really wanted a shot at riding for the GB team and desperately needed some help and advice on what I should be doing to prepare. It looked like I'd need to be a multi-sport athlete to stand a real chance of getting in. It was going to be difficult to instantly become a world-class athlete. I run like I'm being chased by a dog.

Rather self-consciously I got details of the Team Manager, Peter Griffin, and wrote to him asking what the selection procedure was. Basically introducing myself, in case the cycling category had been forgotten, and reminding him that I'd won the bike race in my age category. Cheeky, I know: it was paramount to inviting myself to join a national representative team with only the flimsy excuse of being alright on a bike. All the same, I was determined not to be overlooked by a closed shop of batters, paddlers and joggers. There, anybody who wasn't upset before certainly will be now.

Shortly afterwards, I got a standard letter from Peter. 'Dear (insert name), having won (insert sport) in (insert venue) you are cordially invited to (insert venue) the (insert number) training session for the GB Transplant Games team going to (insert country)'. Wow! Fantastic! Looks like I'll get to show my face at a training session then on (insert date in 1999), with a view to going to Budapest to represent my country. Brilliant (insert joyous expletive)!

In the November of that year I went for my first Sunday ride with Wrekinsport cycling club. This was my first introduction to club cycling. After spending some years

132

in it now I can confidently say, all life can be found there. Some of it human.

Cycling clubs are a wonderful microcosm of British life. People join cycling clubs, and I think sports clubs in general, for a multitude of reasons. One thing they all have in common is that their ultra-talented and competitive athletes tend to be the least demonstrative. The lesser lights are there because they love to participate in their chosen sport with like-minded company. There is great honour in being a clubman. It shows a passion and enthusiasm for a sport that transcends the desire simply to compete to win. Thousands of cyclists all over the country pin numbers on their backs and enter competitions they know there isn't a chance in hell of them winning. They do this because they love the sport, the fun and the camaraderie. I'm proud to number amongst them. It is from this cadre of sportsmen and women that the greatest characters are often drawn. Anybody holding pretensions above their station is quickly brought down to an appropriate level and I'm sure this is the same in all clubs and teams no matter what the sporting focus. It encourages the club's more colourful characters to come into their own, often their notoriety being inversely proportional to their talent.

I think the Wrekinsport lads fairly quickly worked out I was daft (it was cold and I had no leg warmers on) and rubbish, as I was struggling to ride in the prescribed close formation pairs as we rolled along. When I say close, I mean 6 to 12 inches from the rider next to you and the same distance from the rider in front. Pairs of riders behind you will be at similar distances. It is expected that this formation be maintained, with small adjustments in speed and direction made without squealing like a 6-year-old girl.

You may recall you are not allowed to be *told* any of this, again the principle of osmotic telekinesis applies, the non-verbal absorption of information. Riding in this, or in a similar formation, is fundamental for all cycling on the road.

I think it may be time for some more do's and don'ts, this time for group riding, don't you?

Do

Take your turn at the front every now and again. You may think staying at the back on your first few runs is only polite (no please, after you, I insist, etc.) but not doing your share of work at the front means you may get left at the next café stop.

Try to ride as evenly and smoothly as possible, it makes everybody a touch less nervy.

Make pretend rhythmic squeaky or 'pssssss' noises and look around quizzically a lot.

Be first out of the café.

Refuse to attach mudguards to your bike in the winter because you're a racer, not a bloody tourist.

Complain bitterly about how much time you've spent on the front of the group helping everybody else out even if you've only just got there. There's no time like the present to get some moaning in.

Don't

Expect to be able to see where you are going. Unless you're at the head of the group, you have to rely on the guy in front of you. Trust him. You might as well.

Brake hard, or at all, if possible.

Stop to adjust your shorts, or anything else for that matter, without telling everybody very clearly what you intend to do. You may well have seen the glove you dropped last week at the roadside but, unless you want tyre marks all over your back and to be covered in vented spleen, it will have to stay there for a bit.

Swerve or make sudden moves or noises. Shouting "Snake!" may seem like good fun, and indeed it is, but it can upset people very easily.

Eject snot directly out of your nose unless you are absolutely at the back of the group.

Be last into the café.

'Half wheel' your riding partner. You should ride in a parallel pair or your mate will get faster trying to chase you as you move in front of him. He may well punch you in the ear if you do this for very long.

Ride in the winter without mudguards.

Expect to hear anything more than 20% of the conversation you are having with the guy next to you.

On the subject of conversations whilst riding, two club mates of mine were part of a bunch ride on a breezy but sunny day in Majorca. One of the guys is famed for his ability to talk constantly. He has developed a technique for drawing breath whilst continuing to waffle making it impossible to find a natural gap to interject, or escape. His riding partner at this time had switched off from the conversation and couldn't really hear anything being said anyway. He'd grown accustomed to the constant low drone in his right ear. Recognising slightly belatedly the droning had stopped he looked to find he was being expected to react to a statement or question. Of course, he fudged it and gave a wide-eyed expression of surprise and shock; a reaction he hoped might be appropriate in the circumstances. Seemingly satisfied, the drone continued for another 30 minutes or so only to stop again and look expectantly once again. This time my club mate used the universal hand sign for 'meh' or 'not really bothered' opening his hand palm down and wobbling it hoping a non-committal response would suffice. Seemingly satisfied once more, the drone droned on for some hours until the ride was complete.

Later that evening over dinner in the hotel it was established he had firstly been asked how long he'd been riding a bike: to which he had expressed surprise and some shock. Subsequently, his riding partner had apologised for the presumptuousness of his question before being bemused to discover he was 'not really bothered' about how old he was.

Learning basic bunch riding skills by osmosis does work over time as long as you are prepared to stick at it and, in fact, it only happens this way because of the extension of normal British reserve. Riders within the group assume you know what you are doing and are reluctant to offer advice. The fear of intrusion overrides their fear of hitting the tarmac because of your inability to ride evenly.

As a new boy in the bunch, assumptions will be made about the reasons behind any transgression of the unwritten rules and these can be summarised into four categories:

1. You know what you are doing and you're pulling a fast one to avoid doing your turn or putting in a fair share of the effort. You are therefore a slacker.

2. You know what you're doing but you're being deliberately or unthinkingly awkward. You are therefore a dick.

3. You know what you should be doing but lack the necessary skill to execute the manoeuvres correctly. You are therefore a pillock.

4. You have no idea what you are doing and never will. You are a danger to yourself and everybody around you. You are therefore a chopper.

Falling into the pillock category means that at least over the years you may receive some instruction. After a long period of frustration this will be delivered by another rider at volume and speed and will universally be prefixed by the expression 'for God's sake mate'. The advice will be, say, 'close up a bit'. Thus: 'for God's sake mate close up a bit'. This will not mean anything to you of course but it's a start as it is at least verbal rather than metaphysical communication.

It would be more helpful if it was along the lines of 'I say old chap, if you select a gear that's slightly easier to pedal and increase your leg speed a little, you may find not only do you become a more efficient rider but you'll also be able to adjust your speed more easily. This will help you react in a timelier manner to the actions of the rider in front of you, allowing you to safely stay close to him ensuring a smoother and more harmonious ride for us all.' Of course, even if somebody did say this you wouldn't be able to hear most of it and may well have responded indicating you are either shocked or not that bothered. This will reinforce the understanding that you are a pillock.

The simple rotation of riders taking a turn at the front is known commonly as 'through and off'. Not 'throwing off' as I heard a coach once call it. Everybody takes a turn at the front and the effort is shared. Unless it's windy or you're in pairs, or if it's a race and you're trying to save energy or trying to protect another rider, or trying to slow the group, or set it up to make a break. Actually, perhaps it is a bit more complicated than I thought.

There is a massive amount of information to take in but really there is no great mystery, just some basic principles to get hold of that can, as I have mentioned before, be taught to a new group of riders on a car park with some cones. You don't even need bikes: sometimes it's easier without them. You can just walk through the exercises to establish the principle. Just don't tell anybody.

The Wrekinsport guys were good to me and let me into the secrets relatively painlessly and I shall be eternally grateful to them for that. I have only ever been a member of one cycling club in my life and that's the way I intend it to stay. It's expensive mind, the subs are eight quid a year now, but if you can stretch to it, it's great value for money.

Back in the real world my daughter, Grace, was born on January 20th and my training diary records it as 'cold, no ride'. A little prosaic for the birth of a beloved child I know but it is a training diary not my memoirs. I hope you don't think me callous about my fantastic family and wonderful children, it's just that I'm not writing an autobiography: nobody has ever heard of me so nobody would ever read it. Suffice to say, because of my perceivably looser grip on life, the prospect of not being around to care for my children the way my wonderful parents had cared for me scared me witless. It still does, and I suspect most parents irrespective of their circumstances, share this feeling. So why have another child you might reasonably ask? Well, simple. My life would have been immeasurably poorer without my brother so there was no way in this world I was going to leave Charlie without a sibling. Please don't tell Ian I said that, it would ruin everything.

The excitement of Gracie's arrival nearly put me off the reliability season. Nearly, but not quite. Reliability trials are late winter or early spring mass rides intended to form a bridge between long slow winter miles and the forthcoming race season. Both on my patch, and around the country, local clubs put on one or two rides each, usually hiring a village hall and laying on tea, cakes and the like. A fixed route is set and usually two separate groups, a faster and slower one, go off at different speeds with a broad time estimate for completing the circuit often in the order of 3 to 4 hours. They are not marshalled and do not have lead cars as you would have in a race. In fact, these events are very definitely *not* races. That would be against British Cycling rules. You can't have unmarshalled road races can you? Dangerous. So, everybody sets off together at a pretty frantic pace and the first one back is the, ahem, 'winner'.

My first reliability ride was in February 1999 and was quite an eye opener simply because of the pace. It was another step up from the club rides I had been struggling to complete. There were 80 or more riders at the start and it was quite a spectacle to be involved in, watching all these paired up riders in a bunch, vying for position as the pace went up. After a while I couldn't hold the speed of the guys up front, which was described to me as approximately three quarters race pace. I remember musing how fast a race must be and what it must be like to hold that speed for 3 or more hours. A bunch of riders at the front broke away and left single riders strung out in their wake. We refugees banded together, found others who had been ejected and formed our own little packs to help complete the ride and get back for tea and stickies.

A lot of cycling friendships are formed during these rides and this started me thinking about why cycling appeals to some people. I can't claim any anthropological training. My poorly recorded observations are no more than what I have witnessed, but it did occur to me that there is probably something in the shared effort or suffering theory.

I've asked around after races, time trials, road events and at the track. The simple question was, "Did you enjoy that?" I've had a variety of responses, some of them non-verbal and many of them unrepeatable but I can't recall anybody just saying, "Yes" without some kind of qualifying comment. The satisfaction of completing a physically tough challenge is rewarding, but is the process of getting there fun? Probably not.

I also noted that it is considered good form to get a couple of excuses for a poor performance in before the ride starts. Commonly, these include things like a bad night, cough, cold or the consumption of a dodgy pork pie. A rider can then move on to more 'environmentally specific' excuses during the ride. This is a good time to blame somebody else for your lowly predicament. Here's a good one. You've been working to help out another rider who you sheltered and consistently pulled back to the bunch on numerous occasions only for the ungrateful bastard to ride off and leave you when you were spent. There are, as I'm sure you can imagine, many variations on this theme.

It is cycling etiquette to listen intently to the story of woe, nodding and muttering the occasional empathetic 'bastard' or something similar before launching into your own excuse. You should bear in mind that it is unlikely you will be able to hear much of the excuse or moan but do try to get some kind of flavour for the story. Saying 'bastard' and nodding during a story about your riding companion's mother is unlikely to endear you to him. On completing the ride, more rich excuses (the cows were looking at me funny, anything) can, and should, be employed.

On this particular reliability, our club chairman was handing out certificates to those who had completed the ride successfully. Handing out a rather mutilated one to a well-known local rider he said that he'd cut the corners off it because that's what he'd done to the course this year. I think it may be an old gag, but it was the first time I'd heard it and it still makes me laugh.

There was more of the same in the spring. More intense training rides with distances coming down and intensity going up. I was finding this hard, really hard, but incredibly satisfying. I would have happily done it anyway without the incentive of going to Budapest to represent my country but it gave me added impetus.

Moreover, if I continued to improve and continued to take the constructive criticism of my club mates, I might stop being a chopper and become a pillock by the summer.

Back down to earth

I had got two; count them, two, races under my belt now. I'd won one and come second in the other so, on paper, a good – if very limited – record. Looking back now, I should have quit while the going was good. Nevertheless, I made the decision to twist rather than stick.

In order to have a chance of being competitive on the world stage (get me, world stage) I really needed to sharpen up. I needed to convert the basic strength and fitness I had into some real top-end power and work out what racing was all about tactically. How do you do that? Correct! Race! Race against real people, normal people – people who hadn't had bits of them swapped out.

I had asked my club mates how to go about road racing, where to find details of events, whether any of them raced and what I needed to do to get involved. There were some blank looks, some looks of surprise and some disappointment. They decided I was 'one of them'. Turns out that most of my club mates were time trial riders rather than road racers and, as such, didn't know a great deal about the local road-racing scene.

All the events in the Transplant Games, both British and World, were mass start road races and that's very much what I wanted to focus on. I loved the thrill of racing in a bunch and being surrounded by other riders vying for position. Following another rider who was stronger than you, to try and match his pace: that was where the fun was. Time trialling was really of no interest to me.

Some digging around, a few conversations with some helpful riders probably called Dave, a couple of telephone calls to the British Cycling Federation (BCF) and pretty soon I was completely confused. I established I'd need a racing licence from the BCF as a prerequisite, so I said I'd have one of those please. Sure they said, but you need to be a member before you can have one of those. "Fair enough" I said, "One membership as well please" and out came the cheque book. Of course, it would be too easy for the BCF to send your membership information and your race licence to the same address so one goes to your home and the other goes to the club Secretary. Obvious really. I eventually tracked down my licence at Chairman Dave's house and started on the task of finding out where some races might be scheduled. Back on the phone to the BCF, I established I'd need a race calendar. Right ho, "One race calendar, please". It was mostly in code but I'd got the basics of the paperwork to call myself a road racer. One shiny 4th Category road race licence. Check. One BCF membership. Check. One race calendar. Check and cheques.

All new road racers start off as 4th Cat's. If you are good enough you can then accumulate points by winning or placing well in races and move up through the categories (3rd, 2nd, 1st). Progress past this and you completely do away with the need for your earthly body and become the glowing nimbus of pure energy that is an Elite category rider. An inability to sustain your points tally in the next season and you will come back down the categories, if formerly an Elite rider, presumably there will be an unseemly scramble to become corporeal again. Once the bonds of being a 4th Cat have been shaken off by scoring 10 points or more you will never have to return there. You will only ever go down to being a 3rd Cat however crap you become.

It's a slightly crude but broad and useful way of handicapping road racing. For example, a club may promote a race that is only open to 3rd and 4th Cat riders. This prevents some 20-year-old lean muscled whippet 1st Cat with a glint in his eye smashing up the race before anybody has got started, running off with the prizes and getting the girl. There aren't really any girls, I made that bit up.

Similarly, it stops a no mark 3rd Cat, like me, entering the national championship and weaving all over the road trying to side swipe the girlfriend-stealing bastard 1st Cat from the race last week. It all works pretty well once you have got into the swing of things but nothing, repeat nothing, can adequately prepare you for the fury of your first race.

Not for the first time in my life, I was incredibly lucky. A long-term club member of Wrekinsport was involved with the SSSCCRRL, the catchy acronym given to the Shropshire and South Staffordshire Cycling Clubs Road Race League. This proved to be my ultimate saviour and in moments of honesty I suspect many riders of similar limited ability will attest to the same thing. You see, the league is a handicapped event.

Not that I knew that at the time, in a road race – no matter what category you are, everybody starts together. Hence the tag 'mass' start. The first rider over the line is the winner. The categorisation system simply helps limit the field to riders with broadly similar physiological capabilities. Not so with a handicapped event. Here, riders are put into groups depending on ability as judged by a race official and set off with an appropriate time gap between them. The slower riders go off first then to be chased by the next group and so on.

This does three brilliant things: first, it teaches riders to work together in their groups to catch each other or, if you are in front group, to try and stay away. Secondly, if and when the groups come together it teaches you how to race, how to employ tactics and demonstrates just how fast these things can move. Thirdly and most importantly, it gives everybody, fast and slow, the chance to race at an appropriate level. Even with a 3rd and 4th Cat non-handicapped race, a newcomer is quite likely to find himself immediately out of the back of the bunch and on his own. This, as I'm sure you can see, is no longer a race for him it's just a lonely and expensive training ride past marshals who encourage you to carry on but are secretly hoping you will not delay their tea and cake.

Consequently, the handicapped league event was probably the best and most gentle introduction to road racing a 32-year-old transplant patient can hope to have. It was still brutal and the pace was another step up from training and reliability rides, but at least there was a chance of staying with the bunch for a while.

My first league event was the 13th May 1999 at Ludlow. I started in the first group and managed to hold the pace, in fact, I finished 4th. My group had not been caught by either of the faster groups behind us so it was a bit of a fluke. My racing record to date, 1st, 2nd and 4th, delighted me. Inspired by this, I entered an open road race later that month for 3rd and 4th category riders. This was a mistake. A big one.

It was raining and cold on the day of the race. I had only a short-sleeved jersey and shorts, no arm warmers or gilet so I was freezing cold. I looked for where the other 4th cat riders were starting from as clearly, once the 3rd cats had ridden off, I could stick with them. Wrong. We all went off together, every man for himself. No chatting. I was first dropped in the neutralised zone before the flag had been waved and the race proper had started. I clawed my way slowly back to the peloton using energy I really didn't a have to spare. At best, I made my way to the middle of the bunch and immediately realised I lacked the skill and strength to hold my position there and started dropping back. And back.

Despite my best efforts, and I don't usually give up easily, I came out of the bunch and was on my own. No punctures, no mechanicals, no excuses, just nowhere near good enough. It was a long, cold and lonely ride back to the HQ and, as the race had only just got underway, it was locked – with my race licence, kit and car keys inside. I rode back towards the course partly to keep warm and partly to see just how far I had to go to be as good as these guys. A long way was the obvious answer, but after getting warm and seeing the other riders arrive back at the HQ still excited and buzzing, despite the lousy conditions, I felt inspired to do more. A lot of them were clearly happy with their Sunday morning's work and not all of them could have won, so there must be something bigger and better than just the winning.

I was disappointed with my own performance and a hefty chunk of smuggery had been removed but I was determined to work harder and to become as good as these guys. I was not prepared to put my failure down to the fact I'd had a liver transplant. My liver function was perfect and the doses of drugs were small, I was well recovered and physically fit. More importantly, I was not prepared to use the transplant as an excuse. I might do the, "Well, I've been ill' routine in the car park after a club ride as part of the banter, as a bit of fun, but I didn't actually buy it. Not for a minute. If I was a crap rider then I was a crap rider and I'd have to make sure I was the best crap rider I could be.

It was then it started to dawn on me how true it was, you really couldn't lose a bike race; you could just not win it and that wasn't always a bad result. My record had taken a bit of a dent, adding a did not finish (DNF) to my so far glittering results, but that was unimportant in the scheme of things. These were good quality amateur riders in a real world event. Yes, a tough day for me but a lesson well learned that gave me a greater appreciation of how lucky I was to have the road race league every Thursday evening in the summer. This, I decided, would form the basis of my race training for the World Transplant Games in August.

It was about this time that I attended my first GB transplant team meeting in Edmonton, North East London. I didn't really know what to expect so I went with some apprehension and, on advice, without a bike.

Dad fancied the trip so he came with me for the day and we spent some time getting to know a few people. In particular, I looked for cyclists I recognised from the Belfast Games to get a feel for what competing with transplant riders from around the world was like. I recognised one guy, a larger-than-life and popular character within the team and a long-term heart transplant patient. He had raced in the last two World Games in Manchester and Sydney without medalling. He was encouraging and very funny right from the start of our conversation and, as a veteran of both the British and World Games, I was keen to hear what he had to say. Half tongue-in-cheek, he came out with one of the best excuses for not winning a road race I have ever heard. It has since become my automatic default response when questioned in similar circumstances: Magpie attack. The unfortunate rider claimed he had been dive bombed on a couple of occasions by a pair of magpies attracted to some flashing sliver bits on his helmet leading to a crash and his untimely exit from the race with a broken collar bone. At least, this was his story and he was sticking to it.

Whilst the magical electronic interweb had still to gain popular usage, face-to-face meetings, telephone and fax were the only way to pick up information on logistics for the trip, travel arrangements, flights, costs, kit, insurance and the like. It meant taking copious notes during the day that were backed up by letters from Team Management following the meeting. Unfortunately, the letters almost always contradicted my notes. There was a standard issue uniform of a blazer, trousers, shirts and team ties for travelling, visits and the opening ceremony. Sports kit included a team tracksuit and plentiful running, swimming and batting stuff but, sadly, nothing for the cyclists. In fairness, most standard sports kit suppliers do not stock specialist kit for cycling such as padded bib shorts and Lycra jerseys and the guys, as there were no women cyclists, had to sort out their own stuff. They rode in what they had available, although some had either bought or borrowed BCF kit.

There was no cycling Team Captain, no coaching, no kit, no facilities and no support. The reason I had been advised to not take a bike was because there were no facilities for cyclists. They wanted me to jog around the track to prove I had some fitness: so I ran. I ran the only way I know how. Like there was a dog after me.

The cyclists were truly an afterthought in the GB team and I have to say, I was pretty disappointed by the whole thing. It felt like a loose collection of a few self-motivated individuals rather than the cohesive group I was hoping for. I asked the Team Management and the riders who their contact with the British Cycling Federation was and drew a blank. Other than one rider managing to blag a skinsuit from them there was nothing. I asked the Team Manager if he would mind if I contacted them, I was conscious not to tread on any toes here, particularly as I had kind of invited myself along anyway. He had no objection: or interest, seemingly.

I phoned the BCF and had a brief and non-productive conversation with them as they'd had no contact with the team and didn't even know of its existence. Again, it was disappointing but after understanding the profile of cycling within the team it was not surprising. From then on my contact with the BCF was limited to buying a jersey with Great Britain written on it, so at least I could show the country name when I rode in Budapest. A very small step forwards I know, but a step all the same.

The training and racing was going well. I'd decided any more open races would probably be unproductive but the Thursday night league events were really helping me improve. Whilst riding with the first group off you'd always hear a collective groan when the faster riders caught us. Heads would go down a little and some of the fight would disappear as the faster guys tore through. Often they would announce their arrival with a shout of, "On the left/right!" depending on which way they were coming. I always thought it was rather high handed of them. We were working hard too, trying our best to make a race out of it and stay out of their way. They seemed to be a little, well, dismissive of our efforts. I became rather indignant on behalf of my fellow back markers and got slightly huffy about the whole thing. A few weeks later, after another 4th place, I was elevated to the giddy heights of the second group. There I was trying to get to the front to shout, "On the left!" as we went through these slower guys who risked interrupting our majestic progress. What a terrible sell-out; I hang my head in shame. Having said that, justice was usually served when the proper cyclists in the final group came through and smashed the race to pieces. Sometimes they didn't even bother announcing their arrival. No respect see? No respect.

There were a few more uninspiring GB training sessions in Birmingham and one in the North West, about 2 miles away from where my donor family lived (you're getting used to this now aren't you?) and then it was time to make the final arrangements for the trip to Budapest. The entire Smith family were mobilised, my wife, Charlie, Grace, who was now 7 months old, Granddad and Grandma were all coming.

Arriving in Budapest was the point when I began to discover how unfathomable the Hungarian language is which, as I'm confident you know, is of Finno-Estonian extraction. It has no common structure or similarity to anything other than Klingon as far as I can work out. I managed to talk to somebody at the Hotel Sun in Budapest about whether they could cater for a very young child (I think) who said (I think) "You bring baby". So we did.

For the first and last time, the bike went into a big padded bag ready for its journey. Baggage handlers have their own World Championships in bag flinging and I think the current holder of the title must have flung mine. It sustained some damage to one of the tubes but, being steel, it was fine to ride. When travelling now I use a hard shell bike box. These are cumbersome and a bit fiddly to get a bike into but they offer better protection than a big Jiffy bag. Since then I have become a voluntary consultant to those taking their bikes abroad. Friends and teammates will either call or post pictures on Facebook (other social networking sites are also available) showing progress and I can then talk them in. I think the next logical step is either a live video feed or some kind of remotely controlled device akin to keyhole brain surgery so I can insert the bike into a case safely from a distance. Do you think there's a market for it?

In August of 1999, we set off with the GB team to Budapest. Blazers, ties, chinos, the lot. It was a very special experience to be travelling with over 100 teammates to represent my county. Unreal in many ways. People talked to us at the airport and asked what we were doing, where we

148

were going and wished us good luck. It was not lost on me that, but for the transplant, there was no way in this world I would have been representing my country at sport. Never in a month of frozen Sundays. In hell.

It was pretty special and seeing the whole team together in one place for the first time made me realise what an honour this really was. Okay, cycling wasn't at the top of the list of sports as far as the team were concerned, but with a little work we could make it into something sustainable, raise its profile, get more riders and really make a good show of it.

My family had given the transplant meaning for me, I was doing something, living life, working, trying my best to be a Dad. I was making mistakes for sure along the way, but always trying to be straight and honest. Mentally, I was beginning to make the vital shift from resenting being ill: from being angry and frustrated, towards being happy to be alive and, let's use that awful word again, grateful, for my continued existence. The Transplant Games, and more particularly representing Great Britain, gave the whole thing definition and purpose. It meant I was learning, slowly, to count my blessings, to play the hand I'd been dealt a little better and worry less about the cards I hadn't got.

The hotel we were staying in was basic but pleasant and, as good as their word, 'bringing baby' was fine. They had provided us with a brand new cot and made a real fuss over both Grace and Charlie. The team generally adopted them together with a couple of other children of similar age and they were having a whale of a time.

The bike race course was close to the hotel and my three cycling team mates and I made our way over to have a ride around. Whilst there I had my first encounter with the lesser-spotted foreign Jonny transplant cyclist. A rangy Swedish guy who looked like he meant business. We rode together for a little while, superficially exchanging pleasantries but probing each other for information about which age category we were in, what race experience we'd had and the like. This was my first encounter with a young man by the name of Richard Nordstrum, who was later to become a cycling rival and friend. But right now he was the guy who was going to give me a hard time on a bike in a few days. If they were all like him, I figured I was going to be in for a whole world of hurt.

The morning of the race came around. It was a hot summer's day in Budapest and arriving at the start with my family I saw riders from pretty much all over the world. The Italians and the Americans being particularly well represented amongst a field of 57 male riders in total. It was pretty intimidating. Music was blaring out from speakers and an imposing stage and podium had been erected which I presumed was there to celebrate the winners and dispatch the losers via a short and painless rope-aided drop. Rough game this cycling.

The race was held in a true mass start format with everybody, and I mean everybody, going off at the same time. Although there were no youth riders, the youngest being 17, men and women of all ages started together. Predictably, it was chaos. Whilst the start was broad and flat, the slower starting riders were quickly overcome by faster starters behind them, some of whom were still clipping into their pedals. One of the key rules when starting in a bunch is to ride in a straight line. If everybody does this it's impossible to bump or crash into each other. With experienced riders, a clash of hands, shoulders or wheels is not usually a problem. Provided everybody remains calm the race can continue with only a scowl or a knowing shake of the head. With less experienced riders it's a very unnerving situation indeed. What *does* cause a problem is a rider who, unprepared, sees others moving off and reacts by panicking and swerving violently at 45 degrees whilst looking downwards rather than at the progress of the field. There was, it goes without saying, much swerving and swearing at the beginning of this race, much of it in languages beyond my comprehension. It added an exotic if slightly nervy, international flavour to proceedings.

I started mid bunch with two of my teammates. My third teammate had taken a position at the back: it had been a long journey for him and he had battled all sorts of transplant-related health issues in the preceding 2 years. He knew his chances were limited and his aim was to just finish the race rather than win it. Teammate one went off straight, I went off straight: Teammate two went off straight into teammate one, possibly looking over his shoulder for magpies. Thankfully no harm was done; we all stayed upright. We were on our way.

Bunch riding can be an unnerving experience but with time and familiarity of other rider's skills or lack thereof, allowances can be made and the group can work happily together. In a 'normal' race it's reasonable to assume riders understand the unwritten rules – otherwise they would not be there. Transplant cycle racing was, it appeared, rather different. Some of the riders had not come through any kind of selection process. They were there because they'd had a transplant, were glad to be alive and reckoned they could ride a bike for 20kms.

One of these guys was a young American pancreas and kidney transplant rider. Back then, and now to some degree, this was a rare and a valuable card in Transplant Games 'Top Trumps'. Unfortunately, he got himself mixed up with a well-drilled and experienced Italian team and, as they cornered neatly in a group he basically dive-bombed them. He took four of them out. I did see one of the Italians, with considerable skill, manage to remain upright but disappear off into the trees where he was later eaten by a Hungarian wolf. Actually, I'm not sure that last bit is factually correct but it's strange what goes through your head in those circumstances isn't it?

I managed to avoid the accident and a break of six riders became established. The Swede, Richard Nordstrum, was amongst them, as was a strong looking Spanish rider and a Dane. It became pretty clear, pretty quick, the riders in this group knew what they were doing and in all likelihood this was going to be the winning move. And here was me, in the break, working with the other riders to distance the chasing pack who were now no more than wolf fodder.

We were right behind the lead Police car and a camera bike. Yes, really, a lead car and, even more impressively, a camera bike. This was almost a proper, you know, international bike race and everything.

Accelerations from Richard and the Spanish rider dropped two more from the breakaway group leaving just four of us. I knew from my conversation with Richard the day before that he had figured in the 1995 Games in Manchester, medalling but not winning the race. Quite understandably he was targeting the win here. Around the last corner he moved the three remaining riders over to the barrier just as a professional would, meaning any attack could only be launched on one side. He'd closed a gap and left no way through on his right. He only had to guard against riders coming around his left side. He launched a perfectly timed sprint with the Spaniard out of the saddle right on his wheel and me up against the barrier. I had nowhere to go. Even if I could match his speed I couldn't get past him. The road position he had entirely legitimately created had blocked any threat from me. Richard went over the line arms aloft closely followed by the Spanish rider who, within metres of the line had gone past him. And then, I thought, me. I was sure I'd beaten the Dane but I didn't dare believe that I'd come third in the road race at a World Games.

Two riders who were tactically better and appreciably stronger had beaten me but I was delighted to have finished third. The old adage of the disappointment of winning a silver medal rang true to me then; with a silver you always feel you might have managed one better if you had tried just a little harder, had trained better or had a tiny bit of luck. With bronze, you're bloody grateful you've got a medal and avoided the pain of a 4th place. I fell straight into the bloody grateful category.

As I anxiously awaited confirmation of the positions, the American dive-bomber came over to me to seek reassurance. I'm not entirely sure why he picked me as his sounding board, perhaps I was one of the few English speakers there. He was being eyed up by the walking wounded of the Italian team as one of them was loaded into an ambulance with that classic cycling injury, a broken collar bone. The other rider had been rescued from certain death at the hands of a Hungarian wolf and was still brushing twigs and dirt from his bike and kit. His bearing was one of equal malevolence towards the American and, in the heat of the moment, you could understand why. None of the Italian team had featured in the winning break and, in truth, there was a good chance of some of them being there had Flt Lt Pancreas Kidney not scythed through them after 2kms. Two years of training, travel, expense and endeavour up the pipe because another rider couldn't handle his bike. Tough break.

I went off to find my teammates who had all finished but had not been placed in medal positions. One of them had put a sticker on his handlebars at the beginning of the race with the phrase 'he died for you', a motivational reminder of why he was at the games. It was mentioned to him it was likely many more people would die for him, or because of him, if he didn't improve his riding. His frustration about his run of bad luck, starting 2 years earlier with an unprovoked magpie attack and continuing with a number of further crashes, contrasted starkly with the joy of those people who had managed to avoid him during the race. However, the courage and good humour of this remarkable and inspirational man quickly returned to him with the help of his teammates.

Before the medal presentation began, the Dane who had been in the break approached me. He delivered the first of what was to become a long-running series of mildly abusive assertions about my tactical awareness, riding ability or personal appearance. On this occasion I was, it would seem, a 'dumb bastard'. I had done a number of things wrong, in particular not working hard enough in the break.

Worse still, I had allowed the two riders who had finished in front of me to win rather than going for a dangerously improbable gap on the barrier side of the Swede in the sprint. I didn't really know what to make of this. These were pretty serious charges, but they were being delivered whilst he was smiling and shaking my hand. This was the first, but by no means the last, time another rider would accuse me of not working hard enough or taking enough risks with the safety of those around me to help them win a bike race.

I've got a picture of the three of us on the podium that day. I was in a Great Britain cycling jersey with a Union flag hanging behind me and a bronze medal around my neck. I was, it has to be said, a happy lad.

Back at the hotel, we were sitting outside chatting and I remember having a glass of beer and responding to the polite and kind queries of other returning teammates. They had their stories to tell too, mostly of success. It was great to be able to share a few tales of how close the race was. In fact, it gets closer every time I tell the story. Pretty soon it will be so close I'll have won it.

Before coming home we had some time to look around the city now the racing was done. Just before we got onto a coach for a tour around the city I was talking to a young woman called Margaret Koppejan from the Netherlands who had taken part in the bike race. We had the usual bike related conversation as Margaret, like most of her countryfolk could speak perfect English. She told me she was one of the first bone marrow transplant patients to be admitted into the games. She was painfully thin, had undergone a number of bone marrow transplants and the subsequent chemotherapy sessions had taken a pretty heavy toll on her, meaning she had lost most of her natural hair. She was bright, happy and had an infectious enthusiasm for life despite the fact she knew her chances of living more than a few years were slim.

I have been fortunate enough at meeting a proper real life hero at most World games I have attended and Margaret was the first. Her bravery, her plain speaking and her determination to enjoy the rest of what life had to offer overwhelmed me. Soon we were ushered onto the bus and I set about loading young Charlie and Grace and her pushchair. I lost sight of Margaret who I was keen to continue talking too. I found a seat, dropped in and, rather presumptuously I thought, an attractive blonde girl sat beside me and engaged me in conversation. This is not something that happens too often to me. She was Dutch too and another cyclist. I began recounting the tale of the other Dutch female cyclist I'd had just been speaking to. She registered some surprise: there were no others as far as she was aware.

It dawned on me very slowly that Margaret had put a blond wig on. What could I do? I confessed my stupidity and she laughed for the rest of the trip. I said goodbye to Margaret at the end of the week not knowing if I would ever see her again.

International cycling sign language

Back then, the debilitating condition known as Post-Transplant Games Blues was undiscovered. After the delight of being away with a team representing Great Britain in a world event and winning a medal, I was anticipating things would be different at home.

A substantial amount of effort had gone into training and racing and I'd got the little bronze token of my success tucked away in the pocket of my GB tracksuit. Surely everything would be, well, better? There was a little publicity: the local and regional papers and a local radio interview. My friends and family all warmly congratulated me but quite soon it was back to nappies, bills and the routine of daily life. Back to trying to balance family, work and training with the drugs, worries and ups and downs of living with a liver transplant. Things weren't better. They were just the same. It was an anti-climax.

Towards the end of our trip to Budapest, the announcement of the venue for the next games to be held in 2001 had been made. They were going to be in Japan. There was huge excitement amongst the team and it quickly became clear that everybody wanted to go. The opportunity to visit Japan probably doesn't come around that often for most people; it's not really on the holiday circuit. It's expensive and time consuming to get there but it provided everybody with the motivation to get back to training to ensure they had the best shot at selection.

I definitely wanted to go to the World Transplant Games again. The trip to Budapest had been life changing for me, a suspension of reality. I had been surrounded by hugely supportive people, all of whom had been through similar experiences to me. Much to my surprise, I'd revelled in it. This was no self-help group bemoaning their lot but a bunch of motivated athletes making the best of the circumstances they found themselves in. The event was there to publicise organ and tissue donation and raise awareness of transplantation, not by walking around looking sickly or

157

handing out leaflets but by trying our best to compete. We wanted to beat each other in our chosen sport, going at it as hard as we could within the rules. I was surprised by how little the topic of transplantation was talked about by the athletes at the games. In fact, there are guys I have known for 10 years without knowing what organ they have had transplanted. More particularly, I didn't know which bits my cycling rivals had had swapped and in any event it was irrelevant. I just needed to work out how to beat them and I'd got a couple of years to do it.

At the end of the cycling event in Budapest I'd had a conversation with the Spanish rider who had finished second. Our chat was hampered only by the fact he could speak no English and I could speak no Spanish. Having said that, cycling has an international language involving facial expression, hand signs and pointing to bits of the body or bike. Sometimes referencing particular riding styles by naming known pro riders and the like can be used. It's pretty easy once you've got the hang of it. Throw in a few 'chapeaus' and the odd 'bon chance' and Bob's your mother's brother.

Our Spanish friend had indicated via this international language he was happy with his second place (Me contente…Segundo…) with an upward pout, a satisfied nod of the head and a wave of the medal. I too had expressed pleasure with my result (si, si, si and me mate) thumbs up. Wink. He indicated 'next year' or 'two next year's or possibly he ran a frog farm, I'm not sure. The jumping two fingers sign seemed to indicate a future date some years away followed by some tricky Spanish stuff which he quickly recognised I couldn't understand. There was something of a pause before he did the universally recognised 'fat bastard' charade (cheeks blown out, arms out and round indicating an enormous girth) followed by the exact opposite (cheeks sucked it, eyes popping out, stomach in, slightly limp). Finally he mimed the unmistakable 'holding somebody by the shirt collar and kicking him or her up the arse' with a little glint in his eye.

158

I initially deduced the full literal translation of the show was 'I own a frog farm, some of them have big blowy out cheeks like normal frogs but, sadly, others are a little on the thin side. There's nothing in the frog game anymore and I'm thinking of packing it in'. On reflection I thought it perhaps more likely what he really meant was 'I'm a bit fat right now but in 2 years' time I'm going to be a lot lighter and fitter and I'm coming back to kick everybody's arse'. The glint in his eye implying this was closer to the truth.

This guy was far from fat, he was just built like a sprinter and he seemed fully intent on giving it a good go in Japan. Added to this, I couldn't see Richard Nordstrum giving up his hard won title easily and, of course, any number of new riders could be coming along anytime soon. So, for me, there was no lack of motivation to ride and train hard and come back for another go in Kobe, Japan in 2001.

Back in the UK I raced again at the British Games in Birmingham in 1999, which was a fairly easy win in the absence of Wes Clayton and Dave Sykes who had finished second in Belfast. I was sorry neither of them where there. Wes's absence was unexplained but further enquiry established thankfully it was not down to ill health. Apparently, Dave had fallen out with his team following the Games in Belfast in 1998 and had decided not to attend. Whilst sad, at least it meant he wasn't ill. I recall being asked on the start line by one new rider from a fairly thin looking bunch what kind of time I did a 10 mile time trial in. Now, we'll come to the wonderful world of time trialling a bit later but, at the time, I do remember replying that I had no idea because I'd never done one. Nor, as a paid-up member of the road racing fraternity did I have any intention of ever doing one. Time trial indeed.

I raced again in Newcastle in 2000, which was the first time I had attended the whole of the British Transplant Games. I also revived my childhood interest in table tennis and, for reasons I've still not come to terms with, entered the 4 x 100m race for the Birmingham team.

159

My claims that Tinky Winky has an excellent turn of speed and runs a good bend often falls on deaf ears when I tell people I ran at Gateshead International Athletic stadium and was comprehensively out run by a guy dressed as a Telly Tubby. Against my better judgement I was coaxed out of retirement in Leeds in 2001 only to be beaten by the same guy dressed as a pirate, complete with fake cutlass between his teeth. Will I ever learn? Permanently hanging up my aluminium baton, I had confirmed my place in the team for Japan by winning in Newcastle. I could look forward to the winter of 2000 and the summer of 2001 to get some miles in and hone my fitness with racing in the local league again.

Having established I was in the team, my thoughts turned to a new bike. I have previously gone through the thought process of buying a new bike and I won't repeat it here. Whilst my Reynolds 653 had been upgraded and the addition of new equipment made it lighter and more race worthy, bike frame technology was advancing quickly. Much greater use of aluminium and carbon fibre meant durable, comfortable super light frames at prices that would only cause a divorce rather than bankruptcy were now available. My purchase of new levers and wheels was predicated on the basis that when I bought a new frame, they could be transferred on to it whilst the 653 could be reassembled with the old stuff. Voila, a winter training bike *and* a race bike for half the cost. In fact, I'd be losing money by not getting a new bike and, for the good of all, shouldn't delay my purchase any longer.

The object of my desire at the time was a Bianchi EV2 XL frame. The same as Marco Pantani had won the scandalous 1998 Tour de France on. If it was good enough for the 57 kg Marco it was good enough for 80 kg Richo. I bought the frame, at a bargain price of £1350 and built it up myself with matching Campagnolo and ITM componentry using the wheels and levers from the 653. It was a thing of great beauty. Bianchi, a prestigious Italian frame builder had been painting their bikes in a trademark Celeste blue-green colour since they began making them in the 1920s. Mine looked resplendent with its yellow stem and matching yellow flashes on the saddle. It was light, stiff and super responsive and frankly a much better bike than I will ever be a rider. Again. I hoped it was going to be the machine I would ride to victory in the World Transplant Games in Japan, but first it was going to be put through it's paces in the league in the summer of 2001.

I lacked the tools (and more importantly the skills) of a professional bike mechanic. Equally, I didn't having a fully equipped workshop (or the skill to use anything in it even if I did). Notwithstanding this, there were a number of adjustments that needed to be made to make the bike work better. Or at all.

My first mechanical mishap came to light after a local race when I followed the owner of a Shropshire based bike shop back to the car park. Coincidentally, he was also riding a brand new EV2. As I rolled past I shifted into the small ring on the chainset only for the chain to drop ignominiously onto the bottom bracket with a loud and expensive sounding mechanical clatter. This allowed my legs to spin freely, uselessly and embarrassingly in thin air. The guy looked at me and said, "Mine doesn't do that". I offered to adjust his Bianchi so it performed just as mine did but he declined the offer and rode on allowing me to put the chain back on. The grease and oil from the chain seemed to help stop my fingers bleeding quite as much as they might have done after I removed them from between the chain and big ring.

Soon my Pantani replica was working perfectly. This was more than could be said for the man himself who had been busted for drugs in the 1999 Giro d'Italia. Later, after his death in fact, it turned out if you or I had taken the same quantities of performance enhancing drugs, we could have probably won the 1998 Tour too. On reflection, it's probably best not to have professional cyclists as heroes; it was certainly a dangerous business during the last couple of decades, as it seems many of them were there due to taking some kind of dubious preparation. I was lucky, aside from

Marco, my other hero was Chris Boardman. He was regarded by many of his peers at the time as a bit odd because he *didn't* take the same drugs as pretty much every other rider of that era. Boardman single handedly gave British cycling a profile in a sport dominated by Europeans and a few Americans and his enormous achievements and contributions are never fully celebrated in my mind.

His contribution to cycling was (and continues to be) multi-faceted, but two things struck me as being particularly relevant to my situation. First, I had to take drugs every day to stop my body from rejecting my transplanted liver. I didn't like taking drugs because of the debilitating effect they had on me. They were effecting my kidney function and my skin. They were giving me cramp, making me burn more easily in the sun, opening me up to infections I shouldn't get, making me shake and a host of other things I could totally live without. Don't misunderstand me, the side effects are nothing compared to the alternative but they are still not something you would choose to have. Many young riders were taking equally powerful drugs through choice to improve their performance on a bike and in doing so endangering their lives.

In fact, a large number of riders had died because their blood became so thick due to EPO abuse the heart was unable to pump it around the body when they were asleep. Part of the irony is that EPO is used therapeutically in kidney patients and some other transplant recipients to improve the ability of the blood to carry oxygen around the body. It's not a drug that should be abused. The issue of drugs in cycling is complicated, endemic and institutional. It's been going on ever since bike racing started and there are people better qualified than I to make judgements on this. Cycling is a professional sport, through reading many of the excellent books on the subject I have an inkling of the pressure riders are under to earn money and keep their sponsors happy. Thankfully, I will never experience that pressure. I do not have any choice but to take drugs to stay alive. If you are in

162

the fortunate position of having a choice, just say no. Like on Grange Hill.

The other reason Chris Boardman was then and remains my hero now is because of a story my club chairman tells. He tells it a lot. The Tour de France started in Lille in 1994 with a traditional short prologue time trial of 7.2km and our Mr Boardman was a specialist in this type of short distance event.

Success in longer stage races eluded him partly because he wouldn't take the same drugs as everybody else but this distance was right up his street. As part of his preparation for this dash he turned up to a local time trial on the Wrexham by-pass although, as he hadn't formally entered, they squeezed him in right at the start of the event. My club Chairman was off at number 18, meaning, he was going off 18 minutes after the two watches used to record the times of the riders were synchronized. Unaware of Mr Boardman's presence, he was pleased to see so many people had turned up to watch him race. Just before he pressed on his pedals to start his ride, Chris flashed past him. Our Chairman was firstly startled by the fact that Chris Boardman was riding and secondly by the fact that he had just completed a 10 mile ride in 17 minutes and 58 seconds.

We haven't spoken much about time trialling and I suspect some of you are waiting to get to the 'good bit' but briefly a decent middle-marking club rider might be happy breaking 25 minutes for a '10'. A really talented rider might make it to sub 22 minutes. Occasionally, supreme riders might, just might, break 20 minutes on a perfect day, on a perfect course with perfect form. That means riding at over 30 mph for 20 minutes. Try it. Reaching 30 mph momentarily on the flat on a pushbike is very difficult. Sustaining it for any length of time is almost impossible for all but a few very talented individuals.

Boardman's ride was outstanding that evening and he went on to win the opening stage in Lille by an enormous 15 seconds and started the second stage in the yellow jersey. Without drugs. Without. Drugs.

163

Perhaps now would also be a good time to apologise. I'd like to say sorry to those kids for nicking one of their pens and pushing them out of the way so I could get Chris Boardman to sign my programme at the Birmingham stage start of the 1999 Pru Tour. I've never done that before. Not push kids, I've done that loads of times, I mean ask for an autograph.

Armed with my new bike and a non-performance enhancing drug regime my training continued throughout 2000 and into 2001. During this time my wife and I had agreed to separate throwing both of our lives into a certain amount of turmoil and, it would appear, curtailing my ability to keep an accurate training diary. It was a pretty difficult period for both of us although we remained on good terms and focused on ensuring the kids were okay. I promised not to write an autobiography, so I won't, but we got married for the right reasons and separated amicably for the right reasons too without any animosity.

My training or riding, call it what you will, had become a necessary escape from the real world. A distraction from the everyday stuff that life's processes are made of, so whilst it may seem odd to say my personal circumstances didn't affect my riding it is, nevertheless, the truth. I hope that doesn't seem unpalatable to you. The training was a tonic for the difficulties I was going through, so my physiological preparation was not interrupted even if my head was probably not in the right place.

Part of my preparation for the 2001 Games was more open road racing. My previous attempts had been less than glorious but I felt I needed to supplement the local road race league with longer more challenging races where I wasn't given a head start. Head starts are something you ask for at the school sports day when you are 6-years-old and you know the big kids are faster than you. I mean, how the hell are you expected to win anything more than a bloody lollipop when you've got 'Big Dave' for competition in the sack race?

I entered a race to be held on a Staffordshire circuit of 6 miles or so in length. The course was used regularly in the league although this race would be run over nine laps as opposed to the normal 5 miles. It was relatively flat which suited me because I have rightly been accused of being unable to ride over anything more challenging than a canal bridge at any speed. To make up for this, I had a mild increase in speed that made do for a sprint.

On arrival, a car boot sale meant the course had to be changed to something rather more Alpine. Those of you familiar with the Cannock area will know, it is famed for its beautiful mountainous geography. The laps also became longer, now being 9 miles rather than 6. It rained, of course, and the break went away early on. Rather rudely, I wasn't told when this was going to happen and missed it by a mile. I tried to bridge the gap on my own and was left stranded in No Man's Land between the bunch and the six or seven riders who had escaped their clutches.

On this particular occasion, the break contained an aging no-hoper by the name of Les West, well into his 60s now and although he'd apparently achieved some success at amateur level in the past, he was clearly well past his sell-by-date. The bunch gave up hope of catching the break and over the next 40 miles riders continued to drop out until no bunch really existed. It was just individual riders, of which I was one, plodding around. Commonly, little alliances are formed with other riders who have paid their money and are determined to finish, partly for company and moral support but also for sharing the workload. I'd found an amiable chap to ride with and was telling him about how unfair my cycling life was when Les overtook us, at considerable speed, on his own. He had broken away from the little group and was riding towards a solo victory, lapping my mate and me in the process. Now, fair enough, I'm pretty rubbish but still, that's some kind of performance on a course with a 9 mile lap. Les was completely in control and whilst working hard he was within his limits and knew exactly what he was doing.

When I got to know a little more about Les and his frankly amazing achievements I didn't feel so bad about being on the receiving end of a good kicking by him. It's happened to loads of riders considerably better than me, some of them proper cyclists from foreign countries and everything.

It's difficult to judge Les's greatest achievements, but being a silver medallist at the amateur world road race championships and 4th in the professionals isn't bad. Winning the Tour of Britain and the Milk Race in the 60s isn't too shabby either. From behind on a bike, Les looks 25 years old, it's only when you get up close to him and see some grey hair and a few lines you realise he's got a few years on him. Don't be fooled for a minute, he is a class act. I wish I could say all this made him a nasty piece of work but it hasn't. I wouldn't claim to know Mr West very well other than to have been fortunate enough to have a few brief chats with him at signing ons and in car parks before and after races. He has always been generous with his time and kind with his comments. He is a gentleman.

The second bloke that overtook me in that race may well have been equally charming but he was riding a 50 quid mountain bike and wearing football shorts and trainers. He may have been on his way to rescue a granny from a burning house or travelling to his voluntary job saving injured kittens. Right then he was a complete bastard as far as I was concerned. Oh, the shame of it! Again. With a considerable amount of effort and with energy we really didn't have to spare, my new found riding partner and I worked together to chase him down and overtake him for the most pyrrhic of pyrrhic victories. We made a silent pact never to speak of it.

Back at the HQ, we came in just as the prizes were being handed out and the marshals were packing up. Maybe I should have been disappointed with my performance but I couldn't honestly say I was. I'd finished. I'd been in a race Les West had won and I'd got another 104 kms and 3 hours 15 minutes of riding in my legs I didn't have before.

Whatever doesn't kill you makes you stronger right? Well, mostly yes.

Hai

By August 2001, final preparations for the trip to Japan were complete. There were a few new bike bits and a tough hard shell case for transporting the bike to avoid a repeat of the damage sustained on the Budapest trip 2 years before. I had also attended a good number of entirely unhelpful training meetings. I say the meetings were entirely unhelpful but that's a little harsh. Although it was fairly pointless from a cycling perspective, it was good to meet new team members and consolidate my friendships with others, as this time I was going without my family.

One guy I was really pleased to meet was Eddie Reynolds. Eddie was a bit of a legend at the Queen Elizabeth Hospital. A big man with a big character, he was one of the three people who had undergone a liver transplant in the early days of the Unit at Birmingham in 1982. Back then neither he nor the surgeons were sure if he was going to come through the operation alive and it must have taken considerable courage to go for a procedure that was little more than experimental. On top of this he was now nearly 20 years post-transplant and still going strong: strong enough to qualify for the GB team and put the shot in the 60 – 70 years of age category.

Eddie was Bilston born and bred, a gentle giant with the full-blown Black Country accent and the dry but warm sense of humour that so often goes with it. That he was healthy and active so long after his liver transplant gave me great hope and on a more basic level he was a lovely man to be around. I suspect it was his open and honest charm that persuaded the Japanese immigration authority to overlook the fact his passport was out of date. Worse still, it contained a self-portrait in pencil Eddie had drawn in the space where the photograph should have been. As an artist, Eddie was a good shot putter.

I was told to prepare myself for a culture shock when we got to Japan, but that's just the kind of thing people would say so I blithely ignored it. It was of course good

169

advice. It was an amalgam of little things that were so obviously different as soon as we got off the plane. The heat, the smells, the light, buildings, the fact there were no roundabouts or graffiti, the way the people dressed and presented themselves, everything. I suppose had we landed in Tokyo it might have been less of a culture shock. All the worlds' major capitals seem to have something in common but we landed in Osaka, Japan's second city. We took a coach around the massive bay area to our temporary home in Kobe, the epicentre of the devastating Hansin earthquake of 1995 and settled into the very glamorous Portopia Hotel. The very same hotel the England football team was scheduled to stay in during the 2002 World Cup. Very posh indeed. We are going up in the world. I remember getting into the air-conditioned room and opening the balcony door to cool things down a little and being hit by a wall of air the like of which I had never felt before. It was boiling. I closed the door and whacked up the air conditioning.

It was very exciting to be in Japan and a much needed distraction from what was going on in my personal life back in the UK. Things at home were pretty rough. Before I'd left, I'd signed the contract to sell the house my wife and I shared and signed another one to buy a little house in town that I had seen precisely once. Some surveyor I was turning out to be. I went for a walk around the hotel to get my bearings and bumped into Eddie who'd essentially been mugged on the plane by some of the younger women on the team. They'd varnished red, white and blue union flags onto his fingers and, he said, his toe nails too. So there I was in posh hotel in Japan with a 6'4" bloke from Bilston wearing nail varnish. I'm sure there's a gag in there somewhere.

Later, as the teams were being herded together for the opening ceremony, I was looking around for anybody I recognised from Budapest, most particularly my cycling rivals. Spotting the Swedish flag close by I walked over to try to find Richard Nordstrum, the man I'd been focused on beating during my training for the last 2 years. I saw him and went over the say hello. He turned towards me and I could see his arm was clearly in a sling. I greeted him pointing at his arm and said that I hoped he would be okay for the race, making some stupid crack about him not being able to steer the bike as well with one arm. He told me he'd broken his collarbone in a training accident a couple of weeks before and it was still healing. Bad news but I presumed, as he was here, he was fit to race? Apparently not. Even though he couldn't race he'd shown up to support the small Swedish team in any capacity he could. I didn't know what to make of this. Ostensibly it made my race easier but that was not the point. First, I wished no harm or injury to this man and secondly I wanted to race to see if I could beat him. In fact, that's what I had based my last 2 years training on.

Other than commiserate with him I didn't really know what to say but I was rescued by the arrival of the Spanish guy who finished second in Budapest. He was walking towards us repeating his 'fat bastard' impression, you know, cheeks puffed out, arms indicating massive girth. It didn't take me long to figure out it wasn't an impression and he was quite genuinely carrying a fair bit of timber around with him. His friend interpreted for us saying he had been ill soon after Budapest and had never really been able to train properly to get back the excellent form he had then. He used international sign language again to indicate by pointing first at Richard (primaro), then himself (segundo) and finally at me (tercera) that I was now favourite to win. He reinforced this by doing the 'holding a bloke by the collar and kicking his arse' mime.

This was not how I'd envisaged this race going at all; my two main rivals were either injured or ill. I went back to my team as the parade started, a little disappointed at how things had turned out so far. Firstly, cyclists form a cliquey brotherhood that tends to transcend teams. People don't understand us. It's a bit like being a drummer or a referee. It's in the blood and being unable to ride for any length of time is pretty soul destroying so I was upset for the two riders.

171

It would be disingenuous of me to say it hadn't crossed my mind having these two riders out of race would improve my chances of winning but that was hardly the point. Without them the race was devalued a little. It was the last year I could compete in the adult (18 –35) category so there was no chance of this race being repeated with the youngest and strongest riders. It was what it was – you can only race against the competition that appears on the start line, not against promises and threats.

I needn't have worried too much. A young Italian looking gentleman was pointed out to me as the guy who was going to win the road race. In his early 20s I guess, this guy was toned, lean, tanned and unacceptably cool and good-looking. I was starting to dislike him already. Apparently he'd told everybody he was going to win and he was right. I could tell he was going to win purely by the way his sunglasses were perched on the top of his head. That evening I sloped off to the team meeting in the sure and certain knowledge I was going to be thrashed by this rider who, if rumour was to be believed, had ridden the Giro d'Italia only a few years earlier.

To make matters worse, I found that an armchair I had selected to sit on for the duration of the Team Meeting had also taken the fancy of the Team Manager. He eyed me up but I was in no mood to move so he sat on the arm, over balanced and fell on top of me. Peter wasn't very nimble so I was pretty much flattened under him for a few minutes until he was helped up. I figured if he wanted it that badly he could have it so I found some space on the floor that, in all fairness, was where the rest of the 100 strong GB team were sitting.

Things weren't going well. In the last few minutes I'd been flattened by a hefty team manager and learned I wasn't going to be racing with the guys who had beaten me last year. Worse still, I was about to have my arse handed to me by some ex professional that would probably have pinched my girlfriend; if I'd had one.

172

That was when the earthquake struck. I really was going up in the world in a very literal way. The whole team were lifted off the floor like dust being shaken off a rug or a duvet being straightened out with a massive flap. It felt like the whole building had been lifted up and dumped a few feet to the left. There was a good amount of disquiet, some screaming and not a little running around. We discovered later that it was only a tremor; something that happens on a very regular basis in Japan but it felt like a full-blown kick ass earthquake to me. Thankfully one of the team, who was a little shaken and upset herself, had some helpful safety advice at hand. She said that whatever we do, we must not go outside otherwise we'd be killed by the 'Toonarmy'. It took a little while for a friend to explain to her that, whatever danger we were in it was unlikely that a gang of Newcastle United supporters would murder any of us at that precise moment. It did lighten the mood rather.

With the tectonic excitement over, my focus was back to the forthcoming race. It had struck me it was a long way to travel and a long time to wait for a single shot at a 35 minute bike race held once every 2 years. It really is putting your massive single egg into a tiny and fragile basket. It had been amply demonstrated by my Swedish and Spanish friends that this was a dangerously risky strategy. I knew my rivals were disappointed but at least they would get another go at it. Imagine preparing for a 10 second 100 metre Olympic sprint held once every 4 years and getting injured just before the race was due to start. It must be soul destroying.

The bike race was to take place early in the sporting schedule on Monday 27th August in Harima Central Park. The men's race followed the women's with, once again, the whole field going off together irrespective of age. The helpful and rather charming race notes told me the 'competitions will be carried out rain or shine' indicating it might be a good idea to go prepared for any kind of weather.

173

The team had decided to go for a training ride on the Saturday preceding the race to get the long plane journey out of our legs and acclimatise to the conditions. It was far too late for proper training. If we weren't fit enough now, 2 hours worth of riding was not going to put it right. I was preparing for the training ride in my room by applying a thin coating of antiseptic cream to, how can I put this delicately, my contact points. You know, the bits you have to sit on. I was bending over – facing the balcony looking effectively back between my legs making sure all the important bits were covered – when there has a knock at the door followed by a gabble in Japanese. In my compromised position I was somewhat startled by the noise and said, "Hi" automatically. In Japanese, "Hi" or "Hai" means "Yes". As the door opened it became clear the maid at the door had asked if it was okay to come in.

Consequently, my first cultural exchange with my hosts was slightly less dignified than I was hoping for and slightly more revealing than they were anticipating. It also meant getting our towels changed for the next week took longer than one might like. The maids fled every time my roommate or I approached them.

The park where the race was being held was a 45-minute coach ride away from the hotel. Monday morning was the first time that all the international transplant cyclists had gathered together, and we eyed each other up in the lobby; looking to see who was carrying more weight than they should, who was looking confident and who was looking particularly tanned: a good indication of hours out on the bike. Not that it really mattered of course. The favoured 'race winner' had just arrived, legs freshly shaved, flip flops, sunglasses, the lot and everybody was now looking at him. He was pushing a Specialized S Works M4 road bike, the very same as those issued to the Festina professional cycling team for use in the Year 2000 Tour de France. During my research before I bought the Bianchi I had looked at a number of other bikes, the Specialized range being amongst them. I was sure you couldn't get hold of these. They were team issue only.

My pre-race preparation had always consisted largely of running around waving my arms in the air panicking. I'd insist people told me everything was going to be okay, not believe them and panic some more. It's far from ideal I know and, try as I might, I can't find it recommended in any of the British Cycling coaching manuals. Nevertheless, it's pretty much what happened to me before every big race.

This time I had gone into overdrive. I'd convinced myself I was going to struggle against this guy before the race had even begun: before I'd even seen him ride, just on the basis of what he looked like and what he was riding. Of course, this is fundamentally stupid and indicates a significant lack of psychological strength on my part but in the heat of the moment, the race looked like it was already lost. It also showed a dangerous lack of respect for the ability of the other riders in the race. They might not have looked as cool but they could be equally, if not more, dangerous.

We loaded the bikes, piled into the bus and I was joined by my teammates. The 'winner' sat opposite me towards the back of the bus with his legs elevated onto the headrest on the seat in front of him. Another rider walked past him heading towards the rear of the bus and said, "You win today?" in heavily accented English. "Yeah, sure" he replied without hesitation. He smiled, put his headphones on, closed his eyes and took a nap. Took a bloody nap! He was napping while I was fizzing with nervous energy, that's how sure this guy was of victory.

When we got to Harima it was hilly and very hot. We got the bikes together, found the course and started warming up. There was some confusion, as I've now learned there always is, as to which direction the course would be ridden in. In the UK we race anti-clockwise making left-hand turns because we drive on the left and, of course, right turns would mean crossing traffic. In Europe the situation is reversed. The Japanese drive on the left so anti-clockwise was the likely direction but it still didn't stop a few high-speed Red Arrow style passes until the direction was confirmed by the Commissaire.

The bikes were electronically tagged with timing chips and after a cursory look at the women's race it was our turn. I muscled my way to the front of the group and lined up next to the prospective winner. At least that way I could see what he was doing and have a better chance at reacting to his moves however unlikely or impossible that might be. My hysterical and unbecoming pre-race nerves always disappear completely when I'm on the start line. I can't explain why but the pathetic panicky feelings and negative thoughts don't drain away slowly they just vanish in an instant. I don't mean to say I become convinced I'm going to win, far from it and with my rather shaky road racing record that would be plain daft. I just know I'm prepared, there's air in the tyres and it's time to start. Maybe I'm just happier sitting on a bike than a sofa. The gun went, we rolled over the electronic start mat and my young cool rival just took off. I mean he really took off.

In lower category amateur racing you sometimes get a few riders who blast off from the start too quickly and realise they can't maintain the effort for more than a minute or two. It's more usual for it to be a brisk rather than aggressive pace and for speed to be built up when the bunch is together. This start was just a sprint from the blocks and there was no choice for me but to try to follow if I was to have any chance of finishing anywhere near him. One thing I knew for sure was I couldn't hold this pace for more than a minute or so.

After 500 metres we were some distance ahead of the bunch already. I was tucked into his wheel chewing the handlebars and searching for extra holes to breathe through. Then, looking over his shoulder, he slowed. Presumably he wanted me to do some work at the front to establish our gap and distance the chasing riders. I came through and, after passing him, moved over so he could tuck in behind my

176

wheel. If I could work with this guy for the race I might be in with a chance of a podium finish and I'd settle for that against this level of competition. I looked round and I saw he'd dropped back a couple of metres, then a couple more. His head was down and his shoulders and back had come up, a classic indication of a rider who had 'blown' or reached the limits of his energy reserves. He was gasping for breath and looked completely spent. His blistering start had not been a well thought out strategy to distance lesser riders but a naively overly confident one launched out of enthusiasm and excitement.

I found out later, he wasn't an ex professional or, indeed, anything like that. He was a great looking cool guy who had got hold of a lovely bike that matched his striking appearance. He had never claimed to be any of the things I'd imagined him to be. I had built him up to be something he wasn't in my own mind which is, of course, terribly unfair on him. Not that it makes a difference but he was an Israeli, not an Italian and had his kidney transplant after his stint of national service in the army. He had not ridden the Giro d'Italia nor had he ever claimed to have done so, it was just a rumour of somebody else's making that I had chosen to believe. Rather than just popping over, saying "Hello" and asking him, I'd swallowed the gossip. His response to the question on the bus about him winning had not been an idle boast but a funny answer to a light-hearted question. Once more, it was my interpretation that was at fault. He turned out to be a nice bloke, yes, a big character but a good guy all the same. I'm sorry to say I have not seen him again since the trip to Japan.

Back at the race, I was sitting up waiting for the rest of bunch to catch up as there was no way I was capable of spending the next 35 minutes out there on my own. The hills were helping break up the field as drafting becomes less useful here. Individual power taking over from bunch riding tactics and principle of shared effort. Soon a break of four riders had been established. A pleasing multi-national smorgasbord including me, a Norwegian, the Danish rider

177

who had called me a 'dumb bastard' a couple of years earlier and a Frenchman. I was quite happy to keep the break going for a while as the riders from France and Norway were in an older age category than me.

At some point, I was going to have to shake off the Dane or take my chances against him in the sprint but that could wait. With two laps left I attacked on the hill and managed to get a bit of a gap, the French rider closed it bringing the Norwegian with him but distancing the Dane by a few metres and once again, we worked together to re-establish the three man break. Out of the break I knew that as long as the three of us continued to share the effort it was unlikely the Danish rider would be able to make it back to us.

At the start of the last lap we had distanced the Dane by 200 metres or so and he was now without the help of any other riders. I knew I was in a potentially race winning position. I didn't have to beat either of my break away companions as they were having a race of their own, but I did want to win the race overall.

Starting the hill for the last time at the back of the three man group I got out of the saddle to attack again only to see the Norwegian's hand come out indicating he would like me to stay where I was. It looked like another guy wanted me to help him win a bike race. He turned and said, "Work with me, I give you the race". He implied that if I helped him to shake the French rider he would not contest the sprint for the overall race if we arrived at the finish together. He *did* want me to help him win but he was offering something in return.

It's not unusual for deals to be done in pro races or where titles are at stake and, for us at least, this *was* a big race. There *was* a World title at stake. The Norwegian dropped behind the Frenchman and me and launched an aggressive attack; I went with him being careful not to offer the French rider any protection or a wheel he could jump onto. Once clear the Norwegian and I worked together as we moved towards the finish line. With 200 metres to go I drew level with him, nodded, got out of the saddle and sprinted for the line. Good as his word, he sat up and cruised in to win his age group. I went over the line with my hands still on the bars but with a smile of disbelief on my face. The finishing straight was slightly uphill and the video of the event shows me taking my hands off the bars and punching the air only to have to quickly grab them again to stop myself from falling off. Stylish. Picking myself up of the tarmac would not have been a great start to my reign as a World Champion. Get me, a World Champion.

I turned to find my Norwegian colleague beaming at me and holding out a hand that I was only too happy to shake. He was particularly pleased because that completed his run of five consecutive wins in his age group over 10 years. Some going.

The next person walking over towards me had a familiar look as well although I couldn't bring the face to mind immediately. I'm delighted to say, it was Margaret Koppejan (sans wig) the Dutch bone marrow transplant cyclist who I'd first met in Budapest. She was still thin but very much alive and had competed and medalled in the women's road race. Being wrapped up in my own little world, I'd failed to watch it properly and missed her. From a pretty nervy start this day was getting better and better.

I shared the podium (well, plastic chair) with the Dane who had finished second and an Austrian rider that day. Please don't think too badly of me for my treatment of the French rider. One of the wonderful things about bike racing is the tactically expedient temporary alliance. Spoken or unspoken deals are made by riders on a minute–by–minute basis in most races and it is very much part of the game. I know it would be unlikely for a centre back and a striker to have a chat and agree not to knock ten bells out of each other for the first half but they don't have to deal with aerodynamics. The Frenchman had finished second in his age category and was delighted with his result. He asked me to sign his programme later during the week; the first time anybody had asked me to sign anything other than a cheque.

179

After going to some lengths to establish he wasn't taking the piss and he really did want me to deface his programme, I was flattered to sign it.

The Dane shook my hand again and this time commented I was a 'lucky bastard'. I suppose this was a step up from being dumb and, in many ways he was right. The result could have been very different if my main competition, the guys who outclassed me in Budapest, had been racing.

With the race now over, its early position in the sporting programme did mean I had a chance to see a little of Japan. I was completely blown away by a visit to Kyoto, the old imperial capital. The scale and intricacy of the buildings and gardens was fascinating and it was impossible not to be taken by the Japanese people who were charming, friendly and always curious to see a load of Caucasians boiling themselves in blazers and ties. The trips allowed the shock of winning to sink in a little and for me to come to terms with what I had achieved.

The GB team had seen a tiny glimmer of the seismic beast that lines the coastal waters of Japan. What we had thought was a significant event hadn't even rattled the teacups as far as our Japanese hosts were concerned. The area around Kobe had been completely devastated in 1995 by a massive earthquake and even that was dwarfed by what struck Fukishama in March 2011. All of us on that trip who are still around felt very deeply sorry for the plight of Japanese people who had looked after us so well in 2001.

I spent one of the remaining days in Japan helping my roommate lose at double table tennis. Thankfully our opponents were not dressed as children's television characters or pirates but they still comprehensively outplayed us. I do recall my partner suggesting it would be more helpful if I aimed the ball at the table rather than Japan. He helpfully pointed to the table, then to anything else surrounding it, then back to the table to reinforced the distinction between the two. Regretfully, his coaching advice had little effect on me and as a table tennis player, I remained a reasonably competent cyclist.

Time trials: a survival guide

At the closing ceremony for the Japanese games, the venue for the next World Games, to be held in the summer of 2003, was announced as Nancy, France. Whilst I knew I needed a decent break from the bike when I got back home, for both physical and mental reasons, I was delighted. This was a chance to go to the home of cycling, where bike racing is the national sport, as a reigning champion and have another go at this rare and fantastic event. Better still, it was rumoured they were extending the cycling programme to include a time trial and, possibly, a longer distance endurance event as well. If true, this was good news as there had always been a feeling amongst the cyclists that 2 years training for one short race, taking into account the number of things that can go awry mechanically or physically was a risk. For at least two of my colleagues this risk had been realised in Japan.

None of us riders had anything like the same level of support a professional cycling team would have when flying to races abroad and transporting a bike internationally on your own is a nightmare. It means things like spare wheels, a turbo trainer to warm up on or any tools other than a portable set of hex keys is out of the question. A track pump to get the right pressure in the tyres is an essential piece of kit for any ride or race at home but a real luxury when racing unsupported abroad. A puncture, a snapped chain or any other kind of routine mechanical failure can mean not even finishing a race where a world title is at stake. Two years worth of training and preparation can disappear in two minutes.

Right, its exam time again, I'm afraid, and whilst you are doing okay, you could try harder and you are easily distracted in class. As with all these exams, they are modular and multiple choice so if you get it wrong the first time simply do it again as many times as you like until you get the desired result. Please show your workings.

Question 4

You are a transplant cyclist and after a recent run of good form and some success you are pleased to discover your next important race meeting will be held in France and may include a time trial. Outline the most appropriate short and medium term strategy on learning this exciting news?

1. Oh what luck! France is lovely at that time of year and it being much closer to home you could take the children and make a holiday of it. Perhaps taking a leisurely tour around the wider area soaking up the bucolic pleasure of the wonderful countryside. A time trial is a welcome extension to the bike racing programme and will allow those riders who specialise in this discipline the opportunity to compete for a medal.

2. Think wisely. The route to success in Japan has been an arduous one which, in some small part, may have contributed to the breakup of your marriage. You should enjoy your recent success and take a little time to settle into a new home. After a healthy period of reflection and rest you could then consider how racing and training might fit it with a hectic schedule of work and your revised family responsibilities.

3. A time trial you say? Interesting. Once it has been positively confirmed there really will be a time trial at the next World Games, maybe you could look at whether training for two quite different events is possible. Some clip on aero bars for the road race bike would be a modest and appropriate investment perhaps allowing you to try a few short time trials at home to see if you like it.

4. Brilliant! Before confirmation of the existence of the time trial event, you realise you could drive to France rather than fly. Consequently, a decent sized car could be crammed with cycling equipment if things like children were not taking up valuable space. The plainly obvious opportunity for world cycling domination at two events dictates the immediate purchase of a new time trial specific aerodynamic bike designed to eek out the fractions of a second that will undoubtedly separate the top riders. You should ignore your pledge to never to engage in any form of cycle sport other than road racing and start time trial based training without delay. There is no need to check the rules as aero equipment is bound be allowed in the time trial.

Yes, of course, you guess it. I dusted off the $n + 1$ formula once again and decided pretty much instantly, I needed to start getting into this time trial thing. It was another opportunity to compete in a different genre of bike racing and a great excuse for my club mates at home to justify the need to join them in their painful lonely rituals. It wasn't even my fault was it? I'd been forced into time trialling by the organisers of the World Games. Damn them, damn them I say. Now, where's the number for the bike shop.

To put things into context it's important to understand that time trialling is radically different from road racing and an enmity exists between proponents of the two disciplines. Using the analogy of British geography to help illustrate the mutual suspicion road racers view time trialists with, and vice versa, think of it like the relationship the English have with the Scottish. Or the Welsh. The countries are very close neighbours living side–by-side, sharing borders and much common geography and they talk to each other quite happily for most of the time, yet there remains an underlying mistrust and an unwillingness to communicate on anything more than a superficial level or to try and

185

understand each other's cultural differences. Rather than share facilities or administration they would much rather set up their own smaller structures. These attract the most ingrained and partisan officials who will adopt uniforms and arcane customs to fully establish the divide.

Within the cycling community all will be well, provided a healthy distance is kept and nobody comes up with any crazy ideas like sharing things or acknowledging each other's existence. The two (or three or more) disciplines will rub along just as our geographical neighbours do, with only the occasional border skirmish. Should a war break out over something fundamentally important, like how many spokes you are allowed in a wheel or whether you race together or individually, the battles will be fierce and bloody. Grudges will be held for at least one eternity and the blood feud will be passed down to other family members so the fighting can continue for generations. There will be rules and laws governing the two codes, yes lots of rules and laws. And blazers. There must be blazers with important looking gold badges on them.

The historical and political differences between 'testers' (a pejorative description of time trialists often used by road racers) and 'road men' (a mildly pejorative term used by time trialists to describe road racers) go back into the mists of time. It makes unpacking and explaining the Middle East crisis look like child's play and I am acutely aware that even trying to explain it impartially is likely to make me vulnerable to some kind of cycling fatwa.

However, and very briefly, racing on the roads in Britain was administered by one particular bunch of blazer wearers known as the National Cycling Union (NCU) from around the 1880s when cycling and bikes were still in their infancy. There was no established statute governing the use of bikes on the road, let alone whether racing was allowable. Digging into the history you'll find stories of the police interrupting bike races by charging at cyclists with horses and using sticks and batons to put through their spokes. Very much like today really.

The NCU, the organisation developed to help and support cyclists, seemingly without an ironic bone in their blazer bedecked bodies, decided to ban cycle racing on the road and limit it to velodromes and circuits closed to traffic. A questionable decision leading to the establishment of a breakaway organisation known as the Peoples Front for the Liberation of Cycle Racing. Okay, I made that up, it was actually called the Road Time Trials Council but you get the point. These guys promoted individual racing against the clock on the road with riders meeting in secret at dawn and using codes to identify the course to be ridden.

For many cyclists who didn't have access to one of the few velodromes or circuits, this meant they could no longer race in bunches and, if they wanted to continue to compete, they would have to do so against the clock. I appreciate this might seem like a big 'so what?' to non-cyclists but it's akin to banning tennis and excusing it by saying you can play badminton instead. Not earth shattering in global terms perhaps but pretty upsetting if you're a tennis player.

The World cycling governing body, the Union Cycliste Internationale (UCI), also threw their own stick into the wheels of British cycling (big 'B' and small 'c') just before the Second World War. They declared that the World championships would be held as a mass start as opposed to an individually timed event. This made the selection of British cyclists a tad tricky as the British national representative body had recently banned it and most cyclists either didn't do bunch racing any more or were learning to play badminton.

The only logical thing to do in these circumstances was to form another breakaway group claiming to represent the nation's cyclists called the British Cyclists Front for the Liberation of Cycling in Britain or 'British League of Racing Cyclists' for short. This lot promoted and ran illegal mass start bunch racing on the roads, the most famous and inaugural event being run from Wolverhampton to Llangollen in 1942.

You have to give this lot of rebels some credit, as without them it's entirely possible British road racing wouldn't exist in the rude health it does now, if at all. The NCU felt obliged to demonstrate its open, liberal and forward thinking policies by banning those riders who had taken part in this or any other event they deemed illegal.

The whole thing was unpleasant and deeply divisive but eventually, the NCU and the BLRC merged acrimoniously, if there is such a thing, in 1959 to form the British Cycling Federation. Even in 2009, at the 50th anniversary of the merged organisation, former members of the BLRC were still demanding letters of apology for past insults complaining their contribution to the sport has never been properly recognised.

But at last one body with a single voice now represented all cyclists right? Yes, of course, apart from the Road Time Trials Council who still look after time trials. And the Older Peoples Front for Cycle Racing or League of Veteran Racing Cyclists as it's more commonly known. Or the CTC (the Cyclists' Touring Club) whose website claims they are the UK's national cyclists organisation. It's embarrassing but the list goes on. Sadly, there are still numerous governing bodies representing different factions of cycling.

The logical conclusion is that each cyclist will one day have his or her own organisation with increasingly bizarre and pointless rules to establish some kind of distinction between each other. In microcosm I have seen cycling clubs quite literally spilt in two with the dividing line being whether they engage in time trialling or road racing. Some towns that aren't really big enough to sustain one cycling club have three because the riders won't talk to each other. It's all pretty unedifying, rather unhelpful and very funny.

Party because of the historical dominance of NCU, time trialling is still proportionally more popular in the UK

188

than any other form of competitive cycle sport and the 10-mile club time trial is the bedrock of club cycling in Britain. Most clubs hold one mid-week time trial. The season starts in early April and usually carries on until early September.

Time trials are probably the most accessible cycle sport event available, as you don't need a race licence or even a helmet should you choose not to wear one. You just turn up, sign on, pay your 3 quid, pin a number on your back and get ready to go when it's your turn. Somebody will hold you up so you can start with both feet clipped into the pedals, count you down and off you go around a set course as fast as your legs will carry you.

Somebody will set off a minute in front of you and a minute behind until all the riders are out. Club stalwarts and non-club members alike turn up to these things and as specialist equipment is not needed, you can ride one on anything you like. The fact that many riders do turn up on bikes with the latest electronic gears costing ten thousand pounds or more with pointy lids, disk wheels and shoe covers is neither here nor there. You can ride one on your mountain bike if you want.

The guy who completes the 10 miles in the fastest time is the winner; unless you are not the fastest and then you're only racing against yourself and anybody who says otherwise should bloody well grow up. Anyway, you're still getting over a cold. And a tractor held you up.

You'll see now how the evening club '10' comes very close to an ideal British day out: travelling somewhere, wearing silly clothes and drinking tea in a village hall. Often a local pub replaces the village hall and the tea is a cola but you get the idea. The village hall really comes into its own with the much posher open, as opposed to club, time trial where the propensity for pointy headwear and expensive equipment is much higher. Despite the plusher surroundings and extra equipment, it's satisfying to note that the speeds and times are pretty much identical.

All sorts of riders turn up to time trials, provided you are more than 12-years-old and your bike is roadworthy, the

189

course is all yours. Should you choose to attend one of these, and I strongly recommend you do, you will see people exhibiting some of the characteristics set out below. If you are really lucky you will encounter the full-blown 100% pure and genuine article that fits smack bang into one of the categories harshly stereotyped below.

Aero Boy

Aero boy has worked out the greatest obstacle to going quickly on a bike is to overcome the resistance of wind. Accordingly, he has invested in a bike and clothing that will give him every possible advantage. The bike will be made of carbon fibre with the tubes profiled to reduce drag. The wheels will also be made of carbon, the rear one being a solid disk and the front a 'deep section' of at least 80mm depth. Ideally, he would run a disk wheel at the front too but this is against the rules as a gentle sideward's breeze would see him tacking into the middle of a main road with all the deft control of a small sailing boat in a hurricane. His lid will be extra pointy and his position on the bike will be extreme with his head below the handlebars and his bum up in the air. His ensemble will be topped off by an impossibly tight one-piece lycra skinsuit that will leave nothing, repeat nothing, to the imagination.

He will be drinking branded sports drinks and consuming energy gels whilst warming up on a turbo trainer using his spare wheels to avoid the possibility of a puncture. He will have a strip across his nose to aid his intake of air and will alternate his attention between his MP3 player and the power meter attached to his carbon handlebars. If you listen very carefully you may catch him uttering snatches of words or phrase that sound like 'Brad' or 'Cav' whilst he wipes away beads of sweat with his team issue towel and visualises the course.

He may or may not have missed the fact that at between 14 to 18 stone he will be providing the wind with its greatest tool in slowing him down and that the biggest impediment to his speedy progress will be his body mass

190

irrespective of what he is riding or wearing. If he is aware of this seemingly ironic position, he will also know that, because of his equipment, he will be pound for pound faster than the other 14 to 18 stone blokes at the time trial. Do not let this lull you into a false sense that this guy has 'all the gear and no idea' as he might be blisteringly quick even if he is at the upper level of the weight limit. Not that it's about winning here, you're just racing against yourself, remember?

Tri Girl/Tri Boy

Increasingly common at club events now are triathletes training for the bike leg of the event. There is a common misconception that triathlons include a run, a ride, and a swim but it seems to me they are in fact a four, rather than three, event sport. A triathlon begins with a swim, either in a pool or in open water, before transitioning to a bike ride of between 20k and 112 miles depending on the type of event.

The third and often unnoticed leg involves being scraped off the road from amongst the tangled arms, legs and bikes of the other triathletes you've just crashed into. You will then be assessed for damage. Presumably, light damage such as road rash and broken sunglasses will be given a 1 minute time penalty whereas more serious injury including broken bones may attract a penalty of 10 minutes or more. Assuming you are able to continue, the event finishes with a run or hobble depending upon how badly injured you are.

You can spot a triathlete attending his or her first time trial because they watch it rather than compete in it as they have turned up wearing the sleeveless singlet used when they race (presumably you get rid of more skin that way). The Peoples Front for the Liberation of Time Trialists bans these for reasons nobody understands. You may also find they may not be wearing any socks and will sometimes choose to ride in swimming trunks. Don't be surprised if they run off as soon as they have finished.

Triathletes are not considered to be cyclists by other 'real' riders who will be enraged when they record slower times than those who spend just as much time running or swimming as they do training on the bike. It is considered a form of cheating.

The Big Gear Masher

Now hear this. This chap will tend to be a larger gentleman, possibly getting on in years and whatever his name, the initials HMS, as in Her Majesty's Ship, will prefix it. Due to his choice of gearing it will take him a long time to get up to cruising speed and he will be unable to change any parameters like speed, distance or direction during his voyage without written notification sent several weeks in advance. His leg speed will be similar to that of a torque heavy marine diesel engine slowing imperceptibly when riding up a gentle incline and increasing marginally when descending. Under no circumstances will he change to smaller gears as he will not acknowledge their existence. His average speed will remain completely constant, no matter what distance is covered, from 10 to 100 miles although it is quite likely he will be pretty quick when at full steam.

His style of riding and, more particularly, the fast times he records will infuriate those who coach cycling who know, for a fact, that fluid and fast leg speed is a far more efficient and faster way to ride. That is all.

The Wobbler

It is written into most club's constitutions that they must have at least one wobbler on the books at any one time. This unfortunate rider cannot be blamed for his inability to either ride in a straight line or in close proximity to other cyclists. Irrespective of the fact he will strike fear into all concerned, he must be catered for within the club environment. Think of it as cycling's contribution to care in the community. His predicament is caused by a genetic defect rendering him unable to absorb the etiquette and practice of cycling in close proximity to others by normal osmotic telekinesis despite being called a pillock on regular occasions.

192

He is identifiable by the twigs in his helmet vents and grass stains on his cycling garb from when he ploughed headfirst into a hedge or ancient woodland that has jumped out on him. If he goes around corners at all it will be in the shape of a partial hexagon, octagon or other multi-sided object but certainly not anything resembling a curve. He will do this whilst emitting an involuntary low rumbling noise indicating fear of the unknown.

It is likely he will be dishevelled and his bike will be in a constant state of poor repair. Despite this he will be one of the strongest riders in the club because, unable to ride safely in a group, he effectively rides everywhere on his own.

The Slobberer

You should be able to hear one of these coming a mile off. It will sound like you're riding your bike accompanied by an asthmatic St Bernard sucking a lemon. Spittle will be flying with abandon and hanging string-like from its nose and mouth whilst it draws in massive gulps of air through its breathing hole located towards the front of its terrifying face.

Whilst off the bike it will be identifiable by a slobber tidemark on its scaly skinsuit at waist level. A dry rasping sound will be emitted from its throat before its soul-troubling roar begins. These beasts should not be troubled whilst feeding or taking on water and under no circumstances should you be tempted to put your hands or fingers anywhere near their digestive mechanisms.

It is important to check your time before the slobberer checks his as the timing sheet is likely to be unreadable after he's had his paws on it.

The Professional

The professional is actually unlikely to be a professional cyclist although it is possible he has been in the past. He may ride a variety of machines from the ultra new and sleek to something rather more utilitarian but whatever he rides he will be much faster than you.

He will be recognisable because whatever time he started he will be back at the finishing point before you and may well have slowed down for a brief chat or to offer a word of encouragement as he passed by. You shouldn't feel too bad about this because he will be appreciably faster than everybody else too but won't actually look like he's trying that hard.

He will have an excellent riding style and is unlikely ever to be seen sweating. If you're really unlucky he will also be ruggedly good looking and generally a bloody nice chap.

You want to hate him don't you? Well, you can't: he's too nice and you know it. Whilst he knows he's quick he won't make a big deal out of it. He will often congratulate you on a time that is 6 minutes slower than his as being 'pretty quick' and commenting you are only racing against yourself. Just to rub it in, he'll sacrifice his ride sometimes to marshal for the club in the rain before going off to the sickly puppies and kittens charity where he helps prepare meals. For free.

There will be a whole host of other guys and girls who will turn up and fill the spaces between these recognisable characters who could be termed clubmen or clubwomen. They come in such a variety of shapes and sizes it's impossible to define any really distinguishing characteristics. Some take it more seriously than others but they are all there because of the shared suffering that makes time trialling what it is. They will be barfing up a lung in the pub car park with everybody else when they've finished.

I love club time trials. You get to have a chat with your club mates in the car park beforehand and find out the gossip before getting a good 25 minutes or whatever of good quality high-intensity racing. You can follow this up with a collective moaning and excuse-making session if you feel so inclined. Nobody believes you had to stop to dispatch a wounded badger (kindest thing to do: couldn't bear to watch it suffer) and nobody really cares, it's just a good evening out and the thing that binds many clubs together. Everybody is interested in the times to a greater or lesser extent and some people like to compare themselves to their self-perceived cohort to see how their form is progressing. Some check the results just for interest.

I had a lovely time specifying and buying a new bike following the announcement of the inclusion of a time trial in the French Games. My local bike shop built me a Giant TCR Aero frame with Campag equipment and Mavic wheels to launch myself onto the time trial scene in front of my experienced club mates. They found the whole thing very amusing. Bloody testers. I was lucky and I grew to enjoy time trialling nearly as much as road racing. My first time trial was in April 2003 and I did just under 25 minutes for the mid-week club 10, which is distinctly average, but it was really windy and the traffic was awful. And I got held up by a tractor as well as getting used to a new bike all whilst getting over a nasty bug. And I've been ill you know? Have I mentioned that before?

By the time July 2003 came around I'd managed to get a few more time trials and road races under my belt. This followed my first experience of going on a warm weather training camp on the Costa Blanca, Spain, which gave me the luxury of escaping the worst of the British winter weather. I'd managed to bring my 10-mile time trial time down to 23.30 by the summer and was as ready as I was prepared to admit to take on the Games in France. I was beginning to get a feel for both road racing and time trialling now and at risk of becoming a jack of all trades and a master of none. I was starting to understand the differences and distinctions between the two disciplines. It might be useful to highlight some of the less obvious differences between them so should you choose to engage with either, you can safely blag your way through the basics. There's no point in you making an arse of yourself if I've already done it for you now is there?

With road racing you are in a bunch or peloton with other riders and trying to use them to help you move along more quickly than you would be able to on your own. You'll know how you've got along with this at the end of the race. If you're first over the line you'll have won, if you finish anywhere else, you haven't.

Time trialling, with certain specific exceptions, is an individual event where you get into the most aerodynamic position possible and use your own strength to cover a standard distance as quickly as possible. The winner is the one with the fastest time but many riders are really trying to beat their own personal best times rather than be the fastest which, for all but the super human, is virtually impossible anyway.

Testers refer to time trialling as 'the race of truth'. Superficially, this is taken to imply it's a true and genuine test of a cyclist's strength. It also implies that anything other than time trialling is a 'race of lies' and is a deliberate dig at those who aren't hard enough to handle the ultimate challenge.

You can read any cycling coaching manual and it will contain a simple prosaic checklist for the differences between road racing and testing but I think a little insider knowledge might be useful. After all, the coaching manuals don't always cover the really important stuff.

Moaning

One of the reasons people choose cycling as their sport is for the excellent opportunities to whinge about how crap or unfair everything is. The style, timing, content and delivery of the moan differs depending on which discipline you are engaged in.

With a time trial, you get the opportunity before the event to complain to your fellow riders (who don't care) or to the organisers (who don't care) or to the crowd (who aren't there). Most commonly, riders moan about how they have not been able to train as much as normal, how they have been plagued by colds or how they have only just finished work.

You then have to ride the event before getting back to the finishing point when you can launch into another tirade. Popular topics include traffic, tractors and farm vehicles, nutters in cars, drivers in flat caps, wildlife; anything in fact that may have slowed you down. Stand in the car park waving your arms around moaning if it makes you feel better, ask other riders if they saw the combine harvester chop you up. Nobody will care but it's considered good form to try.

You have these 'before and after' opportunities with road racing as well but, because you are in a bunch, you also get to grumble *while* you race. This is why entry fees are usually higher. You should take full advantage of this mobile opportunity to bitch although it is unlikely the guy you are droning on to will either hear what you are saying or care about it if he does. Pointing vaguely at riders or groups of riders implying they couldn't stay in a bunch if they were bananas is always a good one.

Please don't let being ignored put you off. You've paid your money so make the most of it.

Excuses

Ask a cyclist how he is feeling immediately before he rides a race. If he says 'bloody brilliant actually, my training simply could not have been better and I'm fully prepared for this event. I should also mention I have perfect equipment on which to compete' I will send you a prize. No cyclist would ever say this and mean it.

The list of pre-emptive excuses is endless. Some riders have favourites, a non-specific chest infection/virus is a good one, others are more exotic but they are all preparation for a potentially poor result.

Post-race excuses are more varied but should have the ring of plausibility. With road racing you simply blame other non-specified riders for cutting you up, leaving gaps or cornering like a sponge. Time trialists probably have the easier job because they are riding on their own. So long as they check nobody is near them, they can make up more florid excuses, alien abduction, hexed by local witches and the like.

More experienced riders will be able to employ a fully-fledged 'excuse matrix' involving the use of partial excuses both before and after an event. These will be carefully layered to create an unchallengeable web of deceit deployed to explain away anything from a delay of a few seconds to a DNF. Some guys are so good at this you may even find yourself fooled for a while. It won't be until the drive home you suddenly go, "Naaaaaaa ..." and shake your head.

Equipment

One of the great things about being a time trialist is equipment. For starters you'll need a winter training bike for all those mucky wet weekend rides just like a road man, but you can't really train in the summer on your aero time trial bike. It's not comfortable enough and the wheels and tyres are not really suitable for riding on lanes and the like. This means you need another 'best' road bike to ride in the summer. Bonus.

On top of this, time trial specific equipment tends to be much more expensive than stuff you would normally ride on the road. It's all the aero carbon and the odd shaped lightweight titanium bits and bobs that are so essential to the sport. It doesn't actually make you any faster but it's lovely anyway.

A pointy lid is prerequisite. This should cover your ears preventing you from hearing anything, especially other people's excuses and gripes. This makes the most used words at a time trial 'what?' and 'eh?'

A clubmate of mine used to ride team time trials with his right ear sticking out of the helmet. He claimed this allowed him to hear what the team were saying during the ride. Despite riding on the same team, I don't know if it worked or not, but the comedy value of riding with somebody resembling a damaged wing nut made it worthwhile anyway.

Occasionally you should put your pointy lid on backwards and flap around the car park emitting loud screeching noises pretending to be a seagull.

Clothing

Standard uniform for the tester is a skinsuit, a one piece (very) tight-fitting lycra outfit that makes anybody with a less than perfect body look like a vacuum packed box of frogs. Unfortunately this does not discourage those with less than ideal physiques from donning a spray-on skimpy mankini that leaves nothing to the imagination. I apologise if this has put images in your head that have no business being there.

Tight-fitting shoe covers are common; lycra 'booties' are stretched over cycling shoes to further reduce drag by smoothing out the buckles and straps and letting the air flow more efficiently over them. It's as much part of the uniform as anything, as it seems the big fleshy blob on top of the bike is likely to provide more air resistance than an uncovered size 9.

Roadies will wear normal (if you're prepared to concede cycling attire can ever be referred to in that way) separate shorts and a jersey in both road races and time trials. They do this to make it clear that they hold testing to be a poor relative and something they do when there's no 'proper' racing on. It also allows them to include non-specific clothing within their carefully constructed excuse matrix if they come in with a lousy time.

Road racers tend to spend almost as much time bouncing down the road on their arses as triathletes, so having separate shorts and jerseys means replacement following the inevitable crash is less expensive. It's a good job they've shaved their legs because, as we know, this reduces road rash and promotes the healing process.

Cheating

All time trialists think road racing is basically cheating. The very concept of using somebody else's effort in order to advance your own chances of going faster is alien to them. Drafting another rider in a time trial is against the rules and could result in disqualification if caught. The High Priest of Peoples Front for the Liberation of Testers will then ceremonially remove your pointy lid and shoe covers and banish you to a lifetime of riding sportives in the wilderness. Road racers think this is nonsense and that proper cheating is taking drugs to make you faster. Unless you are taking drugs yourself, then it's only cheating if you get caught.

When riding in a bunch it's entirely right and proper you should spend most of your time taking a draft off other riders, it is also incumbent upon you to take your turn at the front even if it kills you to do so. Avoiding this is the equivalent of not buying your round in the pub: you might get away with it for a while but sooner rather than later, you'll find yourself without friends. Remember, you must play nicely with the other kids. And no biting.

Time trialists occasionally cut off part of the course on longer races, particularly those over 50 miles in length. Usually this happens where there are no marshals. This isn't cheating, it's an honest mistake.

Distances

Time trials on the road are run over set distances, usually starting with 10 miles to 25, 50 and 100. You need to be certified clinically insane to compete in 12 or even 24 hour events where you ride as far as you can within the allowed time.

There are some odd distances on hilly courses in the early season, known as 'sporting' events and some intermediate distances like a '30' but these are less common.

I rode a 100 mile time trial. Once. I completed it in just less than 5 hours and it was the only time I have hallucinated since I came out of hospital all those years ago. I convinced myself I could smell colours and had an irresistible craving for blackcurrant jam on toast and ginger beer. I will not be doing another one.

A former club mate of mine is exceptional at these longer distance events, completing 100 miles in not much over 3 hours 30 minutes. This superman-like performance means he not only needs to drink but also eat during this length of effort. He does this by consuming rice pudding in ice cream cones handed up to him from the side of the road. By doing this, he doesn't even need to slow down from his 25 mph plus pace.

Before I did my one and only 100 mile test, I questioned a rather less athletic club mate of mine about his own hydration and nutrition strategy for the event. He told me he was going to pull over at the service station after about 50 miles, have a stretch, a pee and a bacon and egg butty whilst he had a sit down for a few minutes. I laughed, shook my head knowingly whilst rolling my eyes. And did the same thing.

Road races are held over a variety of distances, the transplant ones being ridiculously short at 20k. Weekend races are normally over a 100k and get longer the higher up the category rankings you go. Roadies measure distances in kilometres rather than miles because it's more European and makes it sound like you've raced further. In the handicapped league events that are my bread and butter, the distance is normally 55k although, because the starts are staggered, the later groups have to ride much faster than the front markers to cover the same distance. That's the whole idea: everybody gets a chance and you get to ride with people of a similar ability.

At one event I saw Group 1 ready to roll out behind the lead car when there was an almighty bang. The unmistakeable noise of a tyre blowing out. As Group 1 left, one of their number was digging out a spare tube from his pocket and looking to borrow a track pump. He knew he had approximately 4 minutes to fix it so he could go out with the quicker Group 2.

201

He was looking slightly anxious and fumbling the tyre levers somewhat, a little irked I suspect by the prospect of having to ride with a faster group. All the same, he didn't look unduly concerned until he realised he was going to miss that group as well.

There was a look of considerable concern on his face buried beneath a blurred frenzy of pumping arms as it dawned on him he was going to have to hang on to the coat tails of the third much faster group on the road when bang! Another tube went. Just as I rolled out he was making whimpering noises and had the pale terrified expression of somebody who was going to have to ride with the Elites, the ex-professionals and the young aspiring athletes in the final, fastest group. Assuming he still wanted to get a ride at all that evening.

I heard later he'd managed about 600 metres with them before being blown out of the group. Apparently those 600 metres had nearly killed him. I half expected to see him dangling from a roadside tree by his bib shorts, his crow pecked corpse left dangling in the wind as a warning to others who might consider trying something so foolhardy.

Nancy

July 2003 came around and, with two bikes stuffed in the back of a Focus, I picked up 'Matt the Bat' my roommate from Japan. He made me promise I would never ruin a game of table tennis for him again and we drove over to Nancy, France.

The town was amazing and the people fantastic. It felt like the whole town had turned out to greet us at the opening ceremony. After what seemed like a long wait on a tree-lined boulevard, we walked through the gates to Stanislas Square to where we assumed we would find the Mayor and some sandwiches on trestle tables. How wrong we were.

They had created a barriered walk-through and the teams were parading towards a huge stage area where Michel Platini was greeting the captains and managers. Most of us had given away our uniform and kit to the kids in the crowd before the games had really started. A wonderful example of civic pride by this marvellous French town and not something I have ever experienced before or since.

They loved cycling and cyclists and had created a wonderful town centre circuit complete with a tree-shaded boule lawn in the middle for the road race and the time trial. I was delighted to renew my acquaintance with Richard my Swedish rival and check out the other competition. The Dutch came armed with team cars in full livery, sets of rollers, spare bikes, the lot. They even had gazebos to keep the sun off while they warmed up. It was great sight and a wonderful setting for bike racing.

The time trial was first. A proper start ramp, count down and a knowledgeable and enthusiastic crowd (yes, really, it could honestly be described as a crowd) greeted us. Richard Nordstrum set the fastest time of the day at 7 mins 30 seconds. Pretty quick for a 5k blast. I went a few minutes after him.

I'd trained for the distance and knew the effort level involved in a race this short. The games organisers include it because they imagine a short distance will be less taxing on us poor transplant patients. The opposite is true. 5000 metres is 1000 metres further than the standard pursuit distance on the track and is an horrific lung buster. It's the cycling equivalent of running a 500 metre sprint, giving you very little time to work your way into the ride.

Overcook the start and in less than a minute the initial burst of power has drained your muscles of energy. Your legs will slow, your speed will drop and the more you try to fight it the harder it will become. Getting it wrong could cost 20 seconds – the difference between winning and just making it into the top 10.

Go off just a little too slow and drop a few seconds and it could make the difference between a gold and a silver medal. It's a difficult balance to judge when the pressure is on.

After the start you settle into a 'red line' ride for 7 to 8 minutes depending on the course. If it isn't hurting like hell, you're not going fast enough. I held an average heart rate of 190 bpm and had a fantastic ride covering the distance in 7 min 10 seconds to win. I overtook my minute man and his team car in the process. I have only ridden that distance quicker once in perfect conditions on the track and then only by a single second.

The road race came around 2 days later, this time eight laps of the almost flat circuit used for the time trial. With no hills it was always going to be a fast attritional race. Sheer speed left a few riders out of the bunch within the first couple of laps. Once again, a break formed with the Norwegian I had worked with in Japan, John Moran, a super Irish rider, both of whom were in the older age category, and Richard.

Whenever the pace slowed even slightly, the chasing bunch was too close for comfort meaning it was possible for riders to jump across to the break. It meant pushing hard, taking a few risks and keeping the speed up through the corners. I remember grounding a pedal at one point, losing a tiny piece of metal from the bottom plate. Another few millimetres and the pedal would most probably have dug in and left me spread all over the road. Another slice of luck.

The time trial had proved that I was probably stronger than the Swede but I knew he had an excellent sprint on him – I'd seen it 4 years previously in Budapest as he disappeared over the line in front of me. I couldn't risk leaving the race to a sprint finish so I attacked with half a lap to go and managed to stay clear to win. John Moran, the Irishman, coming in second place overall. I have a picture of me looking disgustingly smug as I go over the line with my arms up. However, I *was* delighted to be the first rider to win both events.

I got onto the podium twice with a very gracious Richard Nordstrum taking two silver medals and a familiar Dane who shook my hand. He smiled and advised me I was a 'fat bastard'. Within 4 years I'd gone through dumb, lucky and fat which is not a great mantra for life I suppose but however dumb, lucky or fat I was, I'd finished in front of him on three occasions. I could put up with a little banter.

I also felt guilty. I had trained hard for this event and used a time trial specific bike. Only one or two other riders had done this and I knew it gave me an advantage. It was entirely within the rules and nobody had even raised an eyebrow but I had gone all out to win these events. The plan had been well and truly executed. It felt a bit clinical and not really plucky or indeed British. A strange feeling.

I read an article later by a successful female Olympian, the sentiment of which was 'You think it's hard losing? You want to try winning something sometime'. I know it must sound odd but targets and plans drive me. I like the process and engineering of getting to a destination as much as reaching the goal itself. It's almost like saying goodbye to a treasured friend once the goal has been reached. Then, unfaithful rat that I am, I go looking for another.

Before I raced in France I had decided to ditch the BCF jersey I had worn in Budapest and Japan and proudly wore my Wrekinsport club kit instead. During those Games, eight British Transplant cyclists had won 11 medals, five of them gold. All this in the heart of a country absolutely passionate about bike racing.

Our racing had been reported in the national press and television in France, the UK national and local press and most of the cycling related media. We had raised the profile of organ donation *and* British cycling and had once again been completely ignored by the sport's governing body in the UK. This remains the case to date. Almost makes you want to establish a breakaway national cycling body doesn't it?

Things that try to kill you

2004 started well for me, physically I was okay and only visiting the Queen Elizabeth Hospital once every 6 months. The liver function test results were coming back showing a healthy blood chemistry. I had managed to get to Costa Blanca again for a sunny week's riding in the February of that year and learned the most useful Spanish phrase ever, 'Donde esta cycliste por vafor?'In English, 'where have the other cyclists gone please?' And, after returning home and launching into my training once again I managed to actually win a road race. I think it was maybe just my turn at the front when we happened to go over the line to be honest but it meant I could send my 4th category racing licence back swapping it for a shiny new 3rd category one.

The beautiful Bianchi that served me so well in France developed a crack in the fork and needed replacing. Of course, I used this as a lame excuse to buy a new bike and ended up with a Colnago equipped with Campagnolo Chorus equipment and Mavic super light wheels. It was a lovely looking bike but unfortunately not a race razor. On reflection a great 'Sunday' bike but not suited to the type of racing I was doing. It's not a great leap to work out I managed to convince myself it would make a great winter bike when the time came to replace it.

I really stretched myself in the summer and entered my first stage race. Not the Tour de France, not even the Tour of Britain. It was the far more modestly titled 'Tour of the Wrekin'. Even then, this was quite a grand title for what amounted to three stages over a weekend in Shropshire.

The first stage was 3 mile prologue time trial in the morning, an undulating road stage in the afternoon and then a long hilly stage of 67 miles around my Bridgnorth home on Sunday. I was in the top third after the time trial; it was my kind of distance and pan flat. I rode well in the afternoon and was pleased to stay pretty much in same position in the overall classification after the first road stage. I took a

207

complete battering on day two and finished second-to-last overall on Sunday. Result eh?

I was second-to-last, rather than dead last, by less than a second. By busting a gut to outsprint my riding companion that day, I cost myself a tenner: the prize for the last man or 'lantern rouge' as it's known. Many riders had dropped out before the finish but I rode with a guy who'd driven up from Cornwall in his camper van and was determined to have his money's worth. I was keen to finish my one and only stage race so we rode together when the big kids wouldn't let us play with them anymore. Great fun and not a wholly unfamiliar experience for me.

I'd taken a kicking from Les West, an excellent veteran rider in the past but here the tables had been turned. One of the 'big kids' in this race was actually a young kid, then a junior, Dan Martin, last seen winning the 2010 Tour of Poland so I've never felt too bad about that one. I suspect he is now more comfortable in the luxury tour bus of his professional team rather than Worfield village hall although I bet the tea and cake isn't as good.

It was a very tough weekend and had taken quite a lot out of me. I ate and drank properly and metaphorically put my feet up for a few days, returning to race in the league the following Thursday. My efforts had obviously paid off, as it was one of the few times I'd managed to establish a break from the bunch. Two club mates and a rider from another local club joined me. The three of us worked together with the other rider hanging on and not contributing until we approached the finishing straight. I sent the strongest rider ahead to take the win and stayed with my other clubmate who was suffering for his efforts. We managed to shake the other rider, he took third and I got second place taking a one, two, three for the club in the league. Something unheard of from a time trial based club.

My third placed clubmate had gone over the line with one hand in the air and the other trying to free his cramped up thigh muscle. He thanked me for shepherding him home and said he bet I'd never seen anybody celebrate a third place before. I had, I'd been there myself a few years earlier in Budapest.

The season that had started so well took something of a turn for the worse after I sustained an horrific sneezing injury. Please do try not to laugh, it's very serious. Feeling a sneeze coming on at work, I pushed myself away from my desk on my little wheelie chair, turn sideways, sneezed and pinged a muscle in my neck. It was painful and annoying, stopping me from turning my head to the right without discomfort but I kept on riding and training.

Big mistake. I was protecting the injury by lifting up my right shoulder towards my head causing an imbalance lower down in my back straining the quadrates lumborum muscle. This protective action, coupled with having poor core muscle strength from the surgery, meant I got literally bent out of shape. I pulled the right side of my back up and twisted my pelvis. I'd put myself in this misshapen position for a couple of thousand miles on the bike and had ridden the shape into my back. Just like when you pull a funny face as a kid and the wind changes direction, I was stuck. It made riding the bike for more than 45 minutes painful and despite seeking the advice of a number of physiotherapists I couldn't really correct it. Not a very glamorous sporting injury is it?

Real life was starting to intrude on my world again. Had I been a professional rider, the injury would have been spotted quickly and resolved. But I wasn't a professional; I was an amateur trying to train like a professional with limited time and resources, and a replacement liver.

On top of that my then employers, HSBC, asked me to work in London for 2 years and have a go at turning a job into a career. Something I probably needed to do if I was going to support my family as my family had supported me. This would limit the time and opportunity for training meaning that I was unlikely to be in any shape to go to the next world games in Canada in 2005. Even if I went, at best I could only repeat what I'd achieved in France. It felt like it was probably time to concentrate on work and family for a little while.

Two bits of bad news came through putting my injury and deliberations firmly into perspective. First, I learned Margaret Koppejan, the Dutch cyclist I first met in Budapest had died. I shouldn't have been surprised but it felt like a massive injustice had been done. She was such a marvellous spirit it didn't seem fair her light had been extinguished by some bloody awful disease.

Secondly, I learned that Richard Nordstrum, my Swedish rival was ill and back on dialysis. Our friendly rivalry was over. I was upset and frustrated for him. After a brilliant win in Budapest he had been courageous enough to travel to Japan to support his team carrying an injury he knew would prevent him from riding. Following that, we'd egged each other on for 2 years, training hard to compete in France. I'd won; however, it could just as easily have been the other way around. Reflecting, I decided to train when I could, stay fit and get the injury right so I could ride comfortably again but I made the decision not to go to Canada.

Just in case you were wondering, after a few months of physiotherapy I could swivel my head like a bloody barn owl but my back still hurt like hell when I rode a bike. It was a ridiculous and embarrassing injury but it set me to thinking about how, as an amateur racing cyclist there are lots of things are out trying to upset, injure or kill you. Sneezing obviously isn't top of the list of dangerous things and we'll leave aside Leukaemia and organ failure to make it fair. With that cheery thought in mind, let's have a look at the obvious and perhaps not so obvious dangers out there that confront the unwitting cyclist.

Cars

A plentiful and obvious danger. In my experience, most drivers are sensible and competent but the sheer number of cars on the roads means they present an increasingly higher risk to you as a cyclist.

In rural environments like B roads and lanes, there are certain types of cars that present an enhanced risk. Much like aircraft recognition lessons during WWII, it is important you learn to recognise the engine notes of these vehicles so you can take evasive action before they kill you. It is vital you learn to identify the tinny hum (with slight rattle) of the Rover 400. Often red, beautifully polished with full main dealer service history it will be driven by an old man with brown leather string-backed driving gloves and a flat cap. P registration plates tend to be the most dangerous in my experience.

The low rumbly roar of a large German car will also become familiar to you, any model but huge and usually silver, often automatic and with an unintelligible personalised number plate. An older lady with massive hair and permanent blue-tinged make-up will drive it. This represents a clear and present danger.

Neither of these driver/vehicle combinations will recognise your existence, or that of other road users, and will neither speed up, slow down nor indicate as they approach from behind. If anything is coming the other way limiting the road space they will simply roll you into the tarmac or, if you are lucky, the hedge. They will then carry on at the same speed. If you see or hear either of these vehicles coming, it may be prudent to get off your bike and hide until they are gone as it may be the last thing you ever hear.

Vans can also be lethal. You will learn to recognise what type of van you are dealing with and, if you are really good, what colour it is before you see it. For sure, you will grow to recognise the intermittent whistling noise indicating ladders are attached to the roof. With time and patience you will also be able to analyse the rattling sound to determine how securely they have been affixed. Should you hear music coming from the van *before* you can isolate its engine note, ladder whistle or rattle you must take immediate defensive action. I would suggest riding in the opposite direction as quickly as possible unless completely paralysed by fear.

211

In urban environments, it's more difficult to detect engine noise, rattles and the like so it's safer to work on the assumption that everything is trying to kill you, including all motorised transport, pedestrians and other cyclists. During my time riding in London I found it to be like gladiatorial combat: very exciting in many ways but always a battle of wits and skill that could boil over into a brutal fight at any moment.

I reckon city cyclists sometimes ride through red lights in because it's safer. It's preferable to take your chances slaloming through traffic coming from left and right because you can see it and take evasive action if necessary. The vehicles behind you are out of sight and you can't defend against what you can't hear or see.

Farm vehicles

Most tractors and farm vehicles are equipped with pointy bits of metal and either blades or skewers. These are specifically designed to impale people who come anywhere near them, usually farm workers, but they work well on cyclists too. I assume a law was introduced at some point to make it compulsory for the drivers of these vehicles to be no older than 13 and for them to be in constant communication with the broader farming community by mobile phone; either text or voice, the choice is theirs.

They often have the appearance of road-going communication satellites. If you come into contact with one of these you may be fortunate and get away with simply being covered in cow shit but, once again, evasive action is often the best policy. Hiding in a hedge can be a good choice unless the farm vehicle is engaged in hedge cutting and then you are in big trouble.

Motorcyclists

These guys used to be our friends. Lone two wheeled comrades struggling against a mass of car drivers who were out to kill our collective kind. Now there are millions of them and they too are seemingly trying to finish

212

us off. Most sunny Sunday's a brigade of people dressed like the purple Power Ranger descend onto country roads for a blast around. Well, the straighter roads anyway they don't seem to like corners that much. Cyclists are the least qualified to comment on how others dress as we parade around with shaved legs in skin tight Lycra but it's got to be more palatable than dressing like the Black Knight.

I was always told by my motorcycling friends one of the joys of riding a bike was the freedom, solitude and isolation of being out there on your own, out of contact with everyday life for a little while. Nowadays they tend to roam in packs so a mini bus would seem more practical if they want to travel around together. Maybe I'm missing the point, but one thing I do know is that if a bunch of them are over-taking a car coming towards you, you can be pretty sure they are all coming round it irrespective of where you are. Come back to the light side my friends, please.

Tools

A surprising one perhaps but I know my tool box and its contents are definitely out to maim or kill me. I only have to look at it and the skin comes off my knuckles spontaneously leaving blood dripping from the end of my fingers. If I make it past this point uninjured the jobs that will absolutely guarantee the use of some extremely bad language and the shedding of skin and blood are:-

Removing or installing a cassette/cog cluster (knuckles)
Removing pedals (trapped thumb)
Removing a back wheel (fingers into springy rear mech and chain)
Rounding off any 4 or 5mm hex bolts (Hex wrench into the eye)

The only person more likely to injure himself with tools than me is my brother. Now a qualified cycle mechanic, Ian once cut off the bottom of a kitchen door in situ with a bread knife because the carpet he'd put down was too thick to allow it to open. He also performed home surgery once cutting off a mole on his forehead with a pair of scissors. After a considerable amount of hopping around in pain, it bled for two days before he went to the doctor to get it stitched up.

With this background I suspect it is easy for you to picture my brother trying to drill a seized bolt out of a SPD cleat affixed to the bottom of a mountain bike shoe whilst the shoe span uncontrollably at 1600 rpm clattering his fingers before shooting off into his groin. The 'shoes of death' perhaps.

Relationships

Sad but true, relationships with the opposite sex, or the same sex I suppose, will eventually have a negative impact upon your cycling. You may think this rather mean-spirited of me but let me give you an example. I rode with a talented cyclist during my first few years in the road race league. He was a stylish rider who used a minimum of effort to maximum effect by never wasting a drop of energy. His back was always still and if he needed a little more speed his legs would move faster but he never pushed a big gear or ground his way back up to the group. If I was struggling to keep up it was his wheel I would look for in the bunch. When he moved in front of you he was inch perfect, you never had to speed up or slow down he just dropped in perfectly every single time. To add to this he rode a very stylish classic Colnago bike and was always impeccably turned out in perfectly clean kit and shaved legs. He had what cyclists admiringly call 'form'.

I saw him at the beginning of one season looking like he'd put a little weight on, in fact, he was a little ragged looking all over. He had stubbly legs and the lovely Colnago was showing signs of use and was, shock horror, a little dirty. How very unlike him I thought. As usual, I was struggling in the bunch and looked for his wheel only to find him suffering at the back as well.

Pretty soon he was out on his own and fading into the distance for the metaphorical early bath. I caught up with him after the race and asked how he was only to be told 'great, I met a woman at Christmas'. It began to sink in then, a stylish cyclist. Ruined by lurve. The red wine, DVD's and romantic Sunday walks had taken the place of long wet and windy training rides and the self-inflicted torture of the turbo trainer. Entirely understandable of course but fatal to the condition of a top quality cyclist.

I'm pleased to report I saw him more recently displaying form more like his old self so I suspect he has put all this silliness behind him and is single again. He'll be back staring at the garage door sweating like a pig on freezing Tuesdays in November doing intervals on the rollers. Phew, that's more like it.

We should not ignore the fact there is a general principal that most sports are designed to give couples a much needed break from each other. Done correctly, all sports take a minimum of four hours to either engage in or to watch live. Golf, football, cricket, cycling, anything, take this time when preparation and donning 'a little uniform' as my other half calls it, is added in. Time for travel to the event, watching, playing or doing and then travelling back should also be factored in.

A 4 hour break from your partner is the minimum time needed to reset the relationship watches allowing a fair restart and reducing the likelihood of killing each other. This is why it is never; repeat never, a good idea for your partner to take up the same sport as you. This destructive process is accelerated if the non sporting partner becomes better at the chosen activity than the original participant creating resentment and leading to the rapid failure of a previously successful partnership.

Animals

We all know magpies can be dangerous but there are other animals out there, dead and alive, that can cause inconvenience and danger to the innocent racing cyclist. A

215

road race league colleague of mine, who is the proud owner of a frankly bostin Black Country accent, once saw fit to complain to the organisers that he had been impeded in the sprint. Not an unusual appeal but on this occasion the impediment had not been another rider but, and I quote, "A dead bodger". Now bodgers, or badgers as they a more widely known, do have the misfortune of getting run over with increasingly regularity and are pretty big animals, so I reckon they are totally capable of impeding a sprint. The Commissaire disagreed on this occasion much to the chagrin of my mate.

Dog attacks seem to be less common than they used to be but horses can certainly be dangerous whether or not they are with their riders; they are unpredictable and flighty creatures prone to sudden mood swings leading to them becoming quickly uncontrollable. Unfortunately the horses are little better. A friend of mine suggested when riding on lanes where an encounter with a horse and rider was likely, you should put some sugar lumps in your jersey pocket. That way you'll have something sweet to eat in the ambulance after the bloody thing has kicked your head in.

A well-known local cyclist once told me, while we were waiting at a finish line, the most ridiculous story I have ever heard of a horse interfering with a race. I, of course, had been dropped and decided to hang around to see what the pointy end of a cycle race looked like: something I rarely see. He swears blind he was in a break in a road race once with five other riders when, in front of the bunch, a riderless horse broke out of a field. He told me the leading riders in the bunch tucked in behind the horse as it ran along in front of them taking a draft from it effectively using it to close the gap on the break away riders. He swears this is true and he's an honest sort of chap so I'm inclined to believe him. Hang on a minute. Naaaaaaa.....

Other cyclists

Again sad but true, other cyclists will try to do you in from time to time although I don't think this is ever a deliberate act as it's just too dangerous to contemplate. Dive-bombers, wobblers, weavers, wheel touchers and swervers all fall under the heading of 'chopper cyclists' these days. They lack the genetic makeup necessary for the osmotic absorption of cycling related skills or the understanding their very presence is a danger to others.

Sometimes you can spot these riders and launch an avoidance strategy (see: hiding in a hedge) at other times fate has already zeroed in on you and a rider/tarmac interface is already written in the stars. I would not claim to be a paragon of cycling virtue by any means. I came to the sport late and, like everybody else I make mistakes. Also I would not profess to be the most skilled bunch rider by any means; I know this because I ride with some people who really do know what they are doing. A skill hard won through hours and hours on the track since they were kids but I can usually spot a chopper and, blimey, did I see one at a circuit race I once rode.

Circuit racing tends to be over a shorter distance than a road race, involving numerous laps of a course that is deliberately tight and around a kilometre in length. Town centre evening events are a great example of this style of racing. I was warming up before one of these, just rolling around a notoriously tight purpose built circuit nodding and saying hello to other riders who I recognised. Then I beheld a truly terrifying sight on the other side of the track. I was confronted by Big Bird who had entered the race aboard an enormous bright pink bike complete with white tyres that I guess must have last seen the light of day in 1984.

Big Bird was wearing something akin to a German football shirt of similar 80's vintage and had finished off his ensemble with a rainbow striped towelling sweatband around his head. He must have been at least 6'6 tall. He was waving, manically, at me and for that matter everybody else. He was warming up by launching short violent sprint efforts at

217

tangents to what most riders would consider a racing line. It was a disaster waiting to happen and we didn't have to wait too long.

One particularly nasty corner on the circuit, a 'P' or hairgrip shaped bend of 180 degrees is very tight and fast. If you go in too quickly or try to pedal through it, you will either be ejected from the bike to be diced by the tennis court 'chicken wire' or you will slingshot around it, accelerate to light speed and make time go backwards. Probably. There is only one racing line through the corner and there is always a fight to get into a position to avoid death by dicing or an inconvenient time displacement incident on the fast straight that leads into it.

I had decided the safest place to be was a long way in front of Big Bird when I heard the unmistakable sound of the bike crash over my right shoulder. This one went on for longer than it should and it sounded like a satellite hitting a scrap yard. Whistles were blowing, people were running, the race was neutralised. I came upon a sight of complete carnage as I rolled towards the scene of the crash on the next lap. I wasn't involved in trench warfare in the Great War but I can imagine how awful the harrowing sights and sounds of sprawled bodies tangled amongst machines must have been. It was only the mustard gas that was missing.

Big Bird had escaped unscathed and made a quick exit to his car never to be seen again. He left ten or more riders spread all over the track. Many were missing a full complement of skin and thinking about how they were going to fund the crash replacement equipment.

It did strike me that perhaps Big Bird was actually an older more experienced rider who had taken the corner particularly quickly during a warm up and had travelled back in time to 1984 before he'd developed any riding skills. On sober reflection I now feel this is unlikely.

The Commissaire later told me a number of formal complaints had been received about Big Bird's riding. One of them specifically concerning his choice of colour scheme. Humour it would seem is alive and well in circuit racing.

Coaching and how to survive it

My 2 years in London were up. After a substantial amount of physiotherapy, core muscle exercises (have you *ever* done anything more boring than that?), free-weights work in the gym and battering around the Isle of Dogs on a mountain bike, it was time to come home. Again.

My last trip back from a spell in London had been rather dramatic and I, being in no rush to repeat the experience, sidestepped the whole liver failure thing this time and returned to Shropshire alive and well in 2006.

If Elvis had my pelvis he'd still be at home deep-frying peanut butter and jelly sandwiches and wouldn't be upsetting Middle America by gyrating anything. He certainly wouldn't be riding a racing bike either. Whilst things were a little better it was still too painful to spend more than an hour on a racing bike without being uncomfortably uncomfortable, thangyouverymush....

At one point I considered selling my time trial bike as I didn't think I could get into the aero position needed to ride it. Nevertheless I wanted to see my old club mates so I rode a few 10 mile time trials on the Colnago to see if there was anything in the tank and if my back would stand it. Including a warm-up, the whole riding process was over and done within three quarters of an hour and I could live with the discomfort for that amount of time.

It was great to be back on the bike. After a few weeks I tried the time trial bike and was pleasantly surprised to find that a short time trial was no more uncomfortable than the same thing accomplished on the more upright road machine. Longer distances were still out of the question, I just couldn't hold the aero position long enough, but it did look like the core exercises and physiotherapy were slowly paying off.

Things had been stable on the liver front with blood results coming back normal from my 6 monthly visits. My donor family and I had continued to build our remarkable relationship via written and occasional email correspondence. I'd kept them up to date with my progress and, more importantly, the development of the kids and my family, swapping pictures of important events.

The prospect of us meeting had been mooted in the past but it felt like the timing was never right. It was something we both wanted to do but mutually understood the delicacy and complexity of such an event happening. Even writing a brief note or a Christmas card required careful thought as the normal letter writing rules don't apply. How do you start and finish them for example? 'Dear and Yours sincerely' doesn't really cut it.

My physical condition continued to improve and was sufficient to win the 2006 edition of the British Transplant Games in Bath. This, in theory at least, meant I could have a shot at the next World Transplant Games to be held in Bangkok in 2007. I was training on a diet of short times trials, club events and opens, but nothing over 25 miles. I was under no illusion I didn't have great form or any road racing under my belt for three years.

2007 continued in a similar vein but I managed a decent winter. I was now able to ride for a couple of hours as long as I stretched my back out meaning some level of fitness returned – I was a least building up some base miles. I reckoned I'd got enough form to go to Bangkok and not completely embarrass myself so off I went.

If you've ever been to Bangkok you'll know actually riding a bike there is impossible. The traffic is dense and as far as I could work out, used both sides of the road depending on where the gaps were. We ended up getting a taxi to a park to train for a couple of hours. The heat coupled with the pollution made riding during the day uncomfortable. We were all relived to discover we would be racing at night under floodlights on a course used for the Tour of Siam.

With the exception of a ramp over the start and finish line, the course was a pan flat broad piece of dual carriageway thankfully closed to traffic for the event and would be used for both the road race and the time trial.

After going to inspect the course, an hour's trip by coach, we had crawled back into the city a few hours later with our driver deciding to use his local knowledge and use a bridge on which coaches were not allowed. We were moving so slowly I can't imagine how he thought he would get away with it and, sure enough, a few minutes later we were pulled over by the police. The driver took the action he deemed most appropriate in those circumstances and ran off. He was discovered by our guide hiding and feigning sickness at the back of a shop an hour later. The crowd on the bus were starting to draw straws to decide who would drive the coach back to the hotel. Thankfully, with the police now gone, he was persuaded to return to the driver's seat and complete the journey.

The lack of a driving licence was his primary motivation for running away although these seemed to be considered an optional extra by most of the city's residents. We saw a family of five travelling at some speed perched precariously on a motorbike at one point. They considered flip-flops and a robust attitude to other road users as adequate safety equipment.

A day later the world's transplant cyclists saw hundreds of thousands of pounds worth of racing bikes lashed into the back of a very old pickup truck with some old rope and disappear off into the Bangkok night. I don't think many of us expected to ever see them again.

Whilst helping to hand the bikes up onto the death trap truck it became obvious my Colnago was old technology and weighed considerably more than the carbon framed machines of my competitors. I remember thinking if my back continued to hold up and maybe even improve a little, it would be time for a new bike. I'd got all the formulas I needed anyway.

Just like in the early days, age categorisation was on my side and as I'd just turned 40 (in my circumstances every birthday is a cause for celebration, even that one). I raced in the 40 – 50s. For some reason, the use of aero equipment had been banned for this edition of the games meaning a few riders were upset as they had brought either time trial specific bikes or aero bars. It was a definite rule change that had been announced some time before the games so there was little to complain about and all the riders would be on an equal footing.

The time trial was first and I recorded a time of 7 minutes and 44 seconds. A long way from my PB but with the limited amount of training, not a bad result. The closest competitor in my age group came in at 8 minutes and 15 seconds meaning a comfortable win. Another British rider in the 18 – 30 category had set the fastest time of the evening at 7 minutes and 36 seconds.

The road race was held the day after. No hills and a straight course, barring a 180 degree corner at each end of the drag strip, meant it was a matter of speed rather than tactics. A break formed and I thought we had got rid of the other riders in my age category. The younger riders started playing about as we go close to the finish line, slowing down and angling for position for the sprint. This allowed some of the riders I was trying to distance to get back in contact with us meaning a big bunch sprint was inevitable.

I led out my younger team mate putting him in a good position for the final dash and he rewarded the effort with an excellent second place to add to his time trial win. I went over the line shortly after him winning my age category. The sprint had been closer than I might have liked and a bit hairy because of the number of riders. Nevertheless, an excellent result for both me and the GB team.

It was not lost on me that many younger riders had given me a proper kicking in the time trial and had finished some distance in front of me in the road race. I'd used my tactical experience to hang on to the shirttails of some much quicker riders and maybe get a better finish than I deserved on strength alone. Winning was nice but it felt a long way short of my victories in France in 2003. Not hollow but a little concave for sure.

After returning home from Bangkok I was delighted to discover my pelvis problem had been cured completely. Cured by moving from my pelvis to my hip but at least the variety of where the pain occurred made a nice change. With more core exercises (oh my God it's dull) I managed to get into a shape where I could time trial on an aero bike for an hour and potentially road race.

I was still unsure what I wanted to do with my riding. I didn't hold out any great hope of road racing again – expecting the guys to wait while I stretched my back out was frankly unrealistic. I figured I'd stick to doing some time trials with the club, maybe I'd even do a couple of 'opens' – if only for the tea and cake.

My son Charlie had taken up rugby I was spending more time helping his team out. I completed the basic rugby coaching badge allowing me to help out in a formal capacity. I loved the coaching bit and working with the kids was great. You still got to be involved in sport with a great bunch of guys but you didn't have to get knocked over and stomped on by 20 stone forwards. Bonus.

It was with some disappointment that Charlie's interest in rugby waned after a while although, without too much encouragement from me, he had started to ride a mountain bike. It took me longer than it should have done to work out how I could combine my newly discovered interest in coaching and my interest in cycling. Hmmm, tricky. Coaching and cycling eh? Cycling and coaching. How would that work? Hang on a minute. Cycling coaching. Yes, a simple recombination of two words took me some months. It finally dawned on me that it was entirely possible I could continue riding myself and do my cycling coaching qualifications at the same time. I might even learn something useful.

I needed to establish my understanding of the coaching process and, if I was to do it properly, I would need to develop an understanding of the branches of cycle sport I'd dismissed as being stupid simply because I didn't know what they were. Like track/BMX/surfing or whatever it was.

223

Anyway, Charlie had expressed an interest in riding more seriously so if it was dangerous or complicated I could get him to do it first and explain it to me as he recovered in the fracture clinic.

I was pretty sure I knew what a time trial was and I'd cut my teeth on road racing but the track was a complete mystery. I got down to my local outdoor track in Wolverhampton and paid a few visits to the velodrome in Manchester for some more half arsed 'research'.
This revealed some interesting stuff and I hope you will find it useful in case you need to blag answers generally or to address the critical 'why doesn't Sir Chris Hoy do the Tour de France' question.

Before you start to absorb any information about the complexities of other types of bike racing it's probably sensible for you to get a feel for your current level of knowledge and attitude to cycling in Britain so, yes you've guessed it, it's exam time again.

Question 5

A friend advises you it's a well-known fact no matter what his other accomplishments may be, any tennis player who has not won Wimbledon is rubbish. Similarly, any professional cyclist who hasn't won the Tour de France is crap. Unless they have won it more than once in which case they're a cheat. Using this inalienable truth as a basis, indicate which of the following statements most accurately reflects your current feeling about cycling in Britain.

1. There has never been a British winner of the Tour de France ergo all the riders in this country are crap Anyway, I've already told you cyclists should be limited to those wooden track things and kept away from my bloody car when I'm trying to drive to places. I pay road tax you know.

224

2. Football's loads better than cycling. It must be, look at how much they get paid and the fantastic performances of the national team in international competitions like the World Cup. Their work ethic and the manner in which they represent our country both on and off the pitch can only be admired.

3. Our British Cyclists are a plucky bunch. Look at that longhaired lad that made his own guitar from a fireplace then won the Tour de France on a bike made out of a washing machine. From Scotland. Later, he went on to represent Great Britain in the ski jumping competition in the Olympics. Big glasses. You remember him don't you?

4. We've had some great British cyclists in the past, multiple world record holders and World Champions in all cycling disciplines and Gold medallists in the Olympic Games. What's more, a new generation of Brits are coming through and making a really big mark on the continental cycling scene winning stages of all the Grand Tours. It's only a matter of time before we produce a Tour de France winner even though the Tour is the cycling equivalent of the Grand National horse race.

5. All cyclists, past, present and future are either rubbish or cheats unless they are Eddy Mercyx.

If 1, 2, 3 or 5 correctly reflect your attitude we may have a little work to do, but stick with me and we'll get there. If 4 rings a bell with you then you share my puppy like optimism about the future of cycling in this country.

If you're a '4' you almost certainly don't need my roughest of guides to other types of cycling following the 'in-depth' research carried out for my coaching qualifications.

However, a blagger's guide was promised and a blagger's guide is what you shall have.

Track

Track racing very broadly splits down into endurance events of over 4000 metres and sprint events which can be less than one lap of a 250 metre velodrome. Endurance in the track world is very different from endurance on the road when single races tend to be measured in multiples of metres rather than multiples of miles.

Track riders use bikes with no brakes and a single fixed gear. Racing takes place on either a banked indoor arena with a polished timber floor with splinters or on an outdoor track surfaced in sandpaper and covered with discarded safety pins, nails and broken glass. All of this makes it extra fun for the baying crowd.

A fixed gear bike means you can't stop pedalling even if you want to when the bike is moving at any kind of appreciable speed. You can try, as I did, but you will need some help moving your hip and knee joints from shoulder level back to where they should be. Good quality tracks have a stretching rack specifically designed to help with this process.

It's hard to blag things like individual or team pursuits as there is a limited number of riders on the track and there is always a certain amount of space between them. With races like the points, 'the Devil' or scratch there are so many riders on the track you are safe making claims about the winning prospects of any of the riders.

At amateur races some of the riders and spectators may not have a truly accurate idea of what is going on. More worryingly the judges and Commissaires may not have the complete picture either. The victory is often awarded to the rider who might make the greatest fuss if not given the win or who had buttered up the organisers with tea and cake. Allegedly.

A scratch race is simply where all the riders start together and the first guy over the line after a fixed number of laps, is the winner. Seems pretty simple but it can get complicated where as often happens riders get lapped by individuals or a group of riders. Further complexity is added when lapped riders unlap themselves making it pretty difficult to keep a handle of what's going on. It's a good place to start unravelling what track racing is about. At amateur events, be wary of experienced riders who throw in a victory celebration as the race comes to a close. It might be genuine, it might not be but sometimes it helps the judges out.

A points race is run in a similar format to the scratch but points are awarded after a set number of laps for being first over the line, at the end of the race and for lapping the field. To be a successful points racer you need to be good at sprinting, endurance riding and mental arithmetic.

One of my favourite races to watch either at an amateur or professional level is called a Devil, short for Devil take the Hindmost. This event is very easily explained but tactically and physically demanding to ride. The simple bit is all the riders start together and every time the bunch goes over the start and finish line, the rear most rider must drop out of the race. This process continues until an agreed number of riders are left who sprint out for final lap. Riders are not allowed to 'undertake' meaning if you wish to move up in the bunch you have to work your way through the other riders or go 'over the top' which expends a lot of effort.

Positioning in the bunch is everything and it's entirely possible the physically strongest rider in the bunch will go out early on due to a lack of group riding skills or tactical awareness. Usually, the winner of last week's race will be first out of this weeks because drop your guard for a minute and the Devil's gonna get ya.

One of the most exciting races to watch on the track is the Madison, where riders operate in pairs. They take it in turns to race and score points by throwing each other below the middle blue line on the track and alternately riding above it circling and waiting to be thrown back in. Actually, what

227

looks like a throw from the guy in front is really a pull from the guy behind making the whole thing safe and controlled. Safe and controlled? Yeah, right. It's one of the scariest things I've ever been involved in but it does make a fantastic spectacle. Nobody knows what the hell is going on in a Madison. To blag it, just point randomly with a pained expression on your face every now and again and people will think you know what you are talking about. Advanced level blaggers nod knowingly when the victorious pair is announced.

Both individual and team pursuit events are relatively straight forward. This involves either a single rider or a team of three or four riding together starting on each side of the track and, well, pursuing each other. This continues until a 'catch' is achieved or requisite distance is covered and the winner is decided on time. With younger riders, coaches often direct them to the Madison and team pursuit disciplines as soon as they become competent to ride the track. If riders can master these events properly then any other racing on the track is entirely with their grasp.

An omnium is the decathlon of track racing and consists of a number of events drawn from both sprint and endurance events with points being awarded in reverse order i.e. getting one point for a win, two points for a second place etc with the rider with the fewest point winning overall. This helps confuse people who don't know anything track racing making it easier for you, armed with this knowledge, to blag.

Sprint races are usually over so quickly you can get away with random shouts and grunts from the stands. If you are watching a motor paced race such as the Keirin you are allowed to do 'the motorbike will win this one' joke once and only once.

Sprints can happen in an individual and team format and can be either timed or be won by the first rider over the line. There is a lot of bumping, barging and jockeying in sprint races as riders try to get into the best position possible to sprint for the line. Commonly this is just behind your fellow competitor. All the tracking standing and painfully slow riding is part of this tactical positioning but it also builds up the tension, making the event very watchable. Generally speaking, if you are brave enough to ride a track race and survive the first attempt, you should hold your bike above your head and seek the approval of the crowd, gladiator style.

Cyclocross

This is a strange hybrid that pre-dates mountain bike racing. Road cyclists who wanted a fast paced event to use as training in the winter to support their summer racing developed it. In theory at least, this kept their fitness up in the grim dark months.

Commonly races last for an hour although they seem to go on for longer than that to any spectators because it's so cold. They are run on an undulating circuit containing obstacles like planks, ladders and stairs and may involve getting off the bike and running in parts. The courses are made up of a mix of on road and off road sections just like going out for a mountain bike ride. Riders still use adapted road bikes with mildly up-rated brakes and thin knobbly tyres presumably because they think the mountain bike, a machine specifically designed for such terrain, has not yet been invented.

Cyclocross is the work of the Devil and should be banned. Anybody caught training for a cyclocross race should be punished by being made to ride with breakfast cereal in their bib shorts. Cyclocross racing *is* training and training for training is plainly daft. Further, any bike race involving running is not a bike race, it's a running race you are allowed to ride a bike in and that, like a triathlon, doesn't count. Finally, road racers need to get their rest in the winter otherwise, by the time May comes around they will be hollowed out shells of their former selves, unable to perform at a meaningful level.

Cycle speedway

See above. Actually that's unfair, nothing is as pervy or as unnatural as cyclocross. Speedway is usually run on shale covered outdoor circuits (although it can be done inside in sports halls or warehouses). Upright single speed bikes with a free hub are used so riders can stop pedalling around corners long enough to push each other off. At least that's what it looks like to me. Riders normally have a leg out like a 'proper' speedway racing that was on after the wrestling on World of Sport with Dickie Davies. Whilst I'm sure there is a good reason for this I'm damned if I know what it is. Similarly, races are usually between four riders at a time and are run in heats with different starting positions on the grid.

Contact between riders is expected, no, demanded actually, and it's all very exciting and great fun to witness. The skill level, bike handling and explosive fitness displayed in cycle speedway is impressive and translates well to track racing.

There is something slightly underground about this rare event and after watching one of these races expect to feel a bit 'dirty'. And not in a good way. Watching one, it feels like you have stumbled across a bare knuckle boxing match or a dog fight and, try as you might, you are unable to tear your eyes away from it. Morbid curiosity I guess.

Mountain bike racing

Mountain biking and mountain bike racing in particular started in the 1970's in California when a group of guys modified single speed 'cruiser' type bikes and raced them down hill. They developed a surfing style culture and a language and dress style that went along with it. Things have come a long way in a short time and downhill mountain bike racing has become a recognised international cycling event complete with rainbow world champion's jerseys on offer for the top riders.

Bikes now have as much as 10 inches of suspension travel at the front and back. They are effectively small motor cross machines with the engine replaced by highly trained pilots. These guys are now unlikely to make a horn sign with their hands and say 'Whooa, that was totally awesome dude' and more likely to say 'pass me my road bike I need to do 4 hours at level 2' or something similar. The courses are now so demanding a significant level of physical conditioning and fitness is required leaving less time to drive your daddy's T Bird to the Drive - Thru or anywhere else for that matter.

Downhill races are organised on a time trial format with riders going off individually and racing over a set course against the clock. This happens at very high speeds and the similarities with a normal club time trial held on the road end here. Downhill courses are lined with fanatical knowledgeable supporters shouting and ring cowbells. Club time trial courses are usually 'lined' with a man and his dog. There are some variations on the theme with things like '4 cross' where riders set off together. The rider with the most blood left in his body at the end being declared the winner.

Mountain bike racing also takes place in a cross−country format over circuits containing mixed terrain, some of it of a technical nature, with climbs, descents and narrow paths. The bikes used are super light and have increasing similarities with road bikes with a little suspension thrown in for good measure.

I have suggested a few times that cross-country mountain bike racing and cyclo cross are merged. A new set of rules and regulations could be developed together with common formats and courses. This would make it easier for both to be banned at the same time.

I am disappointed to say my proposal has so far gained little traction. It has been mentioned, probably fairly, that this simply shows my own prejudices and lack of understanding of cycling generally.

BMX

You may think BMX's are those bikes hoodies ride around on in groups, circling like sharks before they mug you. And you're right, they are, but they're also machines on which a hugely exciting ferocious format of racing takes place. Whilst entirely accessible to any would be mugger with a crash helmet, riders with skill, strength and talent take part in what is now a full on Olympic sport.

The power generated by the top riders over 45 seconds of racing is the highest recorded in any form of bike racing anywhere. Such is the physical conditioning needed to be successful in BMX racing that a direct correlation to sprint racing in the velodrome exists. Excited track coaches now try to tempt riders away from their sideways on baseball caps into Lycra skinsuits.

BMX formats are either time trials or bunch start events, often using a gate to set the riders off. The mass start races are the most exciting to watch.

Sportives

Sportives or sportifs are a relatively recent genre of cycling in the UK but something that has been going on for some time on the continent, particularly Italy and France. They are mass participation leisure rides, akin perhaps to a reliability trial but more formalised. The larger, better established, sportives attract thousands of riders who expect and receive many of the trappings of a stage race. Numbers, a starting grid, feed stations, support vehicles and the like are all part of the package. There is usually a choice of course with varying degrees of difficulty and riders are often timed. There are prizes and mementos, medals and the like for those who successfully complete the challenge,

The best known sportive is probably the Etape du Tour. A stage of the Tour de France is opened to amateur riders the day before the race proper goes past. Despite the massive size of the event, it is usually oversubscribed.

Sportives upset most people who don't ride in them. But, entertainingly there are three categories of people who really dislike them. They deny it of course, but they do. Firstly Audax UK, yes, yet another national cycling body, this time set up to govern people who like to ride really long distances on a bike. They claim they've been organising these things since 1967 and don't need anybody telling them how to do it thanks very much. They certainly don't want a bloody T shirt at the end either.

Secondly, many of the old guard who race on the road don't like them. Or more particularly they have a problem with the people who ride them. Sportives are not races. You tend to get perhaps slightly older riders, some of them on very expensive equipment who like to take part. It's part of the recent rise of the MAMIL (middle aged men in Lycra) where expensive racing bikes have taken over from Harley Davidson's and Lithuanian girlfriends for the man of a certain age. Of course, this allows the hardened roadmen to claim they can go faster on their 1984 Reynolds bikes than those fancy buggers on carbon framed carbon wheeled, carbon saddled machines. They're probably right but there're missing the point.

One of the joys of cycling is you can ride the same bikes as they use in the Tour de France if you've got a few thousand quid to spare. If you're a Formula 1 fan you've got next to no chance of ever driving one of those cars.

Finally, some riders understandably object to paying twenty or thirty quid to ride a sportive. Many who have grown up with reliability trials at two quid including a cup of tea are either priced out or don't want to pay that much. Fair enough.

As part of what I laughingly call 'research' I both rode and organised one of these. I enjoyed the organisation more than the ride. It was the satisfaction of seeing newer riders get a real buzz out of completing what was a tough challenge for them. Okay, a road racer will knock off a fifty mile training ride in a just over a couple of hours, but to a guy who has just bought a bike to get fit, the first ride of this length is going to sting a bit.

After my 'comprehensive' research I realised, as you will have done, that cycling in all its formats is a massive subject. Detailed insider knowledge of all disciplines is all but impossible and we've not even touched on unicycle mountain biking, recumbents, tandems and the like.

Consequently, my image of being issued with a 'Bullet Baxter' tight ass tracksuit and a whistle and to be let loose on elite cyclists as soon as I'd been enrolled on my first British Cycling coaching course was sadly unrealistic. It appeared, after a very intense weekend with some other trainee coaches, that I would be doing over 100 hours of study, tests and exams. In addition I would be recording practical experience and submitting it for analysis and interrogation, attending further courses and being interviewed by an assessor. On top of this I would need a First Aid qualification and an enhanced Criminal Records Bureau check. After this I would be allowed to coach a maximum of 15 kids, on a school playground, accompanied by another qualified coach.

It was a tad more restrictive than I thought and was very definitely starting at the beginning. You cannot, it has to be said, fault the thoroughness of British Cycling's coaching and education programme.

A local primary school lent me some of their children to experiment on and I began on the long journey to becoming a qualified cycling coach, some home truths home truthed themselves within a few minutes of my first session, thus.

As part of the health and safety rigmarole you are required to ask your trainees if they have any impediment, illness or injury that would prevent them from participating. Be careful how you ask this. After one kid told me he'd got over a cold a couple of weeks ago I began to get a full download of everybody's medical history covering the last couple of years – some of it pretty graphic. You don't need to put yourself through this, trust me, you really don't.

Unless you are a qualified mechanic you are advised not to adjust the kid's bikes even if there is clearly something wrong with them. Having said that, it's impossible not to scan across the line of expectant riders and their machines. During one session I could sense something was amiss with one of the bikes but couldn't immediately see what it was. It soon became evident a kid on a new bike had his forks on backwards. This made handling a tad tricky. I shouldn't have been surprised; a big non-specialist retailer had installed them that way.

I discovered during my rugby coaching I am just able to run faster than a 9-year-old kid. Should one decide following a ball into a river or a road is a good idea I can, at a pinch, prevent disaster by chasing and catching him.

I cannot run faster than a 9-year-old kid on a bike, I know this because I tried it once and it nearly killed me. Should a group of 15 kids decide to use their recently gained tactical knowledge of bike racing and ride away from you at speed in 15 different directions you are well and truly screwed. Personally, I think laughing while they did it was unnecessary and cruel.

Kids learn at an exponential rate and their lack of fear, natural balance and willingness to try something new is truly inspiring. After a few weeks of handling and tactical practice on a netball court with a few cones and some simple games, they will be competent cyclists.

I saw two youngsters lock their handlebars together during one exercise and whilst still balancing they simply stopped, looked at each other and agreed which one should move backwards slightly to untangle them. I've seen adult racers touch hands in a race and panic causing a crash. To see kids handle themselves in such a calm manner was fantastic.

After my initial disappointment at the limitations of the basic cycling coaching qualifications I got great satisfaction from spending some time with a lovely bunch of kids and seeing them progress. I began to realise what well-meaning nonsense all this talk of 'giving something back to the sport' really is. Coaching is a privilege. It comes with responsibility and a level of personal risk so it has to be done properly, for the right reasons and with careful thought. All this is worth it because of the buzz you get from seeing people progress towards their full potential, whatever that might be.

It dawned on me with the 2009 World Transplant Games coming up in Australia there was a team of people who might need some coaching support. I had learned over a number of years, like the general population, transplant cyclists come in all shapes, sizes and ages. They have to recognise and overcome the same physiological and psychological challenges as any other rider if they want to be successful but the type of transplant and the balance of drugs has to be factored in too.

It seemed with my background as a transplant recipient, a cyclist and a coach it really was time to give a little back, if they'd let me.

The wizards of Aus

A small team of five GB transplant cyclist went to the Gold Coast in Australia in 2009 and came back with five medals, one gold, three silver and one bronze. In some ways it was back to the old days. Three riders were chosen for their cycling ability and performances in previous British and World games and two others who were riding as a bit of a side line. They had been selected for their ability in other sports but decided to ride and very welcome additions they were to the under strength team.

One of the principle barriers to transplant athletes attending the World Games is funding or, more to the point, the lack of it. It's an expensive business and it's hard to go back to the same of sponsors and ask for money when there are so many other worthy causes. Add to that the logistical issues of transporting a bike to Australia, training injuries and illness and we had a compact and bijou unit rather than a sprawling country pile of a team.

By this time the Colnago had been replaced by a more functional and well equipped carbon Giant TCR. A weapon far more appropriate for racing than the more leisurely Italian bike, beautiful though it was. The Giant would also take clip on aero bars allowing it to double up as a makeshift time trial bike: less than ideal perhaps but taking two bikes to Australia was logistically impossible.

You may recall in 1994 I attended a celebration of 1000 liver transplants carried out at the Queen Elizabeth Hospital in Birmingham. In June 2008 I attended a similar occasion at Edgbaston Cricket Ground following the 3000th. There weren't 3000 of us there: a lot had not made it that far, including my friend Eddie Reynolds, and some had had two or more transplants. The sun shone, Dave Mutimer was there, as was my Dad, Anne, Charlie and Grace and Helen. It was a wonderful day but too emotional really.

On a couple of occasions I did the bravado bit, hugged old friends and made inane jokes whilst choking back tears. Then I'd pop round the corner of the building and cry for a minute until I could get myself back together. It brings back memories of wonderful, strong, people who simply aren't around anymore. It doesn't seem like there's a lot of justice sometimes.

My physical condition had been such that I'd had a good 2008 competing in local time trials. The winter of 2008/9 had started well: so well that I thought my unElvis like pelvis would put up with a summer of racing in the league if I treated it kindly and kept up the Zen like poses I struck during my appallingly dull core exercise routines. Ping. Hoooommm....

Christmas came and went and the standard winter cold bug kicked in. It turned out to be flu and a rather debilitating strain of it too. This was followed by something both voluntary and fully paid up members of immunosuppressed community alike absolutely dread. Pneumonia.

This diagnosis led to a less rapid trip, this time by taxi rather than an ambulance escorted by the police, to the Princess Royal Hospital in Telford where I was admitted to the medical investigation unit (MIU). This is a grand title for a purgatory-like holding area where sick people get to mingle and guess each other's illnesses before an over worked houseman comes and has a go too.

When you take the same kind of drugs as me it does open you up to infections from all kinds of bugs and funky infections that other people are far less likely to get. I was whacked up with a broad spectrum of IV antibiotics that even the doctors were quite excited about administering. I was shown to my bed and was happy to get in it. Along with the antibiotics came an oxygen mask I was also grateful for.

Walking was becoming more difficult, not because of a lack of muscle strength such as I had following the transplant but because I couldn't get enough air into my lungs. Walking twenty metres from my bed to the toilet took some doing: I even needed to plan in a rest break in for half way. For a cyclist used to gulping down as much oxygen rich air as possible it was pretty scary. Just like old times.

I mentioned previously who you should allow, in priority order, to have a go at getting blood out of you. Even if you are unfortunate enough to get Dr Hamfist from the Blacksmith's school of Medicine and Iron-working digging at your arm he will, with time and patience on your part, manage to get some de-oxygenated blood out of you. He may have to mop it up from the floor as you feint away through blood loss but he'll get there in the end. Getting venial blood is relatively straight forward as your veins are pretty big and close to the surface. Getting a sample of oxygenated blood from an artery is a rather more complex task as they are deeper and tend to, well, spurt a bit when you get access to them.

In people suffering breathing difficulties a sample of arterial blood is often needed to see how much oxygen your body is absorbing. If it drops below are certain level you are in some pretty serious trouble. Possibly, using medical terminology, dead. In this case, death would have been entirely unacceptable outcome as I now had kids to look after.

You know that little point on the inside of the wrist where you take your pulse? That's the radial artery and that's where they go to get a small sample of oxygenated blood. The dashing Dr Hamfist arrived and had a good dig around in search of my radial artery, sliding the needle in using my wrist bones as a guide. He had the delicate touch of man who had shoed many Shirehorses as part of his rigorous training.

After taking the sample off for testing a number of people came to my bedside to witness for themselves the miracle of a man who could survive with so little oxygen in his arterial blood. Yes, he'd missed, got some venal blood by mistake and fancied another go.

Now, it had been a long time since I'd been admitted to the Queen Elizabeth Hospital. A remarkably long time bearing in mind my chequered medical history. This was only the second time I'd been admitted to hospital so I was a little rusty. I wheezed a few suggestions and confirmed that, yes, I very much wanted to 'abandon the test' until they found a doctor who could do this with a reasonable chance of leaving me with a working arm.

They were on the cusp of transferring me to intensive care when the antibiotics really started to kick in and my breathing eased significantly. I had the standard bug that caused pneumonia and not any of the more exotic pathogens that could have been far more problematic to treat.

As I recovered, and before my transfer to a general ward, I began to notice my fellow MIU inmates. The guy opposite me was advancing in years and suffering from something similar to me. At visiting times his extended family came to see him en masse. It incorporated all ages from babes in arms to pensioners and included a healthy dose of kids, I guess, between the ages of eight and fifteen. It must have been a boring couple of hours for the older kids but they did find entertainment in playing with my colleague's power adjusted bed.

Designed for the safety of nurses when they needed to move patients, these had moveable head, back and leg rests all of which could be moved simultaneously via a remote control device. He had been in various shapes: knees up, legs up, knees and legs up together, back up, back down and bent double before he remarked 'it's like bloody Alton Towers in here'. There is humour to be found in hospitals.

My recovery was rapid and I was out of hospital in few days. I remember thinking it was not an ideal way to start a cycling season that involved a world games. Once again, I completely missed the point. I was lucky to be alive and should maybe have had a bit of chat with myself about my priorities.

I had expected the first post pneumonia bike ride to be pretty ropey although it wasn't that bad. I'd lost a chunk of fitness but, although I wouldn't recommend it as means of weight loss, I was leaner than normal through a week of not eating very much. I was puffing and blowing a bit when the

Sunday club run from Wolverhampton went past me in the Corvedale valley wishing me a cheery new year but I was rolling along at a reasonable rate.

I was fit enough to have a gentle stab at my club's reliability trial in February although this time I was accompanied by my brother. Ian approached his first reliability trial with a degree of nervousness. He had become a competent mountain bike rider and was strong on the road, commuting to work on a regular basis and enjoying road rides with me and other cycling friends local to him. He had not raced nor did he have any intention of doing so. He was concerned about whether he could hold the pace of a big group of riders who were making the conversion from winter training to race pace.

Ian told me he'd developed a touch of exercise induced asthma and told me he now carried a 'loud hailer' with him (now hear this, now hear this …) although I couldn't conceive why. The reliability ride started on a crisp bright winter morning and we settled in to a well sheltered mid pack position only for Ian to realise he had not used his inhaler. His breathing appeared to be fine and he wasn't having a problem keep up with the speed of the bunch. Just in case, he thought it would be a good idea to get some precautionary Ventolin in him. He started rummaging around in his jersey pocket.

For the competent and skilled rider, taking food or small items from the voluminous rear pockets in a cycling jersey is a simple task practiced routinely. For Ian, who I think we have established is neither of these things, it was all a bit much. Whilst he was fumbling for his breathing apparatus various tools, hex wrenches, tyre levers, spare tubes, chain splitters and a mini pump came out. In fact, pretty much everything came out apart from the inhaler. Metallic objects were pinging off the road surface and around other rider's wheels and bikes. It sounded like an ambush. Bits of shrapnel were flying and riders were taking it in turns to run over the mini pump, chain splitter and tyre levers, flicking them up in the air and spinning them past people's heads as we took cover. Ian was dropping further back in the group as riders went around him giving him and his home made cluster bomb as much room as possible. He wheezed his apologies as the previously dormant asthma attack struck – I suspect mainly due to the panic he had created. He stopped to get his breath back and have a couple of puffs of the inhaler without killing anyone.

His breathing restored, we set off again with me pulling him along. We managed to get back to the group of riders in front of us as we approached what is known locally as the Muller Island. It is adjacent to a yoghurt factory.

80 plus riders took the main road at the island heading towards the intended destination of South Cheshire that day. One rider took the long tarmaced driveway to the yoghurt factory.

Although he disappeared from view every now and again behind parked lorries and trailers I could see him, riding at some pace on his own behind the 12 foot high chicken wire fence. Later he mentioned the startled looks of the bemused yoghurt workers marvelling at a lone cyclist flying through their yard at upwards of 25mph in frantic pursuit of a bunch, casting worried glances over his shoulder.

I suspected his detour had not, in fact, been either an impromptu inspection of the yoghurt facility or a clever tactic to break free from the group and solo to some kind of pro-biotic victory as he claimed. Nevertheless, it was quite impressive to see him emerge at the next roundabout at the same time as the group complete with an 'I'd rather not talk about this now' look on his face.

The ambush he'd launched on the bunch and the dairy de-tour had been too much for the man and we rode the rest of the reliability alone. I could hear him gently wheezing behind me, praying he didn't need any tools or get a puncture.

It was a marvellous day out on the bike, unforgettable and funny for all the right reasons and one that makes Ian a wonderful riding partner.

My fitness returned quickly on a diet of more training rides and early season hilly time trials. After a couple of weeks, it was like it never happened.

I'd been on numerous warm weather training camps before my back injury – principally to mainland Spain to get in some much needed miles in the early part of the year. I always looked forward to these even though I'd gone on commercially organised camps without my clubmates. After a long dark cold wet British winter the prospect of feeling some warm sun on your back whilst riding the bike was irresistible

I wasn't sure if my back would hold up to 4 and 5 hour rides. The maximum I was managing before it became unbearable, was 2 hours. It was with some trepidation I decided to go to Majorca with my club in the March of 2009 – I was just praying my back wouldn't let me down.

I have already mentioned the replacement of the Colnago with a more utilitarian Giant TCR and it arrived the day before I was due to fly. It came straight out of the shop and into the flight case without me ever sitting on it.

It was my first visit to Majorca for what is very definitely a training camp, not a holiday. It's an important distinction. Holiday. Training camp. Holiday. Training camp. See, they already appear totally different, don't they?

Should you ever feel the need to go on a training camp and believe me, whatever level of cyclist you are, you do most definitely feel the need to go on a training camp, it is vital you get the distinction right. This becomes particularly important if you need to demonstrate the difference to a partner or significant other who feels you are simply nicking off with your mates for a good time in the sun. Nothing could be further from the truth and you should show righteous indignation as your default response.

243

There are a number of differentiating factors you may find helpful should you be challenged.

Fun

Holidays are fun. Loading the kids up in the car and driving for hours on Britain's quiet and well maintained road system to your destination is a good start. Alternatively, you can pay very reasonable parking charges to leave the car (in complete safety) at a regional airport and fly, stress free, to some island paradise. A week or more with the loved ones without a single cross word or argument in beautiful surroundings is a certainty and a refreshed and reinvigorated return assured.

Training camps are not like this at all. You have to leave your loved ones at home and be subjected to the company of nobody closer than your club mates. There's no time for lying around the pool or enjoying long leisurely dinners here – even if there were, which there isn't, it would be a hollow and empty experience without being in the bosom of your loving family.

Let's get this straight once and for all, training camps are not fun. They are a painful necessity.

Cost

Holidays are very expensive, sometimes I'm told thousands of pounds. Training camps, because they are not holidays, are very cheap but represent great value for money at probably only a few hundred pounds for a week. Plus your flights. And parking. And the cost of flying with your bike. In a case.

I overheard two training camp regulars explaining to each other how it was actually cheaper for them to spend time in Spain in the spring than it was to be at home in the UK. They'd be losing money by not being abroad when factoring in living costs, fuel bills, petrol, food and the like. I believed them and maybe you should too

Stories

When you are on holiday you come back with loads of either funny or fascinating stories about all the things you've done and all the wonderful and exotic sights you have seen and diseases you have contracted. Capers are aplenty on holiday (see above: Fun).

Nothing even remotely funny or unusual happens on training camps which is why you never hear any stories from the people who attend them. They tend to by dry affairs, just a bunch of clubmates putting the hard miles in during the day and retiring early to bed to recover for the next day's hard effort.

It was once suggested to me the reason any more lurid stories are not heard on the return of these finely honed athletes is the old adage of 'what happens on tour, stays on tour'. This is ridiculous. People should be ashamed of themselves for even thinking such a thing.

Beer

Not applicable. This is training camp remember so there may be some carbohydrate drinks whilst out on the road and recovery drinks when back at the meagre accommodation we'll refer to as 'the hotel' but not beer. Or wine. Some of which can be really nice and at reasonable prices. Apparently. The consumption of a certain amount of high calorie fizzy cold muscle/brain relaxant is recommended at the end of a hard day but this is locally produced and known as 'cerveza'.

Sports doctors recommend a couple of pints of this should be consumed after a long ride together with food. When I say recommend, perhaps more accurately *will* recommend when they have fully investigated its restorative effects with the same thoroughness as my club mates.

Any similarity to what we know as 'beer' is purely coincidental. This can be safely consumed on holiday but not on a training camp.

Cake

Yes, okay, cakes are often consumed, in fairly hefty quantities at 'feedstops'. This is because the quality of 'feedstops' in many of the areas popular for spring training camps like Majorca and Italy are so poor.

The needy and unfortunate cyclist is forced to make do and stop at local cafés and eat what is available. Out of necessity this can include cakes, with local jams, cream, cherries, apricots often with almonds and sweet tasting sugary fillings. Hardly ideal for a cyclist in training I'm sure you will agree but when the facilities are so poor, what's a person to do? A cyclist in training must get sufficient calories simply to continue pushing him or herself to the limit every day. If cake is the only thing available then, regretfully, cake it has to be.

It's important that non-cyclists understand that when eating these local baked delights we are not enjoying them, or the frothy coffee that goes with them, it's simply a less than ideal way of restoring the calorie balance. You might enjoy a cake whilst on holiday but certainly not on a training camp. Shame on you for thinking otherwise.

Celebrities

This is pretty embarrassing really. Some people think cyclists go on training camps simply to spot or hang out with professional bike racers who train in similar areas during the late winter and early spring months.

Frankly, this is pretty insulting as many who go on these camps are slightly older men who are hardly likely to want to spend time with these younger, fitter guys who are getting ready for the Pro season. Similarly, they are unlikely to be impressed with riders who can do really cool track stands for hours on end or ride into the hotel, through reception and press the lift call button without getting off their bikes. Childish.

No way would anybody rush down to the local 'feedstop' for a chance to have their picture taken with a pro rider and maybe get one of those cotton race caps with the team name on it. For the kids you understand.

Fatigue

Most likely you will return from a holiday refreshed in mind and body if not wallet. With a training camp you are going to come back home knackered and with a cold. Who in their right mind would subject themselves to this if it wasn't absolutely essential?

You see, the truth is, a week, or possibly a little more if you can squeeze in a Bank Holiday, of training means a rider actually saves time. By putting himself through this agony the selfless cyclists has to spend less time training at weekends at home. This leaves more time for fun stuff like shopping and gardening.

It's not easy but it's a sacrifice many of us are prepared to make for the well-being of our families.

Weight

Many cyclists return from a camp weighing a little more than when they went away. This is entirely normal and is down to the conversion of fat to muscle, a much heavier and denser material, from all the riding done during the week. This should dispel the ridiculous idea the increased mass is down to an over consumption of cerveza, cake or second/third helpings from the buffet at both breakfast and dinner.

It is considered rude to mention any possible weight gain to a rider returning from a camp. It is likely he will be sensitive to criticism about his shape.

Weight gain is not unusual on a holiday which, I think you will now see, is a very different thing from a training camp.

Partners

It has been suggested on occasion that other halves could come along to training camps to provide help and support and, whilst they are there, maybe have a little holiday themselves. Do them a big favour by advising against it. It's pleasantly warm riding weather but rarely is it warm enough for sun bathing, swimming in the sea or spending days visiting exciting Roman remains. Probably best they stay safe and warm at home and just let the rider get on with suffering. With his or her clubmates.

A week in the sun with the lads had done me a power of good, mentally and physically. My recovered lungs were getting properly full of warm clean air.

Taking a new bike was a risk but it paid off – the Giant was slightly more upright and it made a huge difference to how my back and hip reacted to long hours in the saddle. A change of position could have crippled me but in this case, more by luck than judgement, it had helped. A lot.

My legs had got 600 miles in them and had gone through the normal sequential colour changes of blue to white to bright red to creamy off-white to red to slightly brown. This is as close as I get to a tan.

In the summer it was great to get back to the road race league. I found it fit, well, expanded and full of much younger riders ready to rip my legs off and beat me to death with the soggy ends. I settled back quickly into group 2 and was foolish enough to win a race and get a few top 10 positions meaning I won the Veterans Trophy for 2009. Well, that's nearly true, I actually came second but the rider who beat me also won the overall league so, as is traditional, the second placed man takes the jersey or trophy. Why foolish? Well, you're not really supposed to win anything from the second group - it implies you are good enough to ride with the third group. But this was me right? You know, the transplant guy. No way were they going to put the local 'disabled' in with the proper cyclists. It was a great way to finish off the season and I got prepared for the long trip to the Gold Coast in August knowing I was in good shape, despite the week's bed and breakfast in the Princess Royal.

It was good to meet up with the GB team again at Heathrow airport. There were 100 of us, all tracksuited up and creating a bit of commotion. I wasn't honestly looking forward to spending 24 hours travelling despite a mid-point stop over in Singapore airport. I found my seat in the middle of the row of five towards the centre of the Jumbo and unloaded the iPod, books and magazines I hoped would keep me going for the first 12 hours.

I'd experienced long night flights before when I'd travelled to Japan and Thailand and I'd always thought they were the closest thing to being in intensive care you could get without actually being tubed up and surrounded by nurses. There is constant low level lighting and noise and although it's difficult to get any proper sleep, you fall into a semi stupor. For me at least, it's an unpleasant disorientating experience made worthwhile only by what lies at the end.

I was surrounded by team mates, some of whom I knew well as friends, others who I recognised but was less familiar with. There were some new faces amongst them who were travelling to their first World Games. I wasn't able to get a good look at the new guy who sat right next to me because of the construction of the seats and headrests. I could see people further away from me on either side of plane but not the people immediately adjacent.

This young man had already dropped his hand luggage on my head a couple of times before somebody who wasn't quite as packed in as me could raise an arm and help stow his bag over head. He sat down and we introduced ourselves as best we could without actually being able to see each other, reaching awkwardly around the seats to shake hands.

This guy could talk. I mean really talk. He was talking to everybody at the same time. Picking up snippets of conversation and engaging part way through, he was constantly distracted by everything that was going on around him. Whilst momentarily talking to one passenger, irrespective of whether it was somebody on the team or not, he would point towards where other sound was coming from

249

with the flat of his hand up. This implied they should pause and wait until he was ready to give them some attention. He was randomly saying 'what?' and 'eh?' for clarification. It was chaos.

When he responded he was funny, irreverent, edgy and often, as far as I could see, completely off beam with what was being talked about. I was delighted – there was no way I was going to get to sleep anyway. This bundle of energy next to me was clearly going to deliver the equivalent of a 12 hour 'Bestman's' speech detailing the Brides sexual predilections at an evangelical Christian wedding. And so he did. Even later on in the flight when everybody was asleep, or at least pretending to be asleep, he would comment loudly on the film or programme showing on the headrest monitor. He richly demonstrated a full understanding and comprehensive use of expletives. For those around him it was similar to being in the front row of a show with a live stand-up comedian who was using audience participation as his principal prop.

Time flew and I lost sight of him when we disembarked at Singapore. After wandering around the shops and getting some more coffee, I overheard him talking with a group of friends. I'd not really seen him face to face so I went over and sat down next to him only to be comprehensively ignored. Perhaps he didn't recognise me, odd considering I felt we'd developed a significant bond in a short space of time. I asked if he was okay and he responded with an enthusiastic yes, yes, yes, patted me on the leg and we quickly settled back into the irreverent banter.

"Where are the toilets at fat boy?" he said, harking back to one of the many conversations we'd had on the plane.

I responded in a manner sufficiently irreverent and rude to match his question adding as there was a big blue neon sign with the word 'toilet' written on it he must be blind if he couldn't see it.

"Well" he said, "I am blind"

"Right" I said, "You'll be needing some help then I suppose?"

He didn't need any help. He just asked to be pointed broadly in the right direction. He could make out something of a big blue blur and would work it out from there apparently. Off he set. I made an excuse about needing the toilet as well, caught up with him and kept on talking as we got closer. At the risk of attracting comment I hung around outside the door and accidentally bumped into him on the way back.

I usually meet my hero during the week of the games but this time I'd met him on the plane on the way over. Richard (it's easy when everybody is either Richard or Dave isn't it?) had undergone a combined kidney and pancreas transplant that had resolved the type 1-diabetes from which he had suffered since childhood.

His vision had been fine until one day whilst in a shoe shop he had sneezed and blown the retinas out of the back of his eyes. An unfortunate side effect of his long-standing disease. This meant the mountain biking had to go but the sailing stayed, as did his involvement in athletics. He had come to the games to compete in the 100 metres leaving Bates, his guide dog, and his white stick at home. He had come on his own, unsupported and wasn't there to ask for special help from anybody just the support anybody would expect from team mates. I thought then and think now this is one of the bravest acts I have ever come across. It takes some nerve to get involved with any big team or organisation, to do so in Richard's circumstances is remarkable. He'd not mentioned he was blind before because it had not come up in any of the numerous and simultaneous conversations he'd had. It didn't strike him as being relevant.

He showed similar courage/reckless abandonment later during the week whilst buying a round of drinks at a crowded pub and working his way back through the throng to our table complete with a tray of glasses. Admittedly they weren't as full as you'd like. Nonetheless, he'd got there in

251

one piece and laughed like a drain when the predictable complaints about half measures came his way.

My favourite 'Richism' of that week came during a particularly long-winded and frustrating team meeting. The manager was fielding a series of questions that could have been answered easily by looking at the 'analogue website', or notice board, in the Games village. It was drummed into everybody this was the centre point for critical information about transport, timing and changes in events and was an essential 'resource' the whole team had to be aware of. In a peak of frustration she asked for a show of hands by those miscreants who had not seen the notice board. Out of the 140 people at that meeting only one hand went up.

For a country that is so passionate about its sport it came as something of a surprise to find the organisation of the Games in Australia was less than perfect. Some of the events, including the cycling, were not particularly well run resulting in a number of disputes. There were protests over timings and the conduct of some of the athletes was called into question. This was unfortunate and unsettling and not something I had ever really seen at a transplant event before. It reflected the increasing professionalism amongst some of the participants.

The time trial was held on a circuit without the aid of timing chips meaning multiple riders on the course at any one time. Keeping track of what was going on was difficult with overtaking and lapping giving rise to accusations of drafting – taking shelter from another rider. I'd managed to avoid this and won my event recording the fastest time overall with less than a second between me a Norwegian rider in a younger age category. There remained some fairly unpleasant accusations flying around between some of the other nations that were never resolved satisfactorily.

What made it worse was the attitude of one the organisers and member of the Games judiciary who I'd first encountered at the opening ceremony. She had asked me to tell her how grateful I was. How grateful I was to be in Australia, how grateful I was to be at the games and how grateful I was to be alive. I struggle with this because it over simplifies the truly complex and highly personal issues around transplantation to the lowest, laziest and most inarticulate common denominator. It ignores the range of circumstances in which transplantation can happen. In my particular case, my donor had died but this is not always so. More transplants are happening with living donors, with a significant proportion of kidney patients receiving an organ from a living family member. A number of my fellow competitors are bone marrow transplantees. Their bone marrow has been replaced by that synthesised from donor blood often coming from a relative. These people have a different way of thanking the people who have helped them as their donors are sometimes still around to say "Thank you" to.

I understood the circumstances of my transplant and those of my donor family well - we'd been writing regularly to each other for years. They knew I tried to express the way I felt about it through how I lived my life and what I did on the bike. I felt a need to demonstrate that I was worthy of the decisions my donor's family had made. I wanted to make evident my feelings rather than just trotting out how 'thankful' or 'grateful' I was.

Worse still, she was excusing the poor organisation of some of the events on the basis that it didn't matter much. It was sunny, beautiful and we should all be bloody grateful to be alive anyway. My view was fundamentally different. We had all gone through a life-saving transplant of some kind and were paying tribute to that in the best way we knew, through competition at the highest level we could muster. I could do this because I'd trained for 2 years, dealt with the injuries, balanced the drugs, spent thousands on equipment, travel and accommodation and was fully committed to the sport I'd chosen. Just like most of the other transplant athletes.

People choose different ways to honour those who have helped them on the way. For good or bad, I'd chosen to use these Games as a way of demonstrating what I felt. It might be blunt and simplistic but it was easier than trying to put what I felt into words, something I have singularly failed adequately to do.

I suspect I was particularly indignant over this assault on my own view of the circumstances surrounding my transplant because I knew my donor family were in Australia at the same time as the Games. We had discussed the possibility of meeting up during the events but we all thought it might be a bit too much with all that was going on.

The disputes around the result of the time trial continued although this did not directly affect the small GB contingent or me as the day of the road race came around. The course was to be a single 20k lap of a pan flat road circuit in a fairly remote area starting and finishing adjacent to a local primary school. We raced in our age categories meaning the possibility of working with other riders was unlikely unless there were multiple riders from the same country in any one age group.

Try as I might, I couldn't escape from the group. They knew from the time trial results I was the strongest rider so every move I made was chased down. I'm pretty sure if I'd have slowed down and stopped there would have been twenty riders waiting patiently behind for me to get going again. I did mention that perhaps somebody else might like to come up front and see what the weather was like but I didn't get any takers.

The course didn't offer any help either. There were no hills, no sharp corners to hide around or wind to break the group up. It was only the pace that had shelled a numbers of riders out of the group, leaving 15 or so to contest the last 5k's.

I was still relaxed as the finish line approached and as I opened up a sprint to take another win I had good sight of the guys who had finished second and third in the time trial. I was out of the saddle at full gas when an Italian rider whom I'd not seen for the whole race, and who'd not figured in the time trial, came past me like I was standing still.

I'd been lazy and tactically inept. I'd not given my competitors, in particular this Italian, the respect they deserved. I should have done everything I could to either break free of the pack or tire them out in the process of chasing me down. I hadn't done enough. That's road racing.

He beat me fair and square going over the line a couple of bike lengths in front of me and I was lucky to take second place as the other riders closed in on the finishing line. Spanked. Mugged. Clobbered. Yes, all of those but on that particular day, he had the legs, played the game the best way he knew and won the gold medal. A worthy winner and a good guy to boot.

I couldn't be disappointed at winning a silver medal at the World Games bearing in mind the standard of the competition. What's more it gave me an idea for setting myself a target for the next few events before the next World Games. Never satisfied am I?

Da Youf

I put my medals from the Australian World Games, the medals I'd won at the British Games in Coventry in 2009 and the road race league veterans medal in a little display box. I hung it in the downstairs toilet. Lovely.

There are four gold medals in that box and a silver one that twinkles – it attracts the eye as the odd one out. I've moved the box around the room a few times but I can still feel it winking at me irrespective of whether I'm sitting or standing. Sometimes I go up two flights of stairs to avoid using that bathroom. There, I've said it. It's a mark of what I achieved – second in the world isn't bad. But it's also a useful reminder to respect the abilities of others and not become complacent. It doesn't imply I should go back to the pre-race nerves of Japan in 2001 but a healthy balance somewhere between the two would be appropriate.

It set me to thinking about the possibility of holding all the available transplant cycling titles, British, European and World at the same time. This would mean winning six races, three time trials and three road races consecutively.

As part of my coaching qualifications with British Cycling and as a general principle of my working life, I understood the importance of having a clear goal. Provided I have a clear target I can start to work out how to put the jigsaw pieces together and implement a plan to get me there. I'd already established that I found the process of working towards an outcome useful in keeping me focused and out of trouble. My problem was what I did *after* the goal was reached. Without structure I tend to bounce off walls a bit.

I'd experienced various World and British Games but I had never tackled the European Transplant Games. They were a recent creation having been conceived in 2000 and first held in Greece. They were largely ignored by most of the competitors at the World Games. This was partly for obvious reasons, like not being European, but also because it's difficult enough for competitors to finance annual trips to national games and bi-annual trips to somewhere more exotic for the Worlds, let alone another Games in the same year.

Give the European Games its full title, the European Transplant and Dialysis Games, and one can see there is a slight twist on the theme of transplantation. These Games admit people currently on dialysis and awaiting a kidney transplant but who are fit enough to compete.

This opens up a big debate in the transplant community, something that has been the subject of heated discussion and votes at the AGM of Transplant Sport UK, the body governing the British Games. There are sensible arguments on both sides for allowing dialysis patients into what has always been an event exclusively for those who have received a life-supporting organ transplant.

The whole point of the Games is to increase awareness of the issues surrounding donation so why not increase participation and allow those relatively few people who are fit enough to compete whilst waiting for a kidney to get stuck in? Good point, but the Games exist to demonstrate the effectiveness of transplantation not dialysis; surely this would water down the message? If you are fit and 'healthy' on dialysis why do you need a transplant anyway? It's a circular argument made difficult because many of us have been around long enough to compete with people one year only to find they are back on dialysis, and therefore excluded, a year later.

The organisers of the European Games swiftly got around this one by including dialysis patients at the launch so there was no debate. If you don't like it or agree with it, don't go was the simple and clear philosophy. This may have had some bearing on the numbers attending but I suspect it is more to do with the relative newness of the event. Running bi-annually, its 6th edition was scheduled for Dublin in 2010.

If I was to have a crack at holding all six titles, British, European and World in both time trial and road race disciplines at the same time I'd need to win both races in Dublin on the 10th August. Travel to Bath on 21st August for the British Games and win both races there and finally go to the World Games in June the following year to be held in Gotenberg, Sweden. Again, I'd have to win both races.

Just for good measure, I also fancied being the fastest transplant cyclist in the world, irrespective of age, meaning I'd need to record the fastest 'scratch' time in the time trial in Sweden.

Logistically possible and not done before so far as I could establish, but the last piece of the jigsaw would be the World Games road race, the event I lost in Australia. By far and away the most demanding and variable race from a results perspective. It was a bit like needing 53 to finish off a game of darts and deciding to go one, bull, double one: possible, but not necessarily sensible and certainly full of risk.

The challenge was going to be doubly difficult because of my other commitments. I was working full time as Head of Estates for a national company and juggling my family responsibilities. Finding adequate time to train was becoming difficult and, frankly, I wasn't getting any younger. Physically I was well but, irrespective of the transplant, I was 42-years-old and that meant it took a little longer to recover from injuries and hard training

All cyclists can find an excuse for why they've not trained enough, in fact it's a good idea to come up with a new excuse ever year and have a few in reserve in case your primary excuse is insufficient. It's always possible your subterfuge will be trumped by another cyclist's killer excuse forcing you to deploy multiple and rapid excuses in defence.

I'd been working on the whole 'coaching is taking up more of my time – it's time to give something back to the sport' excuse. It was okay but I needed more. Luckily, my son, Charlie, began to show an interest in moving on from mountain biking and wanted to try his hand at road riding. This allowed me to combine my 'coaching' excuse together with the 'my son is riding now and I'm putting a lot of energy into that' ruse providing me with a watertight reason for any dismal cycling performances. I was fully prepared. I had a stretching target for transplant cycling domination and a full-on kick ass excuse for when I ballsed it up.

I guess a child asking to be let loose on the road on a push bike is a fairly terrifying prospect for any parent to deal with but, with local track facilities close at hand, it was feasible. He could learn the basics of riding and racing without having to go anywhere near people in cars for quite a while. Without this I can honestly say I could not have contemplated letting him on the road at 14. It's a potentially dangerous environment and while 99% of other road users I've come across are responsible, it's the 1% that do the damage and much of this is down to the attitude these people adopt towards cyclists.

I think it's time for the results of my anecdotally shabby 'research' into the public's view of cycling. Brace yourself, here comes another exam.

Question 6

A man is driving along a quiet road on a pleasant early summer evening following a day at work. By the side of the road he sees a group of club cyclists dressed in Lycra clearly about to begin a ride, possibly a time trial or a club run. Outline the likely initial reactions of the man to this sight.

1. Oh, I see some form of cycle event is about to take place. Yes, indeed, there are signs at the side of the road saying just that. I'm not that interested in cycling myself but it seems like a harmless pastime. These guys and gals are staying fit and enjoying themselves whilst doing no harm to others. I'll drive by sensibly within the speed limit aware that other vulnerable road users may be in the immediate vicinity.

2. How interesting, a cycling event in my local area. I've got friends and family who may be involved. It

brings a bit of colour to an otherwise dull piece of carriageway. Maybe I'll pull over, find out what's going on with a view to perhaps watching for a while.

3. I bloody hate cyclists me. They always slow me up when I driving my car on the roads. Don't they know the Highway Code clearly says cars have right of way over bikes because we are more important? Well, it probably says that anyway. None of these layabouts pay road tax, which goes to improve roads for cars like mine. Doesn't it? I think I shall sound my horn at them to well, you know. Beeep! Bloody cyclists.

4. Look at that bunch of wankers. Who do they think they are? Wankers. I'm going to speed up, drive much closer to them, wind my window down and shout 'wankers' at them. And I'm going to ring my forefinger and thumb together and perform the 'wanker shake' thing at them. That'll make them think twice about being such a bunch of wankers.

Yes, you've spotted it, it is indeed a trick question and you get full marks for answering either 3 or 4. This does seem to be the response of a significant minority of the motoring public.

If you've been more creative and have thought that sometimes people drive past and respond with answer number 3, then turn the car around and execute answer number 4 on the return run, you may award yourself some bonus points.

I had already coached young kids on bikes and loved it. Taking my boy down to the track so he could mix it up with some youth and junior riders meant I was going to come face to face with the future of cycle racing in Britain. It also meant Charlie wouldn't have to deal with the 1% of nutters out on the road just yet.

I figured I'd have to learn about youth riders the hard way. Let's be honest, we all know teenagers are terrifying would-be criminals who roam around in gangs generally being threatening and unpleasant. At best there will be intimidating name calling and bad language, at worst they'll rob you blind and beat you up just for the hell of it.

With this in mind, I'll save you from the suffering of the initial introduction to this special breed of cyclist with some advice you might not find in the coaching manuals. Young riders are faster than you. Don't try to deny it or fight it. Most youth riders and virtually all juniors are better at most aspects of cycling than you. If they are not already, they soon will be considerably faster than you.

They neither know nor care that it's taken you 25 years to get a 3rd category licence or manage a sub 25 minute 10 mile time trial and will happily beat you at any cycling discipline you care to mention with 6 months riding under their belt.

Even if you are capable of just pipping a young rider I would advise against it. They often travel in packs, news will travel fast and within two weeks they will all beat you simultaneously on the evening your girlfriend has come to watch you ride.

Young riders are better bike handlers than you.

Youth riders demonstrate their handling skills unwittingly. They adopt the carefree abandon of those who are subconsciously skilled at something that you will never be able to master in a million years.

A regular sight at my local track is 30 kids in pairs or threes and fours, stuffed into what looks like an impossibly small pack. They lean on each other, push each other and hold in depth conversations, presumably about the latest mugging techniques, whilst riding at 20mph.

Most adults, even experienced track riders, will ride the track in silence with a certain amount of tension and an air of concentration but the youngsters seem to move as a

262

sentient homogenous body working unconsciously together like a swarm of bees.

During one Winter whilst the assembled youth were waiting in a corridor to see if the track was safe to ride, I noticed one of the older lads had grown substantially. Alarmingly in fact – he was head and shoulders above the others. Even with rapid growth spurts, I remember thinking this was remarkable. It wasn't until the all clear was given and they moved off. I saw he'd been track standing on his bike amid a milling crowd of kids who'd been pushing past him for the last 10 minutes. He rode towards the door, opening it, holding it open for the others to start coming through and then moved off gently towards the track centre. Still chatting. I don't suppose he'd done it deliberately to upset me. I suspect it never even struck him, even for a second, that most of us mortals would have fallen through the door and been upside down covered in bike had we tried that, but it was a cruel, cruel thing he did.

Young riders will absorb information faster than you.

This is deeply upsetting. Kids listen. They don't look like they are listening; they look like they are hatching some kind of evil teenage plot with their strange shrugs, muted grunts and rolling of the eyes. Don't be fooled for a minute. Their propensity to absorb knowledge by osmosis is massive and they can do this whilst appearing to ignore you completely.

Even deploying your best coach Bullet Baxter inspired sarcasm by asking them to repeat back to you what they have just been told will be greeted by a verbatim response or, worse still, a flawless demonstration of the fiendishly complex task you have asked them to complete. Highly evolved well-established packs of roaming youth cyclists will also use the sentry system employed by other mammals like Meerkats. One of their number will be listening to instructions whilst the others spray paint graffiti or whatever they do. Within seconds of starting the exercise

263

the information gathered by the sentry will be disseminated to the pack, again resulting in a frustratingly perfect demonstration of the task.

Young riders will have better equipment than you.

Perhaps more accurately young riders, particularly those related to you, will soon have *your* equipment. This will happen before you realise what it going on and worked out why you are riding around on a bike that's falling to bits despite investing thousands in it.

It is known as the 'yours–those– the– mine' progression and you should be wary of its deployment by youth cyclists. I suspect they plot the purloining of their parents and relatives cycling equipment whilst pretending not to listen to you.

I shall give you a case study so you are fully prepared for the launch of this strategy, although it seems only fair to warn you there is no known defence.

Yours (possessive pro noun 'belonging to you')

Child. "Wow, those recently purchased very expensive but thoroughly well deserved wheels of **yours** look absolutely fantastic. Are they the new Super Fandangle SPL Tri spoke carbon Fandangles?" (Care; distractionary questioning coupled with flattery)

Father. "Yes indeed they are, both lovely and well deserved aren't they? Thank you for taking an interest. You are indeed a dutiful child".

Those (plural pro noun 'objects')

Child. "How are you getting on with **those** new wheels my revered elder? Still happy with your purchase and getting the promised performance benefits befitting the high cost of said equipment?" (Care: probing question encouraging the self-questioning that commonly follows the purchase of an expensive item)

Father. "Your continued interest in my well-being is commendable my beloved progeny, I am indeed happy with my purchase but feel, taking into account my advancing years, I have equipment that is in advance of my receding talent as a cyclist".

You will note the slight but important change from confirmation of your ownership to a state where ownership of the wheels is no longer the principle determining characteristic of their existence. They are wheels, yes, but who owns them is not material within the confines of the questioning. They could therefore be owned by anybody. The undermining of your right to own such high performance equipment in your autumn years is cunning and ruthless but you can only admire its heartless subtlety.

The (definitive article)

Child. "With this important event/race approaching I feel sure, as an excellent and caring parent, you will feel obliged to place me in the most advantageous position possible by allowing me to use **the** Fandangle wheels. These will be returned to you undamaged immediately following the event as you bask in the reflected glory of my achievements which are, at least in part, down to your sacrifice" (Great care: this statement is laced with more trickery than a box of greased weasels).

Father. "Very well, I see you recognise both the monetary and performance value of the Fandangle wheelset and for this particular event I am comfortable you use them providing you exercise great care. I wish you luck and success loyal spawn of my loins".

You will see here, with a singularly brutal yet incisive masterstroke, the shift of the state of ownership from irrelevant to indeterminate has been ingeniously encased in a tangled web of carefully crafted emotional blackmail. Genius.

The implication is now that ownership of the wheels falls to whosoever can make the best use of their performance enhancing characteristics regardless of whoever actually bought and paid for them.

Mine (possessive pro noun 'belonging to me')

Child. "Those Fandangle wheels of **mine** are not performing to the level I desire, not through any fault of my own but because of the inferior tyres you have installed on them. I feel it incumbent on you to replace them with something more suitable such as the recently released Tyrex super race Evopro 14. Here are directions to the shop where they can be purchased. Kindly advise me when you have fitted them".

Father. "You little sod, you've stolen my wheels and are now you are extorting more of my hard earn money etc, etc…."

You might as well give up at this point and remove your hands from the child's throat. You've been beaten and, because you are a cyclist, you will simply have to take the defeat on the chin, try harder and come back to fight another day. Only this time you'll be doing it on the crappy old wheels you thought you'd recently replaced.

Young riders are the future.

Maybe I've been lucky with the young riders I've come across but I hope and suspect much the same thing could be said for any young people who have found a sport they love and want to dedicate time to. You need a level of self-discipline to do any sport even half decently. This is undoubtedly a common factor but I also see fun, dedication and respect for other riders irrespective of their ability. There is a great understanding of what winning and losing really means.

British cycling has a massively bright future ahead of it and I can't wait to see some of the young riders I'm privileged to know make a big impact as they get into the senior ranks. This is as true for the young women as it is for the young men with great strength in depth across both sexes and amongst all age ranges.

They *should* be giving us a kicking out there on the bike, they *should* be gently moving us oldies out the way and they *do* have enough respect to give us a nod when they go through. It's all terribly exciting.

They will, however, still nick your wheels.

My 2010 had started pneumonia free and with the familiar diet of long Winter rides at the weekends, weight training and the dullest most boring core exercises imaginable. This at least kept my aging body in one piece. I'd fit in weekday rides or turbo sessions when I could. March brought a happy holiday/tough training camp, depending on how you want to view these things, followed by the usual early season time trials. I achieved some pleasingly quicker times than those recorded in 2009.

Sadly, the usually flawless organisers of the road race league had made an administrative slip and had put me in the third group on the road. I contacted them to give them the opportunity to correct this glaring and upsetting mistake only to be told there was no such error. They told me if I was daft enough to win the Vets Trophy and score 26 points ranking points from the second group, what the hell did I expect? Fair comment I suppose.

I got properly panned on a weekly basis in the league. I only just about managed to hold the pace of the faster group at the beginning of the season. I progressed to actually being able to do some work later on and, finally, managed to finish with the group by the season close. It was very hard work but enjoyable nonetheless.

I mixed in the normal diet of 10 and 25 mile time trials without any spectacular results but a gradual improvement that, bearing in mind my advancing years, was probably the best I could hope for. I took advantage of Charlie's use of the local track and entered a couple of 5k time trials. It's a distance used at the transplant games but it's unusual to ever find an event of similar length on the road. I was pleased I was going to get a chance to test my form before I raced in Dublin.

To make things extra interesting the organisers of the European games had banned the use of aero bars thus ruling out using the time trial specific bike. I decided to use the road bike at the track event to replicate the forthcoming race.

5k's is a horrible distance. Approximately 11 laps of the track at full chat and my first attempt on a Monday evening resulted in a pretty pathetic 8.00 mins. Okay, it was 7 years after I'd recorded 7 minutes 10 seconds at the world games in France but this was on a pan flat track without any appreciable wind. I felt heavy and slow after what should have been great preparation for short violent events like this. I couldn't get my legs moving at any decent speed. This was not good. I took 5 days rest and had another crack at it, this time using the time trial bike just to see if the worrying difference in times was down to using an aero position and equipment. No such luck. 7.44 and nearly barfing up a lung at the end of it. Maybe I was just old and rubbish and this was as good as it was ever going to get.

August came around and I took the ferry to Dublin with Helen, found the hotel and took a trip over to Phoenix Park. This had been the scene of some pretty high-class bike racing in the past and the venue for the European Games. It contained some decent climbs and descents and there were some tight corners.

On the day of the race there was a bit of drizzle in the air and it was blowing a hooley. Perfect for a road race really.

The time trial was first and I was chasing a time of 8.09 set by the young rider from Norway I had pipped in Australia. Admittedly, the race was not between him and me, we were racing against the riders in our age category. When you time trial, it's the 'scratch' time you are aiming for – the fastest rider overall irrespective of age. It comes with no additional prize or medal but does come with the nodding respect of the other riders. If I was to do the fastest ride in

Sweden the following year, this was the guy I was going to have to beat.

I rode with the same heavy legged, dry mouthed feeling I trained with but recorded 8.13.

Bearing in mind the nature of the course and the fastest time already set it was okay but not really good enough in my own estimation. As on many other occasions when I raced, there was a rider stronger than me on the day. I had done enough to win my age category and that, at least, was the first of six gold medals I'd need to achieve my target. I was going to have to pull something out of the bag next year though.

The road race was held in the afternoon on the same day. This was to be four laps of the same course with riders of all age categories starting at the same time. There were lots of familiar faces and the international standard communication tools used when cyclists meet was fully deployed – checking each other out and lying to each other about how much training we'd done. There were some experienced heads in the group. We knew some of us could work together irrespective of which country we were batting for as long as we had an appropriate mix of age categories. Devious isn't it?

The first two laps were attritional with pure speed leaving some riders out on their own. Then the tactical attacks started. I went first bringing the younger rider from Norway with me. John Moran, the Irish rider and a veteran of the World Games, bridged the gap to join us followed by three others. John is an excellent cyclist and, very usefully, in the next age category up from me.

The leading bunch of six was now well established with a good gap on the remaining riders and contained nobody from my age category. Job done, I could sit in the wheels and watch the race develop. All I had to do was follow the right attacks rather than having to make them myself, a much easier way of racing.

The sprint came down to three, the Norwegian leading it out with me on his wheel and the Irishman behind me. I came out from behind his wheel with 100 metres to go, got out of the saddle and opened up my best Mark Cavendish sprint. I started going backwards. Well, that's what it felt like anyway. Despite a good lead out, as hard as I tried I couldn't get around him and he deservedly won the race overall by a few bike lengths. Again, I wanted the win but I'd got a result in my age category and was happy to tick number two off the list. Apart from establishing I was now rubbish at *both* time trialling and sprinting, the games had been a success. I certainly hadn't performed as well as I wanted to and was going to have to have a good look my preparation. If only I knew a decent coach.

A week later I made the familiar trip to Bath with Helen and both kids, Charlie and Grace, for the British Transplant Games to have a crack at medals three and four. We stayed with the rest of the athletes on the University campus. It was great to be once again surrounded by friends and to catch up with the guys I had been with in Australia. It was also good to welcome some new faces to the most exclusive sports club in the world that nobody wants to be a member of.

We'd had awful conditions for the past few editions of the British Games so it was nice to have some sunshine and warmth for this one. It was also encouraging to see some new riders and particularly more women. When I wasn't too busy indulging my own cycling fantasies I was keeping an eye out for new riders. This was the selection event for the next World Games and, as captain and coach of the GB team, I was on the lookout for prospective Brits to take on the world in Sweden.

There were some excellent rides that day on a challenging hilly circuit with the women putting in a particularly impressive show of strength. I rode an 8.24 for the time trial, which looked initially worse that Dublin, but on a standard road bike over a couple of laps of a tough circuit it was enough to win.

That was half way in my personal medal target of six medals. The road race went well too. A group of four, including me, had broken away and I managed to shake the others off by the time we got to the finish line to win. This meant two thirds of the job was done and now I'd have a long wait, and a winter, to prepare for the World games in 2011.

I was excited for two reasons, actually that's not true, I was excited for loads of reasons, not least because my family were there but also because I was fully absorbed by the friendly relaxed atmosphere common at the British Games. The two specific reasons for my mood were the general quality of competitors to select from and the number of female riders. The GB team had been very well served by Zoe Dixon MBE, a talented and consistent woman cyclist but however good she was she could only ever compete in one age category at a time. I spent the rest of my weekend chatting to riders about their intentions. I was fishing around to see who needed encouragement to commit to the level of training needed to be competitive against the best cyclists the transplant world had to offer in June 2011.

I finished off that season with a lot of long bunch rides, a good feeling about the team and a very clear understanding I'd need to alter my training to find some form. I'd been lucky to achieve the results I had in 2010 and my vain quest for six gold medals could easily have been derailed by poor preparation.

Cycling clubs and how to survive them

The latest incarnation of the GB transplant cycling team came together for the first time late in 2010. It was my job to coach them − one of my favourite things to do. It seemed we had come full circle from my first team meeting back in 1998 prior to the trip to Budapest. Even finding a cyclist back then was a hard thing to do. Now, lots of people wanted to ride and lots of people wanted to know what we were up to as a team. It was just a matter of creating a focus and structure so new riders knew they would be supported.

I recalled my feeling of frustration about the lack of structure around the cycling team in the early days. My reaction was always 'somebody' should do 'something' followed by a loud 'hurrumph'. Well, yes, it just took a while to sink in that that 'somebody' should be me and the 'something' was a bit of pointing in the right direction. I'd done the coaching badge giving me and the riders some confidence the direction of the pointing was right. Setting up a Facebook page and an email list wasn't a complicated thing to do. It had helped with the preparation and logistics for the trip to Australia.

It might seem unimportant but one of the ways we had created a little cohesion was to have our own kit designed and produced for the games in Australia. It wasn't borrowed from British Cycling – they still didn't want to know us, and it wasn't a generic Union Flag jersey.

It was ours, with our name on it: The Great Britain Transplant Cycling Team. There were some great prospects, including more women, and at the first session we started to look at what a winter of training on the bike might look like for the new members. I think it came as a bit of a shock to some of them.

With the team coming along well early in the New Year I had to prepare for the highlight of the social season. I don't mean to name drop here as I suspect many of you have not been lucky enough to be invited to such prestigious events as the Wrekinsport Club dinner.

273

Rivalling Henley, Glyndebourne and Ascot on the social calendar, the dinner had recently been held in the glittering surrounding of St Georges cricket club in Telford. Just like these occasions the evening is fancy dress (optional). I've never worked out why it's fancy dress – it just is. One of my favourite memories is being presented with the road race trophy by a monk, or possibly Robin Hood, it didn't seem right to ask, whilst being heckled by Batman and Scooby Doo.

This year I was honoured to be presented with the Clubman of the Year trophy. I was honestly speechless when it was announced. Its recipient is voted for by their peers in the club, usually for contributing something worthwhile. I done a little coaching for the club, written the standard wildly inaccurate and irreverent road race reports and encouraged a few extra riders into road racing. We all knew the real reason was 'R.Smith' is a short name and it would fit in the space left on the trophy.

This marvellously generous prize set me to thinking about my club, and cycling clubs in general. They are an entertaining and essential part of the architecture of cycling governed by a strict unwritten code worthy of further exploration.

Those of you who have been involved in cycling clubs for years may recognise some of my findings, others may not. One thing for sure is each club has its own ethos and little quirks. My thoughts below represent the shoddy shoot from the hip 'research' you will be familiar with by now.

Committees and meetings

All cycling clubs have committees and there is little point in having them if they are never going to meet. At my club there is a rule that any meeting, but particularly the AGM, should take no longer than the time in which the average club member can complete the local '10' course. This means meetings can realistically last for no longer than

274

27 minutes even in a poor year. All decisions have to be taken within that period including the election or re-election of the club's officers. Personally I think this is an excellent mantra and the wider business world would do well to take note and set its own appropriate time limits.

I know of other clubs where the AGM is governed by sets of rules so arcane they make the House of Lords look like the pinnacle of efficient modern democracy. The meetings often go on for days. Point of order Mr Chairman, etc. AGM's are good places for members to settle scores for the season's misdemeanours and slights. They are also an excellent foundation to start new ones for the forthcoming year. If possible, club Presidents should be upset by something everybody else sees as totally unimportant. There should be numerous threats of resignation by the officers and the most important business of the day should be the unacceptably poor quality of café chosen for the last club run or something similarly earth shattering.

Each club is likely to have its long-running issue of choice that should be dusted off and proposed at the last minute by the same guy that proposed it last year. And the year before. Popular topics to choose from include, the admissions policy for new members and the route of the club 10 course. It is a brave man who raises anything regarding triathletes, junior and women riders. Particularly if this involves advising the committee a 'none, not applicable and none' policy is no longer acceptable or indeed legal.

In accordance with tradition, the meeting should close with a fistfight on the pub car park.

Kit

All cycling clubs must have the colours of the kit in which they intend to race registered with British Cycling to avoid clashes with others in the area. When racing in a bunch it means riders can be easily distinguished and abuse can be more accurately directed without actually knowing their names.

Many loyal club members will be seen in cycling clothing bearing not even the remotest passing resemblance to their ascribed colours, particularly during the winter months when rides tend to be longer, slower and colder. This is because cycling clothing is a very personal choice and the prospect of spending five damp hours in shorts that fit you like a barbwire mankini is not most rider's idea of fun.

The artificial chamois pad common to most club shorts is made out of recycled wire wool scouring pads combined with a hideously abrasive mixture of sand and glass. It's known colloquially as a 'cheese grater'. Some people, often those who have organised its production, are lucky enough to get on well with club kit or at least claim they do and put up with pain.

One of my clubmates got on so well with his kit he wore and washed it to death until the shorts developed their own translucent viewing panel making riding behind him a revealing experience. Others have to find more resourceful ways around its use when racing such as 'going retro' using plain black shorts or even wearing another pair of shorts under their skin suits.

Recently there was talk that our rather fetching red and yellow 'Fruit Salad' themed colour scheme made many of the club's kit adherents look fat. On reflection it was agreed that many of the club members *are* a bit fat and the colour or design of the kit was purely incidental. Tight-fitting Lycra takes no prisoners.

Nicknames

It is forbidden to award yourself your own nickname within a club environment. It will be developed for you, sometimes over a period of time but more often than not through one embarrassing, unfortunate or catastrophic incident witnessed by one or more other members. For example, descending at pace during a wet sportive ride one of our members hurtled head long into a five-bar farm gate, effectively vaulting it and landing in a sheep field. Clearly, to fully earn his nickname of 'Two Gates' he had to do the

276

same thing with a different but similar gate a few minutes later.

The nickname of another friend and colleague, 'Vampire', is a shortened form of the name 'Vampire the Buffet Slayer' given to him because of his prodigious ability to destroy unprotected food left anywhere near him.

My own club sobriquet of 'Three Puds' came about as I was caught going up for my third pudding at a Majorcan training camp. Well, it had been a long day on the bike. In truth, I was lucky to avoid the more accurate 'Six Puds' tag.

Club legends and stories

Whenever cyclists meet, 'tis writ in ancient lore the same old stories should be dusted off and rolled out once again only slightly more exaggerate than last time. Every club has their own but I have a couple of favourites that relate specifically to my own wonderful club.

There is the story of when we put on a 100 mile time trial. An event you have to be fundamentally crackers to do in the first place simply because if you are capable of winning it you will be trying to ride at upwards of 26mph for over three and half hours. Alternatively, if you are 'only riding against yourself' you will be spending the next 5 hours alternating between extreme boredom and extreme pain. Our story was of a cyclist, 'a friend of a friend' who had ridden from South Wales to Shropshire arriving in time for the 7am Sunday morning start. He had then ridden the event and ridden home to South Wales without stopping to enquire what his time might be.

Frankly, I didn't believe anybody would be crazy enough to do this until I was introduced to the guy at another event. He was, it has to be said, as mad as a rat on a tin shit house roof.

During one of the club's annual holidays, excuse me, training camps, the club had ridden a beautiful mountain climb in Majorca stopping at a famous monastery before finding a café for the traditional wedge of cake. A rider notorious for his dubious bike handling skills set off first on

277

the steep descent to ensure the others were not waiting about for him at the bottom. Another rider soon began to catch him and could hear an alarming rumbling sound as he approached each switchback hairpin bend. Keeping a safe distance he had a good look at the bike and rider in front of him to see if he could work out what was making the noise. A grabbing brake or damaged wheel rim perhaps, but no, he couldn't see anything amiss.

After more sharp and steep corners he realised it was actually the rider rather than the bike making the noise. Nervous of the descent he was making a 'whoooooooaaaa' sound as he entered each bend. An experience he described to me as 'off putting'

Members

Seems entirely obvious I know but a cycling club needs members. Many club officials will rightly claim the running of the club would be less problematic without them but they are essential. It needs riders who race and riders who just ride.

Cycling clubs work symbiotically, because they take their turn at organising and promoting events like club and open time trials, road races, sportives and reliability trials. This is likely to involve many of the active members standing at the side of the road in a yellow bib with a red flag trying to slow down and warn motorists rather than riding themselves. They do this for the good of the club and because they know they will end up riding a lot more events than they marshal. Without this system there *are* no events. It's why clubs or more particularly the emerging 'racing teams' who don't put on events, don't tend to last for very long. When events become oversubscribed preference tends to be given to members of clubs that play the game.

Membership doesn't suit all riders but, when asked, I always advise aspiring cyclists and particularly those that want to race, to find one they like and join it. Then you can start listening to the stories, get yourself a nickname and watch the fight on the pub car park.

Meeting

My preparation for the 2011 season was going well. A winter training with a 14-year-old mad-keen cyclist and his mad-keen mates helped. It meant I was riding a freezing cold track when I would normally be sitting at home eating stew, dumplings and sausage and mash. Often it seemed unfair to inflict the agonies of turbo training on the boy without at least joining him in the torture. By the time my Majorca trip came around in March of 2011, I was in pretty good shape for a 44-year-old transplant patient.

The correspondence with my donor family had continued and whilst mention of a meeting had been made in the past the logistical and emotional complexities meant this had never been possible. More than 18 years had passed since those traumatic events in February of 1993 and although time is a great healer there are constant reminders of what had happened all those years back for both parties. The passage of time just makes the whole thing a little more manageable that's all.

Now, the time did seem right and we agreed to meet on May Day of 2011. My donor's parents came to my house and we met for the first time. It was a very emotional for all involved but made easier by the wonderful relationship we had developed through our letters.

Before we met, I'd tried to rationalise my thinking about the whole 'grateful' issue without meaningful conclusion but when we'd talked for a couple of hours, we'd all come to the conclusion it was indeed an inappropriate description. The feeling that came to my mind when sitting with these awe-inspiring people was one of pride. I was hugely proud of the momentous decisions my donor's family had taken at that awful time. It was brave, courageous, and altruistic: completely overwhelming in fact. I felt deeply honoured to be associated with it. I *was* grateful though. Grateful I'd found a simple word that went some way to capture the gut wrenching emotion accompanying the personal circumstances of my donor family and me. Until I can find something better, 'proud' will do.

We finished off the day with a walk around my town coupled with meeting Helen, Charlie, Grace, Anne and possibly most importantly, Dad.

Yes, it was all too much and yes, I shed a few tears the following day but it was fantastic to meet them and I'm sure we will meet again soon.

I have a picture of my donor now and that makes it slightly easier to catch hold of myself every now and again and make sure I'm doing things the right way. It's important I don't waste my second chance and that I'm doing things in a way he and his parents would think made the brave decisions they took worthwhile.

In some ways this is easy. Dad comes from a different background but his morality and values are the same. I don't want to disappoint them or him. They are rightly proud of their son and his achievements. So am I.

When asked, I am keen people have a good think about signing the donor register. I have met hundreds, possibly thousands of valuable people who simply wouldn't be here without brave donors having difficult conversations with their families.

I am not a proponent of presumed consent. I feel people in this country are naturally altruistic and the 90% of the population who think the register is a good idea can add to the 30% signed up to it through persuasion and awareness.

Maybe reading this will make you have a think about it. Thanks for listening. Lecture over.

Sweden

In June of 2011, eight GB transplant cyclists, three men and five women, set off for the 18th World Transplant Games in Gothenburg, Sweden. Rumours of a much needed lengthening of the cycling events to a 10k time trial and a 40k road race had unfortunately come to nothing.

For the first time ever the road race was going to be held before the time trial. Interesting. And possibly to my advantage, as the time trial is a good indicator of form with the faster riders in the time trial being watched and followed in the race. In Australia I had been marked in the road race making it more difficult to escape from the bunch but this wouldn't be possible here. Having said that, I wouldn't know anything about the form of the other riders, many of whom I recognised from Australia. This included the Italian rider who had outsprinted me. Also present was Jean Claude Schurig, a Swiss cyclist who had medalled in both events on the Gold Coast.

I'd got a lot of riding and racing under my belt since the games in Japan and my pre-race preparation had improved a little. Knowing I had a responsibility to help the other members of the team, particularly those at their first games, meant it was inappropriate to show my untempered instinctive reaction and run around screaming like a child. My preparation could not really have gone much better, not that I'd admit that to anyone of course. I'd missed the early season time trials because of my trip to Majorca and my coaching commitments, but I had managed to get to the track a lot. I'd done another couple of 5k time trials recording 7.09 in one, a personal best and a whole second faster than the time I had set in France in 2003. On top of that I was riding well with Group 3 in the road race league and rather than just hanging on. I'd even achieved some decent finishes managing a 4th in a bunch sprint.

Gothenburg was beautiful. A lovely city populated by calm, cool Swedes who made us very welcome. We settled into the team hotel, checked out the analogue website in the foyer and started saying hello to people. The day after, we walked up to Gotaplatsen Square for the opening ceremony. Despite being nearly mid-summer it was raining a little although this didn't seem to bother anybody. I had a walk around the square with Chris, a new rider on the cycling team looking to 'bag' some exotic transplant recipients. We got talking to the Sudanese and the Tunisian teams.

I returned to the British team and found our large junior contingent being herded together so I went over to talk to them. As I turned to leave I was confronted by a group of dignitaries surrounded by security personnel and a young man holding his hand out for me to shake. It turned out to be H.R.H Prince Daniel of Sweden, the recently married heir to the Swedish throne. He'd had a kidney transplant and had come to open the games. What a great start. I was completely unprepared so I whipped my hat off and did a half bow half curtsey thing. I'm sure he was very impressed. We talked for a minute about cycling before I moved on to do some more handshaking. Later, a team mate mentioned an autograph. I told him he hadn't asked for one.

The course in Sweden had been changed from the profile originally published but it was still lumpy, actually bordering on hilly. This made an interesting change from the flatter courses that had been more common in past events. There were some tricky descents on the indifferent road surface and joy of joys it was raining. We learned we would be riding in strict age category groups. Sharing the pace with older or younger riders from other countries when it was mutually beneficial was out of the question. This was going to be interesting.

The race started off into one of the hills. A rider came straight out of the bunch and darted up the hill echoing memories of the race 10 years ago in Japan. This time I waited, only upping the pace a little. Nobody else reacted to this rider's acceleration either and it turned out to be the right choice. He was clearly starting to suffer for his efforts at the top of the first hill being quickly re-assimilated by the group.

Another two laps of the six lap race saw more riders unable to keep the pace. On the third lap I attacked up the hill. I was not expecting to get away, I just wanted to see who was likely to follow and whether we could establish a break. Nobody came. I had a choice. I could either sit up and wait for the bunch to catch me or put my head down and try to ride the remaining four laps on my own. It was a too early in the race to go for it alone but the surface was wet and riders were nervous in the corners – prime for a crash. I put another 400 metre dig in and looked over my shoulder expecting at least the Italian and Swiss riders to be coming after me but as I descended the hill, nobody was there.

The decision was made for me really; the motorcycle escort was right in front of me so I pressed on turning the road race into a time trial. I managed to stay away and win the race with a feeling of great relief and satisfaction. If there was one race I wanted, it was this one. I knew that silver medal from Australia would be twinkling a little less the next time I was in the downstairs bathroom.

Off the bike and getting some warm congratulations from my team and Helen I was quickly into the tracksuit first watching the Veterans category race and then assuming my coaching duties for the women's road race.

We had one of our debutants, Ottilie Morgan riding in 18 – 30 age category. Ottilie is a true competitor, a graduate in sport's science who played football at a high level and excelled at every sport she turned her hand to. Luckily for me, she'd decided to apply her enthusiasm and competitive instinct to cycling. What she lacked in experience in the art of road racing she made up with grit, determination and strength on the bike. The racing was extraordinarily close and exciting. An Australian rider had been away for most of the race on her own but had not managed to establish a lead of more than 50 metres or so on the bunch containing Ottilie. I was standing on the first hill

283

of the course for the last lap as the Aussie rider went past. 'Otts' was out of the bunch and going hard after her.

I summoned all my years of riding and coaching experience so I could help her with some ferociously useful well-delivered tactical gem as she passed me. 'Catch her' I shouted at the top of my voice. 'Catch her' for Christ's sake. Genius. All those coaching courses were really paying off. Nevertheless, catch her she did. She came over the line a few minutes later just in front of the Australian rider to take the gold medal. In total, The GB Tx team took two gold and two silver medals on the first day of the cycling although I fear this may have little to do with my course-side coaching master-class.

Two days later, the day of the time trial came around. We were competing over two laps of a slightly amended course that still included the two climbs used in the road race. We knew the times were unlikely to be fast but of course, it was the time relative to your direct competitors that was going to be important. I'd unpacked the aero time trial bike unsure how much, if any, advantage this would give me on the challenging hilly course. Happily the weather had improved and the Swedish summer had kicked in.

The time trial was potentially the final piece in the jigsaw. I had to make sure I finished quickly but also that I finished in one piece. A crash in the road race 2 days earlier has been partly responsible for my seemingly straightforward escape that day making it difficult to measure form. It also confirmed the twisting course could bite you back if not treated with respect.

The youngsters, including the Norwegian rider who had beaten me in Dublin the previous year, had gone first at 1 minute intervals. He had set a time of 8.28 that looked quick on this challenging course. My primary target was a win in my age category and finish off the 'grand slam' as people had started to call it. All six titles at the same time. But I really wanted to go fastest overall too. No medals, no trophy – just bragging rights. I knew I could ride within myself, take no risks and stand a good chance of winning my age category. If I wanted to be the fastest, I was going to have to push it. Cut the bends, skim the curbs and stay on the aero bars on the tricky descent.

There are no great tactics in the 5k time trial; you ride as hard as you can until you've finished then collapse. If you've got anything left in you at the end, you've got it wrong and probably haven't won. This was slightly different because it was possible to blast up the first hill and have nothing left at the top to power over it and pick-up speed. Against all natural instinct the acceleration from the starting gate had to be controlled.

I felt like I'd had a good ride. I was measured and controlled. I couldn't have gone any faster whatever the result. I was delighted when the team came over and told me I'd ridden the course in 8.24 reversing the four second deficit over the rider from Norway in Dublin.

The 2nd and 3rd placed riders in my age category both came in at exactly 9.00, the medals having to be decided by thousandths of a second. I had a tense wait for the rest of the riders to finish in my age category and wasn't entirely relaxed until I heard my name called for the medal ceremony.

The team put in another fantastic day with the women picking up more medals, including a hugely gutsy ride from Di Higman to earn a bronze medal after puncturing in the road race two days before. It felt like a real team effort. Determined rides from Chris Foster and Mel Slaney didn't earn them medals on that day but the support they gave to the team was immeasurable. Ottilie put in another storming ride to win the time trial and become a double World Champion at the first time of asking. Outstanding.

For me personally, job done. I now held all six medals at the same time, British, European and World at time trial and road race disciplines. I was also the fastest transplant cyclist in the world.

Equally satisfying, the team had won a further two gold medals, another silver medal and three bronzes at the time trial making ten cycling medals in total. From a team of eight cyclists, including five debutant riders, this is an achievement of which they are rightly proud.

The last lap

The World Games in Sweden represented the completion of a significant target for me from an athletic perspective, but it was more than that. Cycling within the transplant community was a useful device to keep my mind on track but the competition, support and friendship that came with it had become a vital part of my make-up.

I'm not under any illusions about my abilities as a cyclist. My position in the pecking order is reinforced every time I ride a local time trial or road race. I compete happily as a middle marking 3rd Cat clubman with a 23.03 personal best for a '10'. Wherever I finish an event, I enjoy the company of other cyclists.

I have ridden against some top amateur cyclists in the UK and I know they are much better than me: I also know they couldn't hold a light to our domestic professionals. In turn, they would not be able to live with the speed and power of the continental peloton.

I've won transplant-related events because I train smart and hard for them and short power-related races suit my physiology. In addition, while there are hundreds of thousands of transplant recipients in the world for some strange reason not all of them choose to race bicycles. The competitive pool is smaller. In answer to the question, "Would I be a top class cyclist if I hadn't needed a liver transplant?' the answer is unequivocally, 'No' but please don't mention this to anybody because I need to play the transplant card sometimes. Particularly after dire performances.

The little medals are no more than a token demonstrating that the sacrifices and brave decisions my donor family made all those years back had been worthwhile. The real demonstration being the existence of my children Charlie and Grace. They simply wouldn't be here without them. Meeting my donor's parents had satisfyingly closed an open circle and whilst this is not going to be possible or appropriate for all transplant recipients, it was the right thing for me.

In truth I get embarrassed by winning things so it's fortunate I spend most of my time getting regularly beaten. Winning something at the transplant games allows me to soak up a little of the pride and honour I feel at being connected with donors, donor families, transplant recipients and, most importantly, my donor family.

I mentioned I meet a proper hero at the Games sometimes. In Sweden I was fortunate to meet two. First, Tashi, the team manager, team physio, team captain, flag bearer, supporter and only athlete in the Bhutan team. How wonderful it is that transplantation can be supported in such a tiny country and what an effort he made to get to Sweden unaided. Everywhere he went he was applauded and adopted by the larger teams

Secondly, Michel. A Swiss cyclist introduced to the GB team by his team mate Jean Claude. Michel suffered from cystic fibrosis for 29 years and had finally had a double lung transplant 15 months prior to coming to the Games.

Michel had ridden 2200 km's from his home in Verbier to Gothenburg carrying his camping equipment with him. When he arrived he hired a race bike, entered the time trial and finished fourth in his age category. He was a complete ball of energy: a true inspiration and somebody who was totally committed to making every moment he had worthwhile. I cannot think of a better of example of a person making the most of their second chance at life.

For my part I was now in a danger of heading towards a targetless purgatory. It was starting to dawn on me that, in time, I would have to look towards what came next. What the next goal could be.

I was saved on the last day of the games. I spoke to one of our hosts, a member of the Swedish team. He told me Richard Nordstrum, his team mate and my cycling rival for the early years of the games, had received a second kidney transplant that very week. I was delighted for Richard – he'd had a long wait but now hopefully he would be on his way to recovery, and back on the bike again.

With 2 years between Sweden and the next World Games in South Africa there's plenty of time for a man of his talent to come back and give me a hard time. Perhaps get one of those medals back, maybe both.

I'd better get training.

Lightning Source UK Ltd.
Milton Keynes UK
UKOW030338161112

202310UK00001B/8/P